Homes
Within Reach

Homes
Within Reach

A Guide to the Planning,
Design, and Construction
of Affordable Homes and
Communities

Avi Friedman

WILEY

John Wiley & Sons, Inc.

Copyright © 2005 by Avi Friedman. All rights reserved.

Published by John Wiley & Sons, Inc., Hoboken, New Jersey.
Published simultaneously in Canada.

Library of Congress Cataloging-in-Publication Data:

Friedman, Avi, 1952–
  Homes within reach : a guide to the planning, design and construction of affordable homes and communities / Avi Friedman.
    p. cm.
  Includes bibliographical references and index.
  ISBN 0-471-46986-6 (cloth)
  1. Housing--Planning. 2. Low-income housing. 3. Residential real estate--Planning. 4. Architecture, Domestic--Designs and plans. 5. Dwellings--Design and construction--Cost effectiveness. 6. House construction--Cost effectiveness. I. Title.
  HD7287.F83 2005
  333.33'8--dc22
                                        2005001373

Printed in the United States of America

10 9 8 7 6 5 4 3 2 1

Also by Avi Friedman

The Grow Home

Planning the New Suburbia

The Adaptable House

Peeking through the Keyhole (coauthored with David Krawitz)

To my students

Contents

Preface

For many homebuyers, the purchase of a home represents the largest financial investment that they will ever undertake in their lives. Ownership will help most accumulate personal wealth and an inheritance for future generations. Once purchased or rented, a dwelling will form a backdrop for the household life. Its location, size, layout, and quality stand to influence the family behavior day to day and year to year.

Along with health care and education, governments generally see sheltering their population adequately as a basic responsibility. They also recognize that an assembly of homes forms a community—a building block of society. Yet, in most nations, it is the dweller's responsibility to acquire one's own housing. It is assumed that portions of a household income will be allocated to lodging, leaving sufficient funds for other basic necessities. Gradual demographic and economic shifts since the middle of the twentieth century shook the foundation of this assumption and made homeownership a challenge for many.

Economic transformation saw low-paying jobs move offshore, making it harder for some to find employment. The institution of job security, necessary for obtaining and paying a long-term mortgage, eroded. Higher divorce rates, increase in the number of single-person households, and an aging population gave rise to the small household that cannot afford to purchase a residence. The swelling size and quality of homes also widened the gap between income and cost of housing. Barriers placed by some communities in front of those who initiated affordable housing projects have not made things any easier. Governments' avoidance of assuming the responsibility for building subsidized accommodations make it harder for the very poor to find shelter.

The cumulative effect of these societal changes and processes led to a severe deficit of lower-cost housing in many communities, propelling the need for more affordable housing to the forefront. At times, finding solutions was left to private-sector homebuilders whose interests lay primarily in the construction of more lucrative projects. Since the overwhelming majority of design practices are focused on custom-built homes, there is also an evident lack of knowledge of how to plan, design, and construct affordable housing. It is this knowledge void that this book is set to fill.

The book does not single out any sector in particular. The material assembled here can be used by individuals building a home for themselves or contracting a builder to do it for them. It can also be of help to planners, architects, and builders designing and planning a large community. It can be used by for-profit firms or non-profit organizations that plan to initiate home or building ownership or rental accommodations. Although some of the standards described in this book are relevant to the North American market, its basic principles can be used internationally. Similarly, despite the fact that many of the designs described here are for low-rise, wood-frame structures, their concepts are applicable to tall and large buildings.

The thrust of planning and designing affordable homes and communities is about innovation and nontraditional practices. Efficient use of limited resources, whether of land or building materials, requires careful assessment of a range of relevant strategies. This book attempts to provide an organized listing and analysis of options in a variety of domains for such projects. The selections described are based on the author's own experience as a researcher and a practitioner and on a review of relevant literature.

The first chapter sets the stage for the discussion that follows. Background issues that cause and affect affordable housing have been listed, as have ways of measuring them. The principal components of the dwelling cost and the process participants and their objectives have been described. Chapter 2 guides the reader through a site selection process. Issues related to preferred location, size of lots, and relevant zoning are dealt with, along with an examination of the site's natural properties. Chapter 3 deals with the home itself. Dwelling forms, attachment to other dwellings, relation to the ground, roof design, and the effect of these factors on cost are some of the principal topics discussed. Chapter 4 walks the reader through the house's interior. Design strategies ranging from conceptual approaches to space design, access, circulation, and finishes are elaborated in this chapter. The construction of a home and the fitting of utilities are the subject of Chapter 5. Following a description of preconstruction phases, various key building components, such as the foundation, framing, window selection, prefabrication, and dwelling's mechanical systems and their cost, are discussed.

Chapter 6 dwells on lot subdivision. Following the introduction of density measure units, the relationship of lots to the homes built on them and to the streets in front of them are discussed. Chapter 7 discusses issues related to the community's circulation system design and construction. Parking arrangements, pedestrian and cyclist paths, and project infrastructure are dealt with. The communal or private area used for outdoor and leisure activities, better known as open spaces, are discussed in Chapter 8. Design strategies for these spaces are also outlined, as well as strategies for landscaping and grading of a site.

Chapter 9 focuses on infill housing, a critical aspect of affordable dwelling. Taking advantage of existing infrastructure promises to contribute to cost savings. The challenges of finding an appropriate site and its possible use with regard to building options, open spaces, and circulation are discussed in this chapter. Finally, Chapter 10 overlaps the lessons learned in the previous chapters and demonstrates their implementation in five projects of various scales. The projects have been selected because of their unique approach to the design of high-density affordable homes and communities. They each shed light on a facet of the design process.

Affordable housing design is first and foremost about trade-offs. Those who wish to become homeowners will have to trade large homes or amenities for homeownership or rental accommodation. Governments will have to amend bylaws in order to ensure that their citizens are housed adequately. Builders will have to build smaller dwellings for first-time homebuyers if they wish to have a move-up market. This book is meant to demonstrate how, through design, these trade-offs can be accomplished sensibly.

Acknowledgments

Designing, teaching, advocating, and researching ways to house people affordably is a central theme of my career. Over the years, numerous collaborators, colleagues, and students shared my quest. I would like to thank them all for making it a worthwhile and enjoyable voyage. I also wish to recognize those who directly or indirectly contributed to the production of this book.

I would like to thank Julie Trelstad, a former editor at Wiley, who supported the project from its gestation; Marylin Berger, head librarian at McGill University's Blackader-Lauterman Library of Arts and Architecture and Jasmine Chouinard for their help in compiling background information. I would also like to thank Vince Cammalleri and Denis Palin, for expanding my knowledge in technical matters; Jennifer Steffel, for providing information about the genesis of cities and suburbs; Michelle Côté for contributing to a study that inspired several concepts and illustrations; Corrine Cornibe, for doing much-appreciated research for some of the chapters; Clara Shipman, for patiently and meticulously drawing all of the illustrations; Nyd Garavito-Bruhn, for organizing the text; McGill University and its School of Architecture for their support of the Affordable Homes Program and for giving me the time to write. The Program, its researchers, teachers, and students were the source of knowledge for many of the ideas that are presented here.

Finally, I would like to express thanks and appreciation to my wife, Dr. Sorel Friedman, and my children Paloma and Ben, for their continuous love, support, and encouragement.

The Fundamentals

The term "affordable housing" has a number of connotations and definitions. Some regard it simply as housing for low-income people. Others interpret "affordable housing" as any form of directly or indirectly subsidized dwelling. The formal definition, however, refers to the share of a household's income that is spent on lodging. An expenditure of 32 percent of a household's gross annual income on mortgage principle, interest, taxes, and utilities has become a recognized measure of how much people should spend on rented or owned adequate and safe housing. Housing is, therefore, affordable when households with income at or below the city, community, or state median income spend no more than 32 percent of their gross annual income on shelter. Along with societal and economic changes, the growing need to house a segment of the population affordably has accelerated in recent decades. These changes and further elaboration of the affordability definition, the parties involved in housing production, and their interests will be outlined in this chapter.

SOCIETAL TRENDS, CHALLENGING TIMES

The end of World War II marked a turning point in the way North Americans housed themselves. Many demographic, lifestyle, economic, and cultural trends that had begun in this postwar period, left their imprint on the residential landscape for decades. To understand the reasons for the emergence of affordable housing as a key societal concern, one needs to recall the causes of the challenge.

The New Family

The transformation of the North American family not only affected society's demographic makeup but also revealed many indirect links to the rise in the need for affordable housing. After World War II, home builders regarded their clients as a homogeneous block. The common household was made up of a working father, a housewife, and their children. This family structure, with its space needs and lifestyle, influenced designs offered by architects and builders. The three-bedroom, single-family detached home with a garage became a recognized feature across the continent. Housing solutions for families who did not fit this social model, it was assumed, would be found in apartments.

Decades later this demographic makeup changed. The proliferation of birth control methods, along with new lifestyle and cultural tendencies, gave rise to a new societal composition. The share of single-person households and single-parent families grew. The number of seniors also increased. These new households, with a single breadwinner could not accumulate the means to purchase a home. They could also no longer rely on publicly funded housing, since in North America, federal and local authorities had limited their participation in sheltering lower income households. Many of these households were left to fend for themselves, often relying exclusively on rental accommodations, the stock of which dwindled in many cities. Acquiring a home for those who had means became an even greater challenge, as the product itself swelled in size and, as a result, the cost became financially out of reach.

Very Big Homes

One of the most noticeable factors to affect affordability was the transformation of the product itself — the home. If the objective of postwar buyers was to purchase a modest, comfortable shelter, the residence, it seems, had now become a mark of social status. The swelling size of homes paradoxically paralleled the decline in the number of people constituting a household. Clients wanted more space, and builders were eager to provide it. The postwar 800-square-foot (80-square-meter) bungalow, with an attached, single carport, that dots North American suburbs gradually expanded to an average of 2,000 square feet (200 square meters) with a two- or three-car indoor parking garage.

Several other phenomena caused the cost of a home to rise. Some had to do with market supply-and-demand cycles and others with buyers' choices. As the size of homes grew, processing and transporting more building supplies made them more expensive to construct. Labor costs also rose, as the increased housing demand put pressure on a declining number of tradespeople. Unfortunately, the homebuilding industry, which was accustomed to an on-site, stick-built construction method, did not switch to construction methods that used prefabricated components for the sake of cost efficiency.

Compared with earlier decades, the science of homebuilding improved. Homes constructed today include higher-quality products and utilities. Windows or heating systems, for example, are superior by far to those installed a few decades ago. New spaces and functions have been added to home design as lifestyles changed. The kitchen has grown in size to become the home's social center and a showcase for costly appliances. Bathrooms with bathtubs, shower stalls, and floor-to-ceiling tiles, at times on each level of the house, have become the norm. Other added functions and amenities, though, have taken a financial toll. Media centers and home offices are part of the homebuilder's new vocabulary. In addition to the initial high cost of building a home, ongoing maintenance and upkeep expenses have grown. The cost of cable TV, Internet hookup, and telephone lines has to be added to the monthly mortgage payments, utility bills, and municipal taxes.

The linking of a single dwelling to more utilities also meant that infrastructure as a whole had to be expanded and, as a result, development costs rose. The tacking on of a large garage to the side of each dwelling meant that lots and the surrounding roads were extended. Their construction quality ameliorated as well. Water lines supplying fire hydrants and homes, storm sewers and house drainage systems, the electrical grid, telephone, Internet, and cable TV are among the services buried below ground. The cost of building infrastructure, which decades before was financed and built by municipalities and recovered by them through taxes, is now taken on by developers. They, in turn, transfer these costs to homebuyers. By the late 1970s, the cost of serviced land rose from 12 to 25 percent of the cost of a typical North American home, making it harder for people to afford them.

New Economic Realities

One of the factors that affected people's ability to own a home was a change in North America's economic climate and the structure of the labor market. To understand the significance of the change, one needs to trace the homebuying process back to the post World War II era.

Lack of housing after World War II initiated government market intervention through economic stimulation packages and other incentives. Loans at favored rates were given to returning veterans and new homebuyers. Gradually, government limited its intervention, and the business of financing and housing the majority of North Americans became a private affair. Banks stepped up to the task by establishing, under government supervision, their own criteria for lending money.

Several principles guided the process. The first had to do with the amount that a homeowner could borrow. It was established that a household needed to be able to save about 25 percent of the dwelling cost as a down payment on the property. It was also decided that the amount borrowed would not be greater than 25 percent of the household income, as other family expenses, such as food, education, and retirement savings needed to be accounted for. To reduce its risk, the lender made sure that the borrower had secure employment. In the stable work environment of the 1950s and 1960s, however, this was not a concern. Traditional households that were headed by a single breadwinner who held a steady job were welcomed by bankers, and this method of privately financing projects and individual homes flourished.

Things began to shift in the 1970s. Several trends influenced the way mortgages were awarded by private lenders. The return of women to the labor force improved the household's financial standing. Since households had more disposable income, bankers, with government approval, raised the allowable borrowed amount to 32 percent of household income. As a result of their increased spending abilities, buyers sought to buy larger, more comfortable, and expensive homes. Work outside the home by the two heads of the household also influenced the family's lifestyle. Maternity leave, for example, had to be shortened, since the monthly mortgage payment could not be paid with one paycheck.

Another more influential process happened as a result of the transformation in the labor market. Foreign competition contributed to the transfer of many labor-intensive, low-paying jobs offshore. Recessionary cycles eliminated another factor that was necessary for a prospective homeowner to qualify for a mortgage—job security. Watching their bottom lines, corporations did not hesitate to lay off employees when profits declined. Long-term, stable, and secure employment in many sectors became a thing of the past. For many young, first-time homeowners, who lacked high-earning skills, it was harder to accumulate the means to own a home.

The widening gap between household income and house price was another barrier to homeownership. In the decades since World War II, income growth in North America has not been distributed evenly, despite an overall increase. In general, a close scrutiny of studies and statistics suggests that those earning the least income saw little change in their net worth. The wealthiest segment of the population, on the other hand, saw a significant increase in their net worth. Put simply, today's entry-level incomes do not allow for the acquisition of a down payment and a home loan to acquire homes in most urban centers. They do not permit low-income renters to become homeowners (Ford Foundation, 1989).

Not In My Backyard

Housing people affordably poses economic and technical challenges. Initiators of such projects have to overcome another barrier — community opposition. Such opposition is often referred to as "Not In My Back Yard" (NIMBY) syndrome.

Most people like to maintain the status of their living environment. A fear of the unknown can make individual citizens unite in a vocal and organized opposition to any development that upsets the status quo. There are many reasons to oppose any sort of development. Increase in traffic, reduced personal safety, and "attracting the wrong kind of people" are some often-heard motives. Construction of affordable housing raises another fear—an economic one. Along with the rise in the cost of housing, the home is now considered to be an investment and savings portfolio as well as a place to dwell. Homeowners not only hoped to use their dwellings but also to see the monetary value of them rise unlike other consumption goods. They cannot afford to put their investment at risk.

Proposing homes with a different density or architectural character is likely to prompt community resistance. Fearing the possibility that lower-cost housing will be constructed in their municipality, some cities write zoning bylaws that make building affordable homes impossible. Wide lots, low density, large footprints, and indoor parking have been legislated in many places, making the initiation of lower-cost housing projects impossible. Despite their desire to see affordable homes built in their community and their sympathy to the cause, elected municipal leaders fear reprisals at election time. "Not In My Term In Office" (NIMTIO) is a sentiment voiced in many places.

Whether a community can prevent an individual, a building firm, or a non-profit group from building affordable housing by legislating zoning bylaws has been challenged at times in the courts. On most occasions, the challengers succeeded, and affordable homes have been given the go-ahead.

FAMILY LIFE CYCLE AND HOUSING

The ability to accumulate the funds necessary to acquire and to maintain a home relate to one's personal value system. Some regard homeownership as an important life goal, whereas others do not see it as a necessary personal milestone and choose to be lifelong renters. The place of homeownership in a list of personal priorities varies from culture to culture. In most cultures, however, the notion of owning a home is highly valued. It affects personal and family life, as well as provides security of tenure. Unlike renters, homeowners can rest assured that they will neither have to relocate upon the expiration of their lease, nor be subject to ongoing increases in rent.

Homeownership, for most, is also a means of accumulating wealth. Homeowners are in a position to build equity through mortgage amortization, which is something that renters cannot do. Over time, depending on location, the property value may appreciate and, as a result, the owner's equity increases.

Homeowners have greater control over their dwelling's environment. More than renters, they can easily have the dwelling designed to suit their needs, and they have no restrictions in modifying it years later. Unlike renters, homeowners can use their property as an income generator. By renting portions of it or the entire dwelling to someone else, they can enjoy a flow of income. Homeownership also benefits the community at large by increasing individual participation in community life and engaging people in the environmental aspects of their neighborhood. Homeownership also lowers the need of local government to support senior citizens when their incomes decline (Habitat for Humanity Canada, 2003).

There are, however, disadvantages associated with homeownership compared to the rental tenure status. Homeownership requires occupants to exercise monetary discipline. Scheduled mortgage payments must be met, and upkeep chores must be respected. Renters are not bound by the same rules. They are free to move whenever their lease expires. In a recessionary cycle, the value of a home can be depreciated and losses can occur. On a community level, the drive for homeownership is often linked to urban sprawl, as land near urban centers becomes unaffordable to people with smaller means (Habitat for Humanity Canada, 2003).

There is also an apparent relationship between life stage and housing needs. Need for a home and the use of its space cannot, therefore, be regarded in a static, linear fashion. Transitions that result from accumulation of wealth and from the aging process affect acquisition and use of homes. Singles people are likely to look for modestly priced, smaller dwellings, preferably close to the town center or to learning institutions. They are likely to reside in a rented or owned apartment. Young couples with small incomes will also look for modestly priced accommodation. The desire to acquire their own place will increase when they consider expanding, or when they have just expanded, their family. They will look for an affordable, ground-oriented, and larger dwelling that is sufficient to accommodate a growing family; as the children grow, buying a larger home will be considered. The quest for privacy by adolescents will also foster a change in the dwelling's interior (Canada Mortgage and Housing Corporation, 1981).

When the children move out to form their own households, the parents will once again consider their own housing options. They may decide to remain in the same dwelling and adapt it to their physical limits or move to a new place. It is this dynamic process that largely affects affordability in each life stage as well. Means are likely to be more constrained in the beginning and the later phases of a household life cycle.

MEASURING AFFORDABILITY

The economic concerns of a would-be homebuyer are considered when housing affordability is calculated. The underlying principle of such a process is that buyers should not oblige themselves beyond their ability to live up to their financial commitment. Since most home buying in North America is done with funds loaned by private lenders, the rules or conditions of such loans are set by them. They are likely to request that two principles be respected. The first principle is that a homebuyer pay to the home's seller 25 percent of the value of the property upon purchase. This amount, known as a *down payment*, can be reduced as part of government assistance programs. In some instances, it can be as low as 5 or even 0 percent of the total dwelling's price. In such cases, the buyer will have to pay to the lender higher insurance premiums as a guarantee that the loan will be repaid.

The second principle relates to the monthly amounts that a buyer will have to pay to return the loan, which is known as a *mortgage*. The monthly mortgage payment should not exceed a limit set by a lender, which in most cases is 32 percent of the household's annual income and is referred to as the "gross debt service ratio" (GDSR). Once exceeded, overpayment to the home expenses portion of the family budget will have to come from other monetary allocations of the household priorities, which is clearly undesirable. Making sure that buyers will keep up with loan payments is, therefore, a priority of the lender.

In calculating the house expenses, the lender will commonly include the estimated monthly property taxes, utility costs, and the monthly mortgage payment. When the dwelling is sold as a condominium, 50 percent of the condominium fees will be taken into consideration as well. The size of the mortgage will be a function of the *mortgage payment factor*, which will depend on the length of time, known as the *amortization period*, through which the homebuy-

Figure 1.1 The relationship between income, down payment, and maximum affordable home price.

$$H = \frac{(A \times 32\% - C)}{E} \times 1000 + G \qquad C = \frac{H \times 1.9522}{12 \times 100} + H \times 0.1\% + J \times 50\%$$

Simplified, this gives

$$C = H \times 0.3\%$$

where

A is the gross monthly income

C is the estimated monthly property taxes, heating cost, and 50 percent of condominium fees, where applicable

E is the mortgage payment factor per $1,000 of loan

G is the down payment

H is the maximum house price

J is the condominium fees

er wishes to repay the mortgage. Repaying the mortgage faster will require larger monthly amounts, whereas stretching the payments over a longer period of time will place a lighter burden on the family. The relationship between the household income, down payment, and the maximum affordable home price is best represented in Figure 1.1. These figures and methods are instrumental in figuring out how much dwelling in terms of cost a homebuyer will be able to afford.

As outlined above, *affordability* involves a relationship between housing cost, which includes mortgage payments, rent, property taxes, and utilities, and household income. In particular, it refers to the ability of homeowners or potential homeowners to make payments on a home. *Access* refers to the ability of potential homeowners to obtain financing for a home. It is largely determined by lending practices set by the lender's conventions and affected by the availability of financing interest rates, down payment requirements, and other borrowing terms and conditions. The *affordability gap* is aonther important term that is commonly used in this context. It is defined as the difference between the amount a household can afford to pay as a percentage of income and the actual rent or mortgage payment needed, which is also set at 32 percent.

WHO BUILDS WHAT?

Affordable housing can be initiated and managed in a variety of forms. In this book, the term *affordable* is related to the share of income that a household will spend on acquiring, renting, and maintaining a home. Affordable housing is, therefore, seen here to be any kind of housing that meets an income target regardless of its occupants, its initiators, their source of funding, or whether the project, its managers, or its occupants received any kind of direct or indirect financial assistance.

The Initiating Party

Affordable housing can be initiated by two main sectors: the *nonprofit* and the *for-profit*. The nonprofit sector can either be a government-run agency or a non-governmental organization. A government-run project will use public funds, and the end product will commonly be referred to as *public housing*. The project will be not only funded initially but also managed or financially supported through its life cycle by its initiators or their representatives. Criteria will be set, mostly based on economic indicators, for admitting occupants to the project who will likely pay monthly rental fees. The project can be an apartment building or low-rise, single-family houses.

Non-governmental organizations (NGOs) have no legal affiliation with any level of government. The organization can, however, benefit from a subsidy program put forward by a government agency. The NGO may organize itself in a variety of legal structures. It can be a cooperative, for example, whose members will be affiliated based on their ideological beliefs. They will be associated to gain from the economy of scale that a large number of members creates. NGOs can be part of the voluntary sector, such as Habitat for Humanity, whose members are unpaid volunteers, or act for their own self-interest, such as members of a cohousing group.

A for-profit initiator can be any private sector firm that sets to develop, build, sell, or rent housing. It can be a land development company that purchased, subdivided, and made land into lots for sale to builders or to be built upon by the development company itself. The for-profit sector may benefit from direct or indirect subsidies as well. In a period of economic recession, government may lower interest rates or award grants to first-time homebuyers. For-profit builders use private sources of funding to support their projects. They will either qualify for a bank loan or use their own in-house funds. The cost-reduction strategies that will be outlined in this chapter can be implemented and used by either the nonprofit or for-profit sectors.

COST-REDUCTION MEASURES

This book examines and outlines cost-reduction strategies for a single home or an entire community. It places planning, design, and technology as key instruments in making dwellings affordable. Design, however, is only one of a number of strategies employed in bringing the cost of housing down. It will be worth-while to review some of them here.

Policy and Regulation

Controlling and modifying public policies and regulations is largely under governmental control. It is an effective tool in ensuring that proper conditions will be put in place to make affordable design more effective. It may include reducing the length of time necessary for the project's approval or modifying development standards. Increasing the project density, for example, may be the outcome of this action. Innovation will be encouraged by permitting dwelling forms that are otherwise prohibited. Allowing secondary suites in large homes or garden suites in the rear of existing or new dwellings for rental purposes or for housing a senior member of the family can be the outcome of changing policy and regulations. Changing zoning to allow mixed-use activities in the same property can help as well. With appropriate permits, a portion of the home can become a business that will generate additional income to support the cost of the entire structure.

Financing and Tenure

Making housing accessible and affordable also can be achieved by creating appropriate financial mechanisms and tenure arrangements. Many federal, state, and municipal authorities have put such programs in place. They include the use of a *Housing Trust Fund,* the development of *Community Land Trusts,* the introduction of a land-lease tenure, or even making public land available at a reduced cost. In some locations, the use of the occupants' own labor, known as *sweat equity,* to build their home is encouraged and supported. Using Equity Co-operative would be an avenue, as well as forming partnerships between public, nonprofit, and private for-profit organizations.

Redevelopment and Renovation

Although this book deals primarily with the construction of new dwellings, affordable housing can be produced by using existing housing stock. A number of programs and strategies exist to take advantage of housing already constructed. The acquisition, renovation, and sale of dwellings is such a strategy. The projects can be initiated by either for-profit or nonprofit groups. The cost will be lower since the first initiator has already paid all or part of the mortgage.

Converting nonresidential buildings to housing also falls under this category. Known as a "brownfield development," these projects take advantage of inexpensive land or buildings, which are likely to be formerly industrial or institutional, for redevelopment as affordable housing sites. Situated in densely populated areas, these conversions offer a cost-saving advantage since roads and utilities already exist next to or on the property. Increasing the density of an underutilized site is another approach that can bring the cost of housing down. A single-family project may become a multifamily one as the building interior is altered or additions are made to the structure. The project's initiators may undertake construction of new dwellings while renovating old ones and connect them to already-in-place utilities.

Operation and Management

Once occupied, a dwelling's operation and upkeep expenses can be indirectly accounted for as part of its cost. Reducing these later expenses is, therefore, considered essential for owners of affordable housing. Selecting good construction products and techniques and instituting a regular maintenance program can assist in this regard. Choosing an efficient heating and cooling system, orienting the home for maximum passive solar gain, and making sure that it is well constructed and insulated will help reduce energy consumption and the monetary burden once the home has been occupied.

Reducing Cost versus Adding Value

When affordable homes and developments are designed, the strategies used in their conception can be divided into two: those that immediately contribute to lower cost and those that add value to the project by ameliorating its quality or appearance. The first, cost reduction, is a straightforward and quantifiable approach. The initiative needs to make the project, or part of it, less expensive compared to a similar design or product. The second, adding value, is less obvious since the outcome is not always measurable. The added value can be manifested by improving the curb appeal of the development or by increasing the occupants' pride and satisfaction. Adding value is important in the case of affordable communities. Past experience demonstrates that projects can be successful in reaching a cost target but poorly regarded by their occupants and neighbors. Affordable design may require reduction of cost but not necessarily lowering the quality and standards of the project. In advocating design strategies, the author will dwell on and advocate ideas that contribute to cost reduction and value amelioration.

Tenure and Legal Title

The tenure of a residence and its type of ownership title will depend on the nature of the project and the initiating organization. The project may be offered as an affordable rental accommodation or sold to individuals. When the project is initiated by a for-profit corporation, the units can be either sold or rented. Depending on the type of project, the legal title can be a *freehold,* whereby the occupants own both the land and structure. Public areas, such as the parks and the roads, will be owned and maintained by the municipality.

The legal title can also be a *condominium.* The occupants own their single-family home or flat, in the case of an apartment building, and the site occupant-owners collectively own the common spaces, such as the stairs, roof, roads, or yard. Condominiums are effective tools for lowering cost, since the cost and the maintenance of the common amenities are shared among many. When a public project is initiated by a government, it will remain government owned. The project can also be owned by an association of occupants, such as in a *cooperative* or *cohousing.* Decisions about project construction and later management are made by the association's members.

THE COST OF A HOUSE

Builders often divide the cost of residential developments into two categories: *hard costs* and *soft costs.* Hard costs are the sums of money that are spent acquiring the site and building the dwellings. Soft costs are the amounts spent on indirect expenses related to the execution and the marketing of the project, which are as essential (Figure 1.2).

Hard Costs

Hard costs may include several components: land cost, development costs, material costs, labor costs, and landscaping costs.

Figure 1.2 Development-cost breakdown of single-family and multifamily housing.

Components	Single-Family Housing	Multifamily Housing
Land	22	6
Materials	31	} 73
Labor	22	
Financing	5	12
Overhead and Profit	20	9
	100%	100%

Land cost refers to the amount spent acquiring land, whether undeveloped or partially developed. The project may be an entirely new development on the edge of town or a project built in an existing community. The cost of land will depend, among other factors, on the site's location, the utilities available, and the designated zoning.

Development costs are the expenses associated with the preparation of undeveloped land or an infill site for construction. This includes the clearing of natural obstacles (such as boulders), the laying of roads, and constructing the necessary utilities. Utilities, which will also be referred to in this book as infrastructure, include hydroelectric power lines, gas lines, water pipes, domestic and storm sewer lines, fire hydrant systems, cable and other lines for TV, telephone, and the Internet. The utilities are essential to the functioning of the community and its houses. They are provided and paid for by the project's initiator, whether it is a public agency or a private firm, and are included in the dwelling cost.

Material costs are the amounts spent acquiring the building materials necessary for the project's construction. Cost of materials may fluctuate with supply-and-demand cycles and the quantity needed. Some builders include rented equipment in this category.

Labor costs are amounts spent on the labor involved in constructing the dwelling and the community. They encompass salaries paid to the trades involved in all aspects of fabrication and include the rough structure, utilities, and finishings, both indoors and outdoors.

Landscaping costs will be spent on landscaping a single house or an entire development. Grading terrain for appropriate drainage, planting trees, and laying sod on the development's public and private areas are included in this category. Often developers may include landscaping costs in their land-development cost.

Soft Costs

Soft costs expended in the construction of a single home or an entire development may include the following components:

The *financing* is the amount that a homeowner, developer, or builder will spend borrowing money from a lender—such as a bank, trust, or credit union—to build the project. It will be paid back over time, according to the terms set by the lender. The borrowed amount, the *mortgage,* is made of capital—the amount lent and the interest costs. Often the lender will open for a builder a *line of credit* from which money can be withdrawn as construction progresses. The amount paid to the lender for its services and interest charged are referred to as financing. It may also be known as the "cost of money."

Professional fees are the monies paid to those who consult the project's initiator throughout the building process. They include land surveyors, who subdivide the site; the project's engineering, planning, and architectural teams; the legal consultants, who prepare contractual documents with the trades or when ownership is transferred to the eventual dwelling owner; and the accountant, who keeps the financial records of the project.

Marketing costs are the monies spent on promoting the project. In the case of a large development, advertisements have to be placed in local papers, project signs mounted, and pamphlets describing the dwelling layout and technical specifications printed. In some locations, this category may also include the cost of building, decorating, and maintaining a model unit—a showcase of sorts—that often doubles as the builder's office during the project's duration. Marketing costs may also include the set commission paid to a real estate agent for the sale of each home.

Taxes are the sums of money that the builder or the homebuyer will have to pay to federal or local tax authorities, and they should be considered part of the cost of the house.

Overhead refers to expenses incurred by the builder throughout the project life cycle. The cost of running the builder's own office, as well as the salaries paid to off-site staff, such as a secretary or bookkeeper, and on-site members of the team who supervise construction are also among overhead expenses.

Profit refers to the builder's own financial gain, which, depending on the type and size of project, may be considerable or limited. Any profit gained may fluctuate along with market supply-and-demand cycles. Traditionally, in residential projects, the profit may be as low as 5 percent and as high as 20 percent.

When financial issues related to affordable housing are considered, the tendency on the part of lenders and homeowners is to examine costs associated with homeownership in the *postoccupancy* stage as well. These costs add to the challenge of owning a home; they can include *condominium fees* as well as yearly municipal taxes. The cost of heating and cooling a residence, which are also referred to as *upkeep costs,* need to be considered as well as any ongoing repair and maintenance expenses. Once the purchase of a home is made, new homeowners will incur additional costs such as *legal fees* associated with the transfer of ownership from the builder, as well as moving, basic furnishing, and decorating expenses.

The categories and components listed above can be divided into two main groups as far as cost reduction measures are concerned. The first group includes those costs over which the project initiator, whether an independent homeowner or a builder, have no control. They include applicable taxes or interest rates, for example, that are set and regulated by governments. Other cost groups will be within the initiator's control and are subject to the project initiator's decisions. Selection of project site, nature and type of amenities as well as dwelling sizes, for example, are all subject to choices made by the property owner. Strategies to reduce these latter costs will be the subject of this book.

When construction costs for a new project are estimated, the type of structure and its methods of construction will be considered. The construction of a low-rise, wood-frame home involves different trades, construction methods, and materials than building a concrete or steel structure. The project will have a different life cycle and duration, which will affect the final cost. The cost will also depend on the project's geographic location and market cycle. Construction in urban sites is often considered costly due to the logistics involved in getting equipment and material into densely populated areas. Similarly, when the market is very active and trades and materials are in great demand, it will affect the cost and labor and materials may come at a premium.

PARTICIPANTS IN THE DELIVERY OF AFFORDABLE HOUSING

The building of a single home or an entire development is a complex and involved task. A number of organizations, agencies, and firms take part directly or indirectly in the process throughout the project's life, which is also known as the *delivery process*. Project participants have their own objectives, interests, and ways of working. These differences are likely to affect attempts to reduce a dwelling's cost. Participants in a housing delivery process can be divided into

Figure 1.3 The participants in the housing-delivery process can be divided into three broad groups.

1. Controlling Agencies	
A. Government:	
i. Federal and State:	Promotes and regulates housing policies and safety through financial incentives, codes, and standards.
ii. Municipal:	Using local legislation, municipal governments reflect their housing policies through a master plan and bylaws, as well as, when needed, a system of incentives.
B. Financial Institution:	Banks, trust companies, or credit unions that lend to the initiator or the home buyer the financial means for the execution or the purchase of a dwelling.
2. Participants in the Supply Process	
A. Initiator:	The party that initiates, conceptualizes, and realizes a project. The initiator can be a single person who plans to build a dwelling for himself, a private firm, or public entity, depending on the source of finance and objectives. Initiators can actually be involved in the building process or can designate a representative, such as a project manager, who will act on their behalf.
B. Design Consultant:	The project's designers, which include an architect, engineer, or interior designer.
C. Project Executor:	The actual party that executes and builds the design according to plans prepared by the design consultants. May be referred to as general contractor, subcontractor, or trade.
D. Product Manufacturers:	The manufacturer and suppliers of the materials needed for the project's construction.
3. Participants in the Demand Process	
A. User:	The party who uses the end product. It can be an individual homebuyer or a group of users in the case of cooperative housing.

three broad groups with specific roles and characteristics (see Figure 1.3). The following sections describe the characteristics of these parties, their role in the project, and their likely effect on the project cost.

Governments

In most countries a government's key political obligation is to ensure that all its citizens are adequately housed. It is often the shared responsibility of all levels of government, each of which contributes to this endeavor in a variety of ways. Governments can also act as developers through the building of publicly funded housing that, once built, is managed by a public agency throughout the project's life.

In North America, governments have traditionally played a modest role in homebuilding. The same is true of government contributions to the supply of affordable housing. Some 95 percent of all homes are constructed by private-sector builders with private funding. Providing incentives through a granting mechanism is the key role that governments commonly play in the construction of privately funded affordable housing.

The tendency of governments in North America in recent decades was to limit their role as residential builders and managers. This tendency often resulted in a lack of affordable housing, primarily for first-time homebuyers. Increased demand for higher-end homes did not make the building of lower-cost residences a worthwhile endeavor for for-profit builders; this lack of interest, on many occasions, led to a housing crisis.

All levels of governments, both directly and indirectly, are involved in the housing process as regulators. By setting building codes, standards, and zoning bylaws, governments exercise control over the end product. The codes decree a set of minimum dimensions and technical specifications to ensure the quality and safety of homes. Zoning bylaws can also help to generate affordable housing. By increasing density limits, for example, more units may share land and infrastructure expenses that can potentially lower the cost of an individual unit.

The secondary role of governments in affordable housing is, at times, stirring interest and educating the parties involved. Conferences and publications that instruct professionals and the general public are often the key means of communication and dissemination of knowledge about a subject.

Financial Institutions

Financial institutions play a critical role in homebuilding through their effect on both the builder's and the homebuyer's decisions. The majority of projects built and homes purchased are financed by private lenders. The guiding principle of the banking industry is to reduce the risks associated with the loan. As a result, careful scrutiny is made of every project and borrower to gauge the amount of risk involved. New design concepts and untried building materials will often be discouraged or not financed. Privately financed affordable housing may be considered "risky" by lenders. The low income of potential homebuyers may turn them into less than prime candidates for lending. It is therefore common for governments to assist first-time buyers by providing additional guarantees to their mortgage.

The Initiator

The term *initiator* refers to the individual or organization that initiates the housing project. It can be a government agency, an association of people who are about to construct cohousing or to reside under cooperative arrangement, or a for-profit private corporation. The terms that are commonly mentioned when a private housing development is constructed is *developer* and *builder*. Developer means *land developer*, which is the individual or entity that options and purchases the land and carries out the necessary administrative procedures, such as subdividing the land, obtaining the necessary zoning, and laying the infrastructure.

Once the site is subdivided and serviced by the developer, lots are sold to builders who then engage a design team, obtain building permits, and construct and sell the homes. In small projects, land development and construction may be done by the same organization. Traditionally, the for-profit building sector was composed of small organizations that built fewer than 20 dwellings per year. Today, there are several building firms that construct over 10,000 units a year in several states and sites.

A fundamental change occurred in the structure of home building firms after World War II. From a firm that executed all stages of construction with in-house labor, now the head of a building firm assumes a marginal role in active construction. Currently, most—if not all—work is subcontracted to tradespeople who are highly specialized in their fields of expertise and execute only a segment of the work. A rough carpentry team, for example, will not undertake finish carpentry work.

Nonprofit organizations—whether quasi-governmental or nongovernmental organizations—that initiate affordable housing begin the delivery process after their funding has been secured. The entire project may be built at once. For-profit builders, on the other hand, follow a speculative process. A model home will be constructed and additional units built as they are sold.

It is common in the private sector to encounter specialization. A builder will have expertise in projects of a certain size or building type with a defined price range. It is rare to see a small building firm that builds low-cost housing switch to high-end, more expensive homes. Building affordable housing is often regarded by for-profit builders as an undertaking that yields smaller gains compared to expensive homes. However, builders who build lower cost housing often enjoy the profit that results from a large number of units built. They also may be known as *volume builders*.

The Design Firm

The planning, architectural, or engineering firms provide the developer or the builder with knowledge about new trends and building technology in addition to consulting services. Yet, at times, design firms are reluctant to work with the for-profit housing sector due to the small budget that is allocated to design. Compromising professional ethics and liability is also a concern, because at times supervision may not form part of the contractual agreement and designs may be changed without notifying designers. Whereas small building firms will employ a "house designer" or use pattern-book designs, large development firms will engage the services of an urban planning or architectural consultant. Design consultants will help interpret zoning and density allowances in a way that permits introduction of change to conventional practice.

Architectural competitions are also an important instrument in bringing about change and new ideas. The years following World War II were such a period. Innovation was put to work to meet the constraints of small budgets and limited spaces. Once published, ideas generated during competitions inspired design concepts that were imitated across the continent.

In 1944, the Veteran's Administration created the Veteran's Mortgage Guarantee Program, later known as the *G.I. Bill of Rights*. Administered by the Federal Housing Authority (FHA), this program enabled veterans to borrow the entire appraised value of an approved house without a down payment. The importance of the G.I. Bill of Rights to the housing industry was in the guidelines set forth for qualified housing. The program limited the price range of the affordable postwar family house from $6,000 (C$7,800) and $8,000 (C$10,500) and the size range from 800 to 1,100 square feet (74 to 102 square meters). The price restriction drove architects into experimenting with cost-reduction strategies (Friedman, 1995).

Economic constraints, material shortages, technological advances, and changes in consumer expectations were reflected in the design of a typical, low-cost family home between 1945 and 1959. The prewar family home was commonly a two-story structure with a pitched roof and a basement. Such a structure was not acceptable under the FHA guidelines, because it was excessive in both size and cost. Therefore, postwar houses, though still traditional in nature, were considerably smaller, yet included more innovative features than their predecessors. Many of these innovations were introduced by the leading design firms of the day.

Interest in technology and modern concepts could be discerned in the West Coast's influence on housing design. Western ranch houses were characterized by their single-story, basementless, and flat-roof configuration. Such designs developed because they were climatically suited to California, but evolution in heating and cooling technology also made it possible to transfer these trendsetting designs to other climates. The popularity of the ranch home grew throughout this period, as the design developed such features as pitched eaves, large expanses of glass, a low profile, and a rambling floor plan. Architectural historian Gwendolyn Wright points to a primary influence on these ranch homes: "These relaxed, comfortably styled homes may be seen as a modification of Frank Lloyd Wright's Usonian House concepts with the addition of traditional elements: clapboard, shutters and a front porch" (Wright, 1981).

Product Manufacturers

Manufacturers and suppliers form a vital part of the building process. For the most part, they are the only particpants in the homebuilding industry with sizable investments in facilities and production equipment. But their greater, more important role has been in the development and the promotion of new products that contribute significantly to cost reduction.

One of the well-known products that revolutionized homebuilding is the prefabricated roof trusses, which forever changed the way roofs on wood-frame buildings were constructed. The development of gypsum wallboard altered the way interior walls are finished by eliminating the need for cumbersome plastering, saving labor costs, and shortening construction time. Another notable example of significant cost savings for labor and materials was a result of the invention of the plywood board. It altered the way roofs and exterior walls, as well as interior subfloors, were constructed by enabling coverage of large surfaces at a fraction of the cost and time.

Construction costs can, therefore, be reduced by employing new techniques or materials. Products, tools, and new technologies, however, are continuously invented. Some inventions hold promise, but they require time to be accepted by mainstream builders before they will generate the economy of scale that contributes to significant savings. However, caution has to be exercised, as past experience shows that a "miracle product" has sometimes resulted in failures that necessitated replacement or additional expenses.

The User

Users of affordable housing may live in a publicly funded project or buy a market home. Yet their ultimate concerns may be identical to other homeowners—to reside in an adequate and safe home. The user's identity and needs may or may not be known to the project's initiator at the time of design and construction. In a custom-designed project, knowing the user's budget and personal tastes will help guide design decisions. In a subsidized project or a privately initiated, multiunit dwelling project, where the occupants are unknown, design decisions will have to be based on assumptions and perhaps fit to the owner's needs during or after construction.

For a homebuyer, the purchase of an affordable home will typically involve the greatest single outlay of a household's financial resources. Home purchase, however, includes more than an economic dimension. The home and its location, more than any other factors, play a major role in determining the day-to-day quality of life experienced by a household. The homebuying process itself is a complex one, especially for people with limited means and more restricted choices. Several factors are involved in such a process. They include the physical characteristics of the dwelling, the location, and the corresponding social connotations; the physical features of the home, such as size and architectural style; and the characteristics of the household itself, such as life-cycle stage, number of family members, and wealth. These factors will combine to influence the home's purchase and use. Once purchased and moved into, the home is likely to affect many household decisions, at least in the period following occupancy. It may require the purchase of another car and additional expenses, such as maintenance and upkeep, that were not part of the homeowner's budget before.

THE BUILDING PROCESS

The participants in the housing delivery process can be perceived as a team formed on a short-term basis around a project. This team is established to manage, design, and construct a project on a specific building site. Despite the fact that the team's members are independent, decisions made by each participant affect the entire team. The relationships among the participants usually take the form of contracts, the prime objective of which is to outline what the contributing parties are to deliver and to receive. However, these contracts do not establish the functional division of responsibilities among the parties. In a large housing project, three major contracts are commonly signed. They can be seen as lines of communication between the user and the initiator, the lending institution and the initiator, and the initiator and the project's subcontractor.

Analysis of the housing delivery process as a system demonstrates that a very efficient way of building homes has been established in North America. Millions of units have been built since the mid-1940s, and approximately two million new units are added each year. The system as a whole performs a routine sequence of tasks, which explains its efficiency. Many of the units built are consistent: similar plans, layouts, construction methods, and finishing standards. Roberts (1970) sees the decision-making process that takes place prior to the building of a home as a "closed system" (Figure 1.4). In the for-profit sector, once a builder decides to build, construction starts are rapidly followed by completion and occupancy. Each unit sold generates profits, which then generate capital for the initiation of a new project. The efficiency of the housing delivery process can be demonstrated by examining the communications that take place after the decision to build has been made. Working drawings are simplified, because the trades are familiar with traditional construction techniques; specification of products are brief and need few details, because manufacturers know how their products will be used and design them to fit conventional construction.

Innovation and fundamental change of the above processes are difficult to introduce since they tend to break down a routine process in which the parties are familiar with the tasks they are to perform. The introduction of lower-cost design strategies in a manner that will alter mainstream process will not be welcome and will probably fail. Innovation should be compatible with current industry customs rather than to try to introduce new ones. Innovators need to

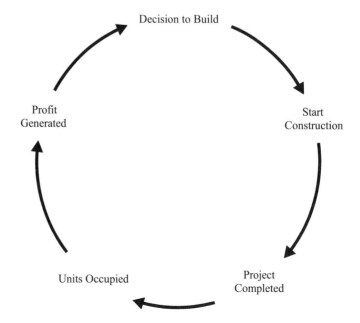

Figure 1.4 The mass housing development process can be regarded as a "closed system," where successes in one project lead to the initiation of the next.

consider the fact that most building firms are small; however, builders will support innovative ideas that are likely to help them either increase profits or save time.

The concepts and terms described in this chapter serve as background for this book. Some of these concepts and terms will be referred to as the various cost-reduction strategies are discussed in the following chapters. Although planning and architecture are the main thrust of this book, one needs to bear in mind that other ways to lower costs must also be explored.

KEY CONSIDERATIONS

- An expenditure of 32 percent of a household's gross annual income on mortgage principal, interest, taxes, and utilities has become a recognized measure of how much people should spend on rented or owned adequate and safe housing.

- The share of small families composed of single persons or single-parent families grew in the past half-century. The households with a single breadwinner had difficulty acquiring the means to purchase a home.

- Homes constructed today have grown significantly in size compared to earlier decades. These homes have also improved in quality and contain more costly finishes, systems, and utilities, making them more expensive.

- New economic realities contributed to the disappearance of job security, which is critical for those who wish to qualify for and obtain a mortgage.

- Fearing the possibility that lower-cost housing might be constructed in their municipality, some cities initiated bylaws that made building affordable homes impossible, fostering "not in my backyard" (NIMBY) sentiments.

- Homeownership is known to benefit the community at large increasing an individual's participation in community life. It also reduces the need of local governments to support senior citizens when their income declines.

- The affordability gap is the difference between the amount a household can afford to pay as a percentage of its income and the actual rent or mortgage payment needed.

- In addition to design and construction, cost reduction in housing can be achieved by altering policy and regulations, creating avenues for innovative financing and tenure, initiating redevelopment and renovation, and ameliorating the project's operation and management.

- Selection of appropriate housing design strategies can contribute to lowering cost or to adding value, which will increase the occupant's pride and satisfaction.

- The key components that determine the cost of a house are land, infrastructure, material, labor, landscaping, financing, professional fees, marketing, taxes, overhead, and profit. Whereas this book will dwell on lowering development and construction costs, known as hard costs, other items, known as soft costs, need to be considered as well.

- The cost of a home is likely to be affected by actions taken by a range of participants in its delivery process. They include governments, financial institutions, initiators, design firms, product manufacturers, and the end user, that is, the buyer or renter.

- The participants in the housing delivery process can be perceived as a team formed on a short-term basis around a project. Despite the fact that the team's members are independent, decisions made by each participant affect the entire team.

2

Selecting a Site

The planning and building of a lower-cost home or an affordable housing project requires careful attention to the monetary implications of each decision. Overall savings will be the result of measures taken throughout the entire process. Selecting a suitable building site holds potential for significant savings. In addition to determining the price of each dwelling, a building site will affect the project's duration and appearance. This chapter will guide the reader through decisions that need to be considered before construction begins. Issues related to location, plot size, need assessment, and zoning will be outlined, followed by a discussion of how to examine the physical properties of the selected site. Additional site issues and their effect on project design will be dealt with in later chapters.

CHOOSING A PROPERTY

Land value is one of the key factors in determining the cost of a home. In most locations, land value will account for 25 percent of the sale price. It has a greater monetary significance when lower-cost homes are planned, and it often determines whether the project will be affordable. In projects initiated by for-profit or nonprofit organizations, the development process will begin by selecting a location and finding out each unit's share of land cost at the outset. Decisions about where to build will be affected by a number of factors (Figure 2.1).

The relationship between location and cost of land has been well-studied by theorists and practitioners. A theory about land location and use was introduced by Johann Heinrich von Thünen, an early nineteenth-century scholar who laid the foundation for regional economics. According to the theory, a farmer's bid for a parcel of land declined as the distance to market increased and, as a result, crop transportation costs increased. Studies that followed also theorized that land would be converted from agricultural to urban use when the economic return from the sale of the land would benefit the farmer more than agriculture (England, 1980).

William Alonso developed a mathematical model of an urban land market. In Alonso's model, a range of economic players competed against each other to own land in the city, where the highest bidder was likely to get the land. The key features of Alonso's model were distance to the city center and expenses one would incur to get there. He therefore valued the central business district (CBD) as having the highest land value and commercial use. The area immediately next to the CBD, plagued by noise and pollution, would commonly be less

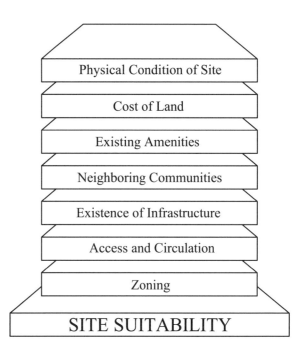

Figure 2.1 Site selection for an affordable housing project will depend on a range of factors.

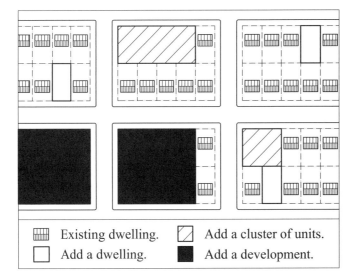

Figure 2.2 To minimize reliance on private cars and to avoid urban sprawl, initiators of affordable housing should locate their project within or next to populated areas.

desired by residents; but the next ring would command a higher land value. The rings that followed were likely to see a decrease in their value (England, 1980).

Choosing a building site for affordable housing corresponds to the above principles. Building on inexpensive land in an outlying suburban area of town is known to have contributed to urban sprawl. Extending transportation links, building on and clearing away valuable agricultural and forested land, and increasing air pollution are some of the well-documented negative effects of sprawl. Yet, at times, building affordable housing can only take place far away from the city center because land costs will be lower.

Choosing to build affordable housing in outlying areas on inexpensive land will impose on homebuyers additional expenses. In addition to paying for their homes, occupants will incur transportation costs. Newly developed areas with fewer homes often do not justify economically the introduction of convenient public transit, forcing residents to rely on their own means of transportation. When the two heads of family work, two cars will be needed, with high fuel and insurance costs. Transportation expenses, therefore, need to be regarded as part of the overall household shelter costs.

The need to curb and manage sprawl led to several initiatives and ideas, intended to see growth take place rationally. *Sustainable development* and *smart growth* projects had higher density, reduced land allocation to roads, heightened conservation of energy and other natural resources, mixed land uses, and provided public amenities within walking distance as some of their main features (Figure 2.2). Those ideas stand not only to benefit society at large but also to bring down the cost of each dwelling by having more units share the same property and utilities.

Lower-cost land for affordable housing can be available on or near the industrial fringes of town. Whether a former factory site, or undeveloped land, what makes the site inexpensive is, unfortunately, its undesirability. Once soil, air, and noise pollutions have been rendered safe and acceptable, careful attention

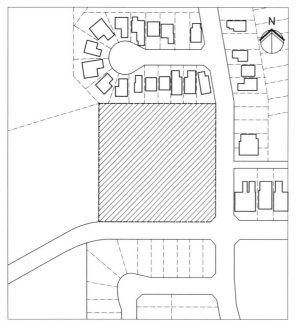

RESIDENTIAL SITE: This site is adjacent to costly single-family homes to the north and semidetached complexes in the east. Residents may oppose the construction of affordable housing in their neighborhood.

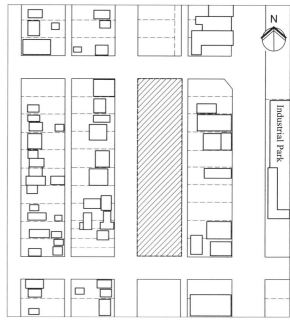

COMMERCIAL/RESIDENTIAL SITE: This site covers a city block and is situated between residential and commercial activities. The land may be inexpensive, yet polluted and noisy.

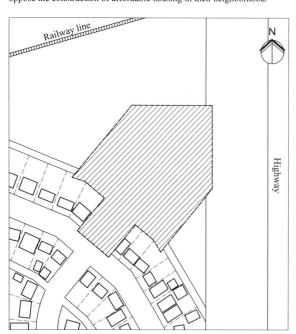

BOUNDED SITE: This site is affordable, because it is bounded by a highway to the east and a railway line to the northwest. It will be noisy and have a limited access.

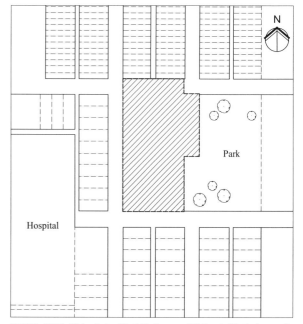

INFILL SITE: This site is affordable because it is located in the heart of a rundown neighborhood. A hospital, elementary school, park, and senior citizen's residential complex are in the vicinity.

Figure 2.3 Each site needs to be evaluated for its suitability for affordable housing based on its merits and demerits.

should be paid to the design itself. In addition to inexpensive land cost, the advantage of such a site will be its proximity to roads and sewage and water lines. Existing industrial buildings on the site can also be converted into affordable units.

The building of affordable housing in populated areas poses a challenge, yet has many advantages. Depending on location, land cost might be expensive, forcing construction of higher density buildings, prompting opposition from local community groups. When the district is rundown, land can be purchased at a lower cost and the project can spark a neighborhood's urban renewal. Building in urban areas, however, is known to be more expensive than building on outlying sites due to the time it takes to negotiate labor and material to the location. Each site, therefore, needs to be evaluated based on its merits and disadvantages (Figure 2.3).

AMENITIES

In addition to the cost of a home, occupants may incur indirect expenses as a result of a lack of amenities in or near a development. *Amenities* is a catchall term that encompasses the services and the community support system a homeowner will need daily and yearly. It includes child care centers, schools, medical clinics, grocery and other shopping centers, and services like a post office, pharmacy, or bank.

Decisions as to which amenities to build are based on the prospective number of users of such facilities, and they are, therefore, a strictly economic venture. New developments built on the urban fringe often do not have enough inhabitants to support such establishments. Several years may pass until the community will grow to justify construction of a school or a shopping center. Such a scenario is unfortunate for buyers of affordable housing. Households made of young, first-time homebuyers with children are most in need of child care centers, schools, and medical clinics. To reach such facilities, they will have to rely on their own transport in the absence of public transit, thereby incurring additional expenses.

As a matter of principle, selecting a site with, or adjacent to, existing amenities is preferred for affordable housing. Conceiving a plan that leaves a place for such facilities to be added in the future is also wise. When a regional master plan is prepared, a proper distribution of such facilities can be made to permit larger numbers of users easy access to them by public transit and to justify their economic viability (Figure 2.4). Developers of affordable housing sites can also verify that the mixed use of residential and commercial areas will be permitted in the future.

Overlapping urban development and transportation networks was the thrust of California-based urban planner Peter Calthorpe's work. "Transit-oriented development" (TOD) is an approach to planning of cities and neighborhoods that attempts to tie them with transportation corridors. Transit nodes are the places where commerce and other amenities are located for the convenience of commuters (Calthorpe, 1993).

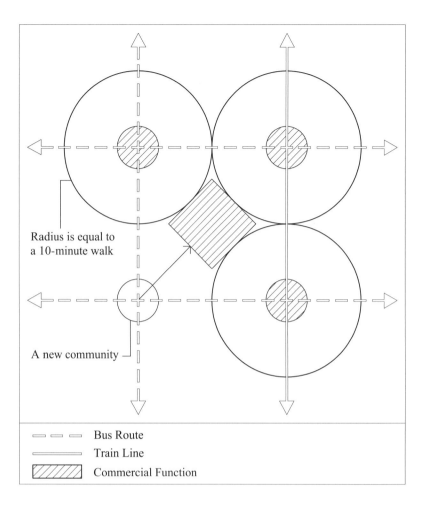

Radius is equal to a 10-minute walk

A new community

Bus Route
Train Line
Commercial Function

Figure 2.4 Locating affordable-housing communities next to existing amenities, enabling easy access to them, or allocating land for their future addition will lead to cost savings for each homeowner.

ADHERING TO ZONING ORDINANCE

Prior to acquiring a site for an affordable housing project, the initiators will have to familiarize themselves with the development process and with relevant zoning codes. When the site is in (or adjacent to) an existing neighborhood, they will also have to determine whether they can expect opposition to their initiative from community groups.

A decision on how to proceed with a new project needs to begin by examining the region's master plan, which outlines the community's own vision of its future. The document designates land-use areas, such as the present and future locations of dwellings, schools, and recreational and shopping facilities, among others. It outlines where future roads will be constructed and which wetlands will be preserved. Developers of affordable housing need to consult the master plan to understand how their project and its future occupants will be affected. Access to basic amenities and public transit will all be paramount in the mind of would-be homebuyers.

Once the project's initiators familiarize themselves with the master plan and its effect on their chosen location, attention is focused on the site itself. Planning can commonly proceed in two ways. The first way adheres to specific zoning reg-

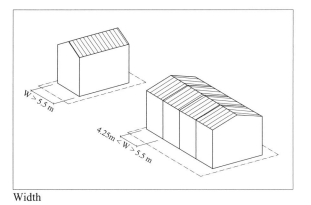

Width

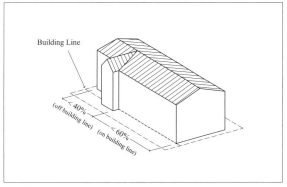

Lot Coverage

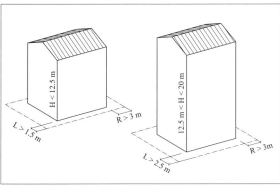

Setback and Height

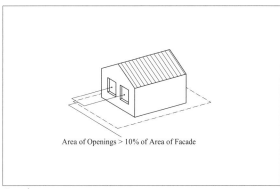

Openings

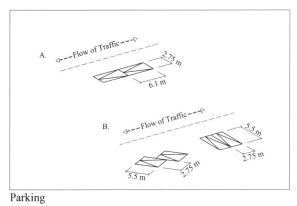

Parking

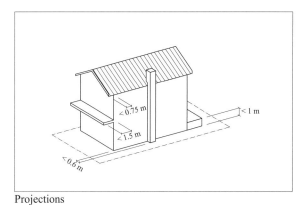

Projections

ulations decreed for the site. The second way is known as "planned unit development" (PUD), or "direct control," and it provides a greater degree of design flexibility to the designer and the municipality.

Zoning allowances affect all design aspects. In the case of affordable housing, zoning will determine the viability of the project. Dwelling density will demonstrate how many residents will share land cost. Zoning will also decree how many parking spaces must be provided per dwelling, road widths, and the exterior cladding material of each home, among other requirements (Figure 2.5). Zoning

Figure 2.5 Each of the illustrated codes and bylaws affect both community planning and dwelling design and, as a result, the cost of each home.

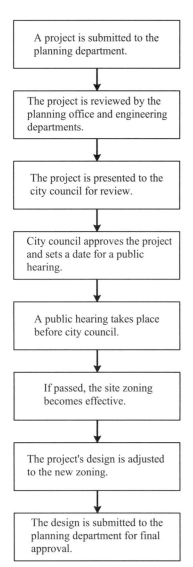

```
A project is submitted to the
planning department.
        │
        ▼
The project is reviewed by the
planning office and engineering
departments.
        │
        ▼
The project is presented to the
city council for review.
        │
        ▼
City council approves the project
and sets a date for a public
hearing.
        │
        ▼
A public hearing takes place
before city council.
        │
        ▼
If passed, the site zoning
becomes effective.
        │
        ▼
The project's design is adjusted
to the new zoning.
        │
        ▼
The design is submitted to the
planning department for final
approval.
```

Figure 2.6 A project review and approval process varies in each location. It has, however, several steps common to many towns. A longer process may also add to the project's cost.

will have direct cost implications that will assist in establishing an initial project budget; these factors determine the cost of each unit.

Even if zoning has been approved for a site, on occasion and with appropriate justification, zoning requirements can be changed. A set process will have to be followed. In most cases, this is a time-consuming procedure that may require a review by the local zoning committee, the drafting of a new bylaw for the site, a formal public hearing, a vote by city council, and the turning of the proposal into legislation. The type of changes that may be required in affordable housing include, for example, an increase in density allowance, reduced road widths and parking standards, or the reduction of lot sizes. Some will be known as minor variances and may proceed faster; others, major variances, will be substantial deviations from the existing bylaws and will take longer to approve (Figure 2.6). In the case of PUD, there will be fewer limitations, yet the plan will have to fit in with considerations of the overall master plan of the area. Significant deviation from the character of already-built dwellings will also encounter opposition by zoning officials and local community groups.

Encountering community resistance to the introduction of affordable housing in or next to an established neighborhood is quite common. The NIMBY (Not In My Back Yard) syndrome—i.e., opposition to development by some in a community—can slow development processes considerably or bring them to a halt. It is, therefore, necessary to elaborate further on the manifestation of the phenomenon and to propose methods of countering or resolving it.

Dear (1992) suggests that typically, a NIMBY conflict follows a three-stage cycle. In the first stage, *youth,* the opponents become aware of a new development, form an organized group, and express their displeasure in private. In the second stage, *maturity,* battle lines solidify. The opponents move the debate to a public forum. The tone becomes more rational, and formal complaints are filed with elected officials and the media. The third stage, *old age,* is the period of conflict resolution; this period is often long. The sides may agree to concessions or one of the sides may gain the upper hand. Past experience demonstrates that the closer residents are geographically to a project, the more vocal they will be. Study of locations of such conflicts shows, however, that inner-city residents are more tolerant and willing to accept change (Dear, 1992). Occupants of single-family homes in suburban areas, on the other hand, will mount strong opposition.

Steps and inquiries, therefore, need to be taken when choosing to build on a controversial site (Jensen, 1984). The project's initiators can find out how organized the neighborhood association is and whether they opposed similar projects in the past. More information can be obtained from the city's planning department. Data can be collected on the history of the site and on attempts to rezone it for other projects. Information also needs to be gathered about the specific concerns of the opposing groups. For the purpose of establishing future lines of communication, it is valuable to know key leaders in the group opposing the project. Knowing the elected representative of the opposing group is useful—that person can act as a liaison and help to reach a middle ground.

At times, community opposition to a project will be strong, rejecting any type of compromise. Yet often a process can be initiated that will lead to a negotiated settlement, with or without amendments. A key feature of the process is communication between the parties. Opposing neighborhood groups may be uninformed about the particularities of the project. Higher-density housing may, in their minds, translate into obstructed views. Information and education sessions, therefore, need to be the first step in the process. Explaining via the media or in public meetings that potential home-buyers of the proposed project are young and lack means to purchase a cost-ly home might affect the outcome.

Presenting the design to a group in a public meeting is another method of mass education. Parking or traffic concerns can be addressed and discussed at that meeting. The project density may be lowered, or the location of a cluster of homes shifted to avoid blocking views. The public green space can be placed next to already-built dwellings to serve as a buffer. Trees can be planted to block noise. Some of these measures may help bring the two sides together. Once the integrity and credibility of the builder has been established, there will be less resistance to the project.

There will also be times when no settlement will be reached and the negoti-ating process will be at risk of collapse. It is the responsibility of the local leader-ship, the city council, or the mayor to convince the opposing party about the effect their actions may have on achieving the greatest good for the community. In recent years, numbers of cities were unable to attract new businesses to their boundaries due to lack of affordable housing. They saw their tax base decline sig-nificantly. Other cities saw young, first-time homebuyers moving away, resulting in communities populated primarily by older people.

NIMBY syndrome and its many facets have become one of the barriers to the production of affordable housing. The need to curb urban sprawl makes it nec-essary to build next to established neighborhoods. Project initiators, therefore, need to be well prepared to encounter opposition. They must argue their case well and engage professional support to help present their concept and case to a doubtful community. The initiators also need to know that the approval may take longer when a project becomes controversial at the outset, and to prepare for this.

NEED ASSESSMENT AND SETTING AFFORDABILITY TARGET

The formal definition of affordable housing designates homebuyers according to the amount that they can allocate to shelter expenses out of their total income. This group of buyers is commonly not monolithic. It can be made of subgroups divided according to their demographic makeup and level of income. *Need assessment* is an evaluation process that helps initiators of for-profit or nonprof-it projects profile their potential buyers and, as a result, know what the proposed design should be for their homes, whether a single unit or an entire community. It can also be a process undertaken by a municipality to find out how many of its citizens are in dire need of affordable housing and whether affordable homes are being produced at all.

Tomalty et al. (2001) group the data sought in need assessment under two main headings: *housing* and *socioeconomic* data. The housing data relates to how the community houses its citizens at present and how active the market is . Each information component can help draw a sketch of the current housing situation. The characteristics and status of the local housing pool can be ascertained by knowing the existing stock and their tenure situation as well as how much of the housing stock is occupied. It will help to determine whether there is a dire need for rental or owned housing. It was often argued that renters constitute the main pool of affordable housing buyers. When rental vacancies decrease and their cost rises, people are more likely to make the move to ownership. Knowing current rental costs can be an indication of how much people will be able to afford as buyers. Studies have demonstrated that renters will often stretch themselves economically and are willing to commit to higher expenses in order to become homeowners (Friedman, 2001).

Valuable data about future design trends can be gathered by knowing the kind of homes that exist in the community. The dwelling standards that home-buyers are accustomed to, such as the number of bedrooms and level of finishes, will all determine the type of proposed products. In certain regions, the practice of selling homes with unfinished interiors is common and accepted. It will be, however, unacceptable in other parts of the country, making homes more expensive. The desired design and construction strategy, the style of the homes, and the community layout can be determined by looking at currently built and sold projects.

Future demand can also be part of the need assessment process. Most municipalities only initiate an affordable housing strategy once the need has arisen. Forecasting market trends needs to be a constant process of policy makers and even for-profit firms. The arrival of major employers with low-paying jobs may draw out-of-town immigrants who will look for low-cost rental or ownership accommodations. The aging of the housing stock is another indication of what the market will be like in the future. If the current stock will require a large investment in rehabilitation, buyers will opt to buy a new home rather than an old one and renovate it.

Socioeconomic data will shed light on the users themselves. It is meant to ensure that the end product will fit the needs and affordability targets of would-be buyers. It will be essential to find the makeup of the household by size and type. It may help to determine, for example, the layout of the proposed homes, the proportion of single-parent households in the district, and the number of people with disabilities or reduced mobility who may require a special design as well as accommodating entranceways to their units. Data about in- or out-migration trends will reveal whether young would-be buyers will leave town to look for housing opportunities in a neighboring city. Knowing the composition of the population by age will also assist in figuring out future housing trends. The result may help determine when the demand will be at its peak.

A question critical to a proposed affordable housing project is how much the units should cost. The cost can be figured out by estimating the dwelling's cost components such as land, infrastructure, and construction. On the demand side, by knowing the level of income of would-be homebuyers, a price range or specific target can be set. When the two figures match, the project will likely respond to a real market need (Figure 2.7). At times, projects are planned and built but end up not providing affordable housing to the group most in need.

Setting affordability targets begins by collecting data about household incomes. Since approximately 32 percent of income is a recommended amount that a family should spend on shelter, one can find out how much would-be homebuyers can spend on housing. The amount of required down payment and

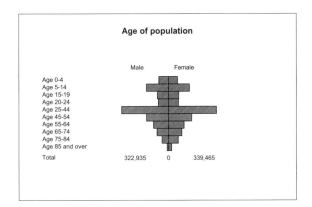

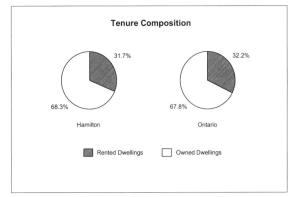

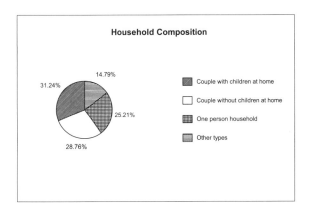

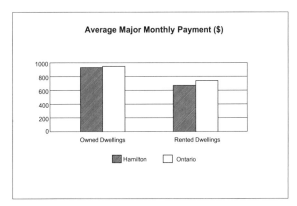

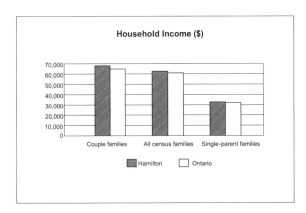

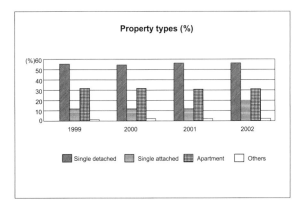

Figure 2.7 A variety of demographic and economic factors needs to be assessed prior to determining a site's suitability for affordable housing and a dwelling's selling price. These charts represent some of the issues that were considered in a Hamilton, Ontario, Canada project.

the interest rate at the time of initiation can help determine what the affordability target will be. As a result, a range of dwelling types and costs can be established. A decision about what to build should arise from an examination of the housing and socioeconomic data gathered. The need will be the result of correlating the data.

Conducting market research is often an activity associated with a government housing authority or with a large building firm. It is assumed that such an activity will be costly and time consuming. This need not be the case. Data required can often be found in easily accessible sources. Income and demographic breakdowns are available on government statistics Web sites. Information about housing trends is made available by housing authorities or real estate associations. It is worthwhile to spend a relatively short amount of time researching income and demographic data to ensure that the project will be affordable for potential buyers.

THE SIZE AND SHAPE OF A SITE

An affordable housing project can be a single home or a development made of numerous units. Prior to the initiation of such a project, questions need to be asked about the effect the size and shape of the considered site will have on cost. Often, the building site is the only one available for a lower-cost project. A vacant lot, for example, will be put up for sale where a need for affordable housing exists. There are, however, times when a builder has a choice between different locations. The size of the project will then have a significant importance in determining the cost. One of the main tools in making a choice between sites will depend upon an *economy of scale*. A larger number of built units will yield discounts on expenses such as materials, labor, and marketing.

The *project life cycle* consists of many steps with a built structure at the process end. The same number of basic steps is needed for a single home or a number of dwellings. Similar trades are also involved in constructing both projects. What differentiates the two is the length of time needed to complete the project. The larger the project, however, the greater the potential for cost savings, due to better management of resources. More units will share the cost of land and infrastructure. There will also be cost savings from purchasing large quantities of building materials as well as from the project's marketing.

It is a challenge, however, to find a large, vacant lot in a densely populated area. Large projects commonly take place away from city centers, and issues related to sprawl need to be considered. It is also difficult to propose an optimal project size for cost-saving purposes. Multifamily dwellings are likely to be cheaper than single-family homes, and a number of built structures will have a greater cost effectiveness than a single structure.

Another factor that influences project cost is the site's shape. Affordable housing sites, primarily in new developments, often have odd shapes. They are built on leftover plots of land at a large site's corner or adjacent to a main traffic artery. They are generally not easy to access and to connect to existing infrastructure. In addition, it is likely that the amount of land devoted to roads and parking will exceed the customary 30 percent of the total site area. Unless the

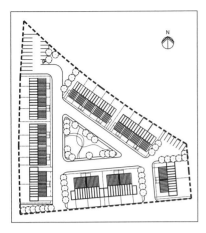 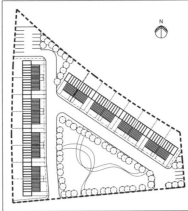 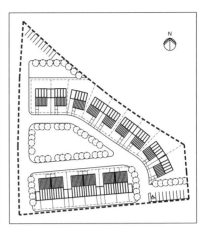

land is very inexpensive, the costs of constructing roads and utilities on the site will render the project unaffordable. In some communities, zoning bylaws will also mandate leaving 10 percent of the site's area for public green spaces. When this amount of land is dedicated, it can reduce the buildable area and further compromise affordability. On the other hand, in the design of a site with an odd shape, unusual corners can become the open public space. To verify what effect the site's shape will have on the cost, the designer needs to study alternative planning approaches and their effect on cost (Figure 2.8). It must be noted that location of main access roads to the site as well as points of connection to the infrastructure will play a significant role in evaluating the site's design efficiency.

When the planning of a large housing development is undertaken, the designer will have to consider the amount of time that it will take to construct the project. Often, depending on market cycles, it can take a number of years for the entire project to be built. During that time, market conditions may change. The demographic makeup of would-be homebuyers will be different than the ones anticipated when the units were proposed. Affordability targets may also be shifted. Buyers with lower or higher incomes will have to be sought, or the dwellings themselves will have to be redesigned since they will no longer respond to the space needs and lifestyle of the available buyers.

Not every site has a potential to accommodate new and emerging trends and needs. Verifying that the site will permit future planning flexibility is essential in large projects since the initiators may have unsold land or units leading to cost increases. An approach to design for flexibility will be to verify first whether a local municipality will be open to later changes of a master plan. The next step will be to divide the site into several subplots, each equal to the number of units that can be sold and constructed in a year or two. Introducing circulation networks for the entire site will then take place, followed by proposing design guidelines for the entire community and the homes (Friedman, 2002a). The objective will be to ensure that despite changes to the dwelling types, the entire community will have a unified appearance. Such a process will enable the development to withstand changes as a result of ongoing socioeconomic, technological, and environmental shifts (Figure 2.9).

Figure 2.8 Prior to the acquisition of a site with an odd shape, the designer needs to study alternative planning approaches and their effect on cost.

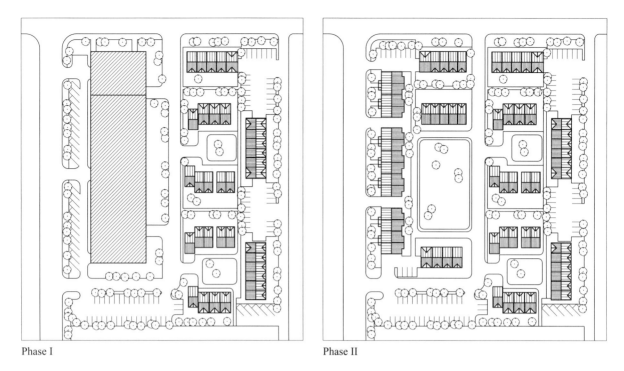

Phase I   Phase II

Figure 2.9 The designer of this project anticipated and prepared for the demolition of an industrial building and the addition of more affordable housing units.

THE SITE'S NATURAL CONDITION

When selecting a building site, the property's natural conditions need to be verified prior to acquisition. Aspects such as soil composition, topography, presence of ground water, vegetation, and orientation will affect design and cost. In an affordable housing project, these issues ought to be given a greater priority. Gains made by purchasing an inexpensive lot can be offset by additional investments in site preparation. The following discussion is meant to help initiators and designers of affordable housing projects to verify what should be their main concerns when selecting a site.

Soil Condition

The word *soil* is commonly used to describe all the fragmented materials in the crust of the earth (Legget, 1966). It includes materials ranging from sand and gravel to fine clay, all of which were derived from solid rock. Each region has its own types of soils that require engineers to adapt foundation designs and the backfill method to the characteristics of these soils. When considering a building site, an initiator should not be deceived by its attractive appearance. Even a pristine greenfield site may pose a soil challenge. With increasing land costs, small building firms often purchase leftover lots, not realizing that more expenses will be needed when design and construction begin.

In general, it makes sense to stay away from sites with soils that "will not adequately support a building through its life or that may damage a structure through soil movement or flooding" (Pope, 1984). Prior to purchasing a site, one therefore needs to follow some steps to ensure that there is nothing wrong with the property. If the site remains unbuilt in a mostly populated area, suspicion needs to arise as to the reason. In a rural area, professionals need to be consulted and soil tests done. Information can also be obtained by inquiring locally about the site's history.

When one is considering soil types suitable for construction, common knowledge is that rock "does not usually present a problem in construction of single family dwellings unless it rests on a fault" (Pope, 1984). A fault occurs where there have been shifts in the earth level as a result of earthquakes, for example. Building on organic soils, those that have been shifted as a result of glacier movements or landslides must be avoided. Examining an aerial photograph of raw land may help spot such a situation.

Groundwater

When rain falls, some of it will flow along the ground into a storm sewer and, on the surface, into lakes, rivers, and eventually into the sea. Some of it, however, will filter into the ground. Other portions will be held close to the topsoil, yet most of it will flow until it reaches a larger body of water that has been accumulating underground from previous rainfalls. This reservoir of water held underground is called *groundwater* (Legget, 1982).

The top of the underground body of water is also known as the *water table.* Whether in a contained state or flowing into a large body of water, underground water on-site will have a costly consequence on foundation design and maintenance. Therefore, when the water table is elevated, the purchase of the site must be reconsidered. Building a home under such a condition will require special piling or careful attention to damp-proofing the foundation to prevent dampness in the basements. Presence of a high water level will also contribute to future ground settlement and, as a consequence of the building process itself, construction faults.

Flood Plains

The lower cost of sites that are located in flood areas may be at times attractive to builders of affordable housing. The wisdom of building on them should be carefully considered before a decision to purchase the site is made. A *flood zone* is an area located adjacent to a river or lake. In springtime when snow and ice are melting rapidly or when there is a heavy rainfall, the area may become flooded. Pope (1984) describes flood-prone areas as one-zone or two-zone. *One-zone* is the land that can be covered by water in a hundred-year flood that can effectively happen at any time. The *two-zone* is the area on which the water streams on its way to zone one, and it can be a more risky area to build.

Each year, extensive and costly damage is reported across North America due to flooding. Building affordable housing in such zones is not advisable because often residents cannot afford the necessary insurance, and they will be bound to lose everything. Most municipalities and national authorities have maps in which they designate areas with the greatest building risks and lands to be avoided altogether. Prior to the site's acquisition, it would be wise to consult such documents. If the site nonetheless poses a splendid building opportunity, the initiator will inquire if measures have been taken to prevent disasters by local authorities.

Slopes

Most building sites are not evenly leveled. Their slopes provide opportunity for creative design through interesting views and grading. There are times, however, when the slopes will exceed a certain norm, leading to additional expenses in fitting the buildings to the site. Slopes of 0 to 8 percent are generally considered optimal for roads and pedestrian paths. In fact, 2- to 8-percent grades work best for buildings (Devereaux and Bedford, 1991), that is, if appropriate grading measures are taken for drainage. Slopes of 5 to 10 percent will be more suitable for small detached homes due to the planning flexibility that they provide. When the slope exceeds 10 percent, site design will be more restricted (Figure 2.10). When larger structures are considered for the site, fitting them will be more expensive. The homes will have to be "broken up" according to the elevation, leading to more complicated and costly designs.

Row housing, known to be cheaper to construct than a detached home will, therefore, incur additional costs. One can also expect higher development costs as roads, complex in elevation, will have to be built and properly drained. In the conception of landscaping plans, one will also have to ensure that rainfall from one lot will not flow into an adjacent lot. It is therefore recommended that when an affordable project is contemplated for a site with a significant slope that the costs of fitting the design to the site be figured out in advance.

Brownfield Sites

The term *brownfield site* refers to lands that have been previously used by industry. Be it a vacant lot or an abandoned building, activities that took place on those properties might have contaminated either the soil or the building. Soil testing and auditing of the site according to standards set by environmental

Figure 2.10 When the site's slope exceeds 10 percent, the homes must be designed to the unique characteristics of each plot of land.

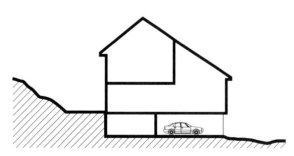

With a gradient of 15 percent, this home is built with a wide and shallow floor plan. A garage is built into the landscape to pick up grade.

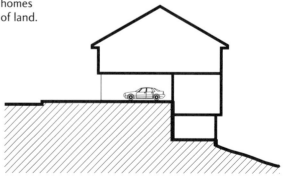

With a gradient of 20 percent, this home takes advantage of the grade change with an entry at grade and space built into the down slope of the house.

Figure 2.11 Abandoned industrial building sites are often considered for affordable housing development. The buildings may be demolished or converted once their environmental suitability is verified.

agencies will most likely be needed before new uses can be proposed. Building on such a site will require replacing the topsoil to a depth found in a test. The sites, often located in close proximity to services and utilities, are frequently eyed by initiators of affordable housing projects. However, precautions need to take place since cleaning costs will not render the building affordable once construction has ended (Figure 2.11).

In the case of an industrial building, conversion to affordable dwelling units has been attempted in North America on several occasions. It was often demonstrated that unless the structure is in good condition and requires minor repair, it rarely yields low-cost dwellings. Replacing old windows, introducing new stairs and elevators, and rebuilding roofs and utilities will surpass the cost of building a new structure. Savings, however, can be obtained by not having to build new access roads, since the projects are often located in an urban area where roads already exist. In recent decades, governments set grants to support building on brownfields; when used, the grants can contribute to the lowering of the project cost.

Flora and Fauna

In addition to the site's soil composition and grading, the natural coverage will affect development costs. Natural coverage is also referred to as *wetlands*. Petrowski (1999) explains that "Wetlands, whether adjacent to salt or fresh water are broadly defined by the vegetation that is found on them, not by the presence of standing water." In past decades, wetlands have become all that remain for building in many areas. These sites hold potential for attractive community design due to their natural beauty. By law, wildlife and trees will have to be kept, and altering the terrain is prohibited. The cost of preserving a portion of the land may increase the cost of each dwelling unit, making it unaffordable.

On the other hand, since land developers are reluctant to develop wetlands sites, such sites may be sold at a much lower cost. Creative design can take advantage of the site's natural conditions. High-density housing may be built, for example, on a portion of the site leaving the rest as green public space. The site, therefore, needs to be examined carefully before design proceeds.

Appropriate Microclimate

Each region has its own unique climatic characteristic. The site may also be affected by factors associated with its location, orientation, and landscape. Appropriate planning may lead to energy conservation in each dwelling and, as a result, to substantial savings in upkeep costs. Prior to selecting a site, the design team will have to figure out in which direction most of the homes can be oriented. The east-west direction will expose the dwelling's longer elevation to the southern sun, enabling passive solar gain. Wind direction can also be of crucial importance as cold wind can lower the home's temperature in winter. When trees grow on the site, their importance in blocking drifting snow and wind can also be studied. Designs that consider the site's microclimate can lead not only to money savings but also to greater comfort (Figure 2.12).

Proximity to Existing Infrastructure

The cost of infrastructure, which is often included with development cost, forms a significant part of the project's overall cost. When selecting an affordable housing site, existence or proximity to infrastructure must be one of the first issues to verify. Infrastructure includes roads and utilities as well as fresh water pipes, drains, electricity, and the like. It will be desirable, therefore, to select a site within an existing development or adjacent to one. Connection costs will be lower than extending services to a site located on undeveloped land away from already

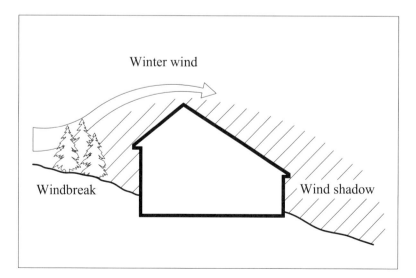

Figure 2.12 Climatic considerations and integration of natural features in the design of homes and communities will contribute to energy savings.

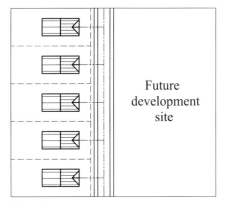

Future development site

Phase I

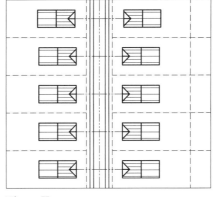

Phase II

Figure 2.13 Proximity to existing infrastructure will facilitate future connection and lower the cost of each dwelling.

developed areas. New roads will have to be constructed and costly utilities included with them (Figure 2.13).

Municipalities commonly pay for the services linking the new development to the old section of town. Extending the infrastructure from the main road into the development and within the development itself will be paid for by the project's initiator, who will include the expenses in the cost of the dwellings.

Building on undeveloped land on the fringe of town can yield savings through the lower cost of such land; yet these savings may be offset when the cost of building the infrastructure is factored in. It also brings to the forefront the negative economic implication of sprawl. Once built, roads and other utilities will have to be maintained at mounting costs. Building denser neighborhoods not only fosters environmental sustainability, it also helps keep costs down for the entire community.

KEY CONSIDERATIONS

- To lower household expenses and a reliance on private cars and to prevent urban sprawl, initiators of affordable housing should locate their projects within or next to populated areas, amenities, and public transit routes.
- An infill site in a rundown neighborhood may benefit from lower land cost and existing infrastructure, and it may also spark urban renewal.
- A "planned unit development" (PUD) design process will offer the designer greater flexibility in decision making and, therefore, more opportunities for cost reductions.
- To avoid conflicts arising from NIMBY sentiments, prior to the start of the project, its initiators should research the site's history, the level of organization of the neighborhood association, the area's elected representatives, and the chance that a negotiated settlement can be reached with any of the opposing groups.
- Prior to the start of a project, its initiators should conduct need assessment research to ensure that the project outcome will respond to the needs of the area's target population and fit the affordability level of would-be buyers.

- The initiators should pay particular attention to housing data that shows how the community houses its citizens and to any socioeconomic data that will shed light on the users themselves.
- When considering a design for a small site with an odd shape, questions need to be asked about how the size and configuration affect the cost. After area is deducted for roads, parking, and open space, there may not be enough land left to create affordable dwellings.
- In general, it makes sense to stay away from sites with soils that "will not adequately support a building throughout its life or that may damage a structure through soil movement or flooding" (Pope, 1984). Building on organic soils, that is, soils that have shifted as a result of glacier movement or landslides, must be avoided.
- The purchase of a site with a high water table must be reconsidered as the need for special foundations and damp-proofing basements may make units too expensive.
- The purchase of a site located in or near a flood zone should be reconsidered despite the land's low cost. Prior to any site's acquisition, the project initiator should consult appropriate maps to verify that the site is not prone to floods.
- Sites with 5- to 10-percent slopes will be more suitable for small detached homes because they allow greater planning flexibility. Steeper slopes will produce higher foundation costs.
- When considering design for a brownfield site, the initiator needs to verify whether the cost of cleaning the site will allow for affordable homes.
- When considering design for an area with a large wetland, the site's flora can become part of the project's public open space.
- Selecting a site with appropriate location, orientation, and terrain can contribute to energy conservation for each dwelling. Siting homes in an east-west direction will expose the dwelling's longer elevation to the southern sun, enabling passive solar gain.
- The site's proximity to existing infrastructure will lead to substantial savings, because the cost of roads and basic utilities will then be avoided.

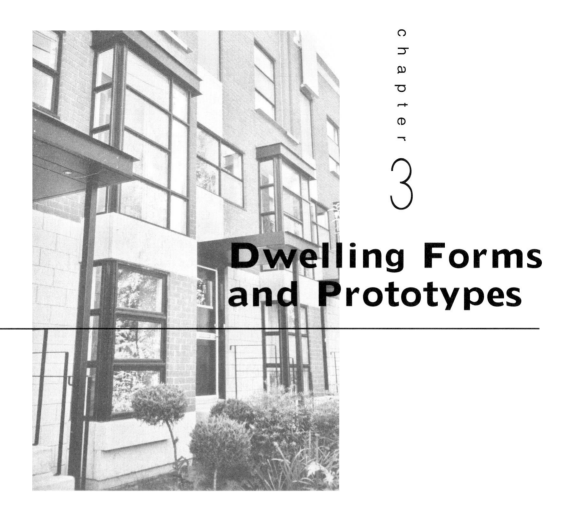

Dwelling Forms
and Prototypes

hoosing a dwelling type is one of the fundamental building blocks of
any residential design process. What to build will depend on a need
assessment or the initiator's familiarity with the site and the clients.
In an affordable housing project, the choice of homes and their price will
relate to the future occupants' income, which will help define a target cost.
In addition to cost considerations, zoning bylaws, demographic makeup,
and cultural norms will also influence the chosen prototype. This chapter
examines issues related to the choice and design of low-rise, wood-frame
homes and their effect on cost. Following a description of the houses' form,
the manner of attachment to one another, and the relationship to the
ground as well as roof design are explored. Then, selected examples of
dwelling types are described and analyzed. The discussion ends with a look
at residential transformation and accessory structures.

FORM

In an affordable housing project, land, infrastructure, and construction costs, among others, will have to be brought down to lower the overall price of each home. These reductions will all have to be made without compromising comfort and livability. Lowering the dwelling's cost will be achieved through efficient use of all material and nonmaterial resources by simplifying the building complexity. Issues related to the dwelling's design and its configurations are listed here (Figure 3.1).

One of the principal issues to affect cost in home and community design is the dwelling's form. Width, length, and height, as well as overall geometry, will likely depend on zoning bylaws. Regulations setting density, land coverage, and setbacks will influence the final design. The chosen dimensions will have a significant effect on cost since they will determine land and infrastructure expenses. The chosen width of a home will be the result of design and construction considerations. Design issues will be affected by the chosen dwelling type, form, and condition of attachment to other dwellings, which will be further outlined below.

Commonly, the proportions of the dwelling's footprint can be either square or rectangular. The interior of a home with a square plan is easier to subdivide. As well, detached units offer greater flexibility in the placement of windows. The disadvantage of a square plan, depending on proportions, is the need for a larger plot of land and, as a result, costly infrastructure.

Guiding interior design considerations in a rectangular, narrow front design will be the number of bedrooms that can be placed on a floor. Two bedroom plan categories can, therefore, be introduced: one bedroom and two adjacent bedrooms. The width of a floor for a single bedroom occupying the dwelling's entire width can range from 12 feet (3.7 meters) to 14 feet (4.3 meters). The footprint of the floor needed to accommodate two adjacent bedrooms will range from 18 feet (5.5 meters) to 20 feet (6.1 meters) (Figure 3.2).

The length of a dwelling will depend on a number of factors as well. In a typical North American subdivision, the common length of a lot is 100 feet (30

Figure 3.1 Aspects considered in this chapter for their effect on the cost of housing.

Form	The chosen geometry and proportions (width, length, height) a dwelling has.
Attachment	The relationship that a dwelling will have to an adjacent unit (detached, attached) and its method of attachment.
Ground Relation and Roof Design	The way the building is placed on the ground, how the roof is designed and used, and the effect of both on cost.
Typology	A chosen dwelling type, either single-family (bungalow, rancher) or multifamily (duplex, triplex).
Transformation	The way the dwelling's original shape can be altered by addition or conversion to other uses and spatial arrangements.
Accessory Structure	Any structure (garage, granny flat) that exists on the property, attached to or detached from the main dwelling unit.

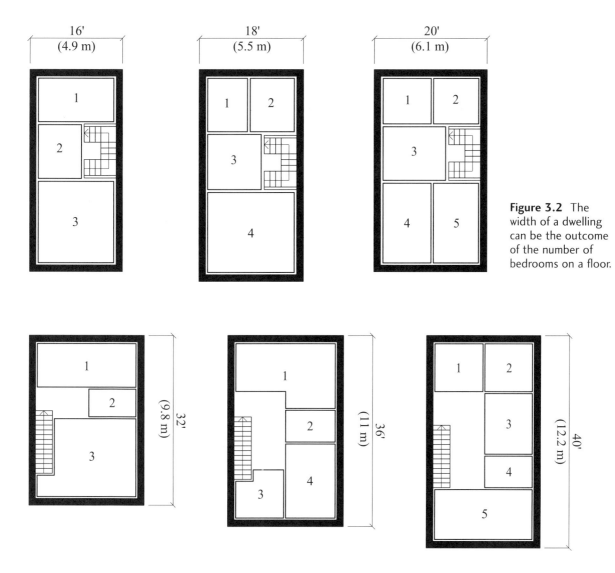

Figure 3.2 The width of a dwelling can be the outcome of the number of bedrooms on a floor.

Figure 3.3 The length of a dwelling will depend on the number of functions that are placed in a row on the floor, either on the lower or upper level.

meters). When front and rear setbacks are considered, they will determine the length of a dwelling. In "planned unit development" (PUD), the length of a structure will be at the designer's discretion, but they will be based in the expected functions of such a unit. When a narrow unit is designed, placing one or two rooms at one end of a bedroom floor and one or two at the other end will be a design option. The middle section of the unit can accommodate the service areas of the floor, such as stairs and bathroom. In the lower floor, placement of kitchen, dining area, and living room will be the determining criteria for the unit length (Figure 3.3). In a narrow unit, when the length that the kitchen, dining, and living functions comfortably occupy is calculated, the overall length of the unit can be as short as 32 feet (9.8 meters) to 40 feet (12 meters). The length of a dwelling can also be affected by the decision about where parking will be located. Indoor parking may require a longer footprint, whereas the length can be shorter when the parking arrangement is outdoors.

The dwelling's footprint will also affect the overall cost of a home and its appearance; therefore, the shape of the dwelling ought to be decided early in the

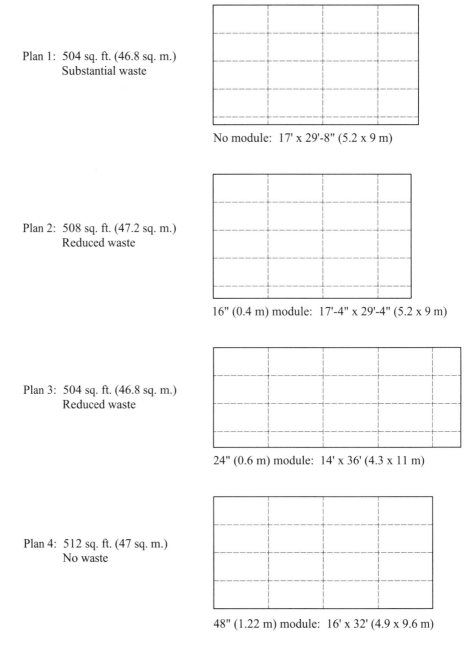

Plan 1: 504 sq. ft. (46.8 sq. m.)
Substantial waste

No module: 17' x 29'-8" (5.2 x 9 m)

Plan 2: 508 sq. ft. (47.2 sq. m.)
Reduced waste

16" (0.4 m) module: 17'-4" x 29'-4" (5.2 x 9 m)

Plan 3: 504 sq. ft. (46.8 sq. m.)
Reduced waste

24" (0.6 m) module: 14' x 36' (4.3 x 11 m)

Figure 3.4 Modular dimensioning of a floor footprint with a similar area can lead to material savings. Eliminating unnecessary corners can save on both labor and materials.

Plan 4: 512 sq. ft. (47 sq. m.)
No waste

48" (1.22 m) module: 16' x 32' (4.9 x 9.6 m)

process. A common way to reduce material use and heat loss is by simplifying the unit's configuration. A more complex building form requires more corners and a greater perimeter, which in turn will require more "skin," or building surface. This results in higher construction costs and increased heat loss. Generally, the ratio of floor area to perimeter should be maximized. Another simple and effective way to reduce material waste is through careful dimensioning of the building to accommodate the modular configuration of materials. At the most basic level, designing within standard dimensions for structural framing members, such as studs, joists, and plywood, could result in substantial savings. Designing for 4-foot (1.2-meter) modules and 24-inch (610-millimeter) stud spacing alone can reduce lumber use by 8 percent (Figure 3.4). Providing for efficient details at corners and intersections of exterior walls and interior partitions could double these savings. With more careful planning and material selection, the same principle could be implemented to accommodate interior finishes such as drywall and floor tiles. Cost savings are achieved through not only efficient use of materials but reduced labor requirements, since less cutting and fitting will be required.

The building's height and the chosen number of floors will be subject to zoning bylaws and will affect the project's cost. While the vertical distribution of a unit's floor area will have the greatest impact on land-use efficiency and housing density, it can also have a substantial effect on the building materials used and, to some extent, the energy efficiency of the building. Vertical designs make the most efficient use of space, since more stacking of essentially the same design units uses fewer construction materials. The cost of a two-story, square house, for instance, is lower than a one-story house of equivalent area, since it has half the foundation and roof area. Floor-to-floor heights, which are affected by such factors as floor thickness, will also affect the amount of raw materials used, especially in the building envelope, that is, the exterior wall.

The form of the envelope's surface is another aspect worth considering. When a building has a number of projections—the upper floor extends beyond the lower, for example—costs are bound to rise. Projections, therefore, need to be introduced where they are most needed. Providing a cover above an entry door or creating a suspended bay are functional uses for a projection. One also needs to bear in mind that the floor of a projected area must be well insulated to prevent infiltration of cold air in wintertime.

ATTACHMENT

When the density of an affordable housing project increases, the cost per unit declines. Attaching units to each other, therefore, serves an important role in achieving affordability. When considering methods and forms of attachment, designers need to pay attention to the project's budget, appearance, and livability. The reason for attaching dwelling units to each other is to give occupants the sense that they live in a lower-density setting than they do. Placing the units close to the street will save on the cost of extending utilities. The method of connecting the utilities to each unit will depend on the legal title of the project. When the project is sold as a condominium, only one connection will be needed from the main utility source to a block of units. When the project is sold as a *freehold,* separate connections will have to be made to each unit, thereby increasing the cost.

An important consideration in attaching low-rise units will be the amount of, and access to, outdoor space. Depending on the plot and chosen housing configuration, there can be common outdoor space, private arrangements, or a combination of both. The method of attaching units can influence that choice. The chosen method and form of attachment may also influence how parking will be arranged and, as a result, the appearance of the project as a whole.

The dwelling's exposure to natural light will be affected by the way the homes are attached. Certain attachment forms will limit the number of walls on which windows can be placed. Units in shadow or partial shade may be a result of staggered units, for example. Attachment can affect aspects related to privacy. Noise transmission is likely to increase when units are attached, and affordable construction practices may not include superior sound insulation. Greater attention also needs to be paid to safety issues. When fire breaks out in one of the dwellings it can easily spread to the next. Therefore, firewalls need to be constructed between units and, in multifamily projects, additional exits provided. Due to their compact form, attached dwellings offer better energy efficiency and greater savings on building materials. Joined units offer less façade from which to lose heat; therefore, the occupants will benefit from lower heating bills.

Detached Homes

Detached homes are the most common type of dwelling in North America. A detached home on a large plot of land attracts homebuyers who enjoy privacy, ample outdoor space, and self-contained living. Yet many of the attributes that make such a home attractive to homebuyers also contribute to their higher cost. Mounting land and service costs forced designers to consider still detached but narrower lots and homes. The detached design provides an opportunity to reduce the size of the home to as narrow as 18 feet (5.5 meters) wide. The homes, built on narrow lots, have small side setbacks. The home can be placed on the lot line to increase the distance between dwellings. Parking will be a prime consideration in small-lot design. When front, indoor parking is provided, the project—with a row of garage doors—may contribute to a poor streetscape. It is, therefore, recommended that parking be placed at the rear, either on a private or common lot with lane access.

Linked Housing

One can take advantage of the small space left between detached dwellings. Linking them in the front or at the rear creates a row effect, yet a portion of the area between the units will remain open, creating a feeling of detached housing. The element that links the buildings can be a carport, a garage, or even an entrance to one or both units. A side entry will leave more free area for placement of windows along the front façade. The link can be a one-story structure, or it can be provided as an upper-floor expansion area. When carports or parking garages are constructed, they can be designed to allow top additions (Figure 3.5).

Semidetached

When two structures share a common wall, they are known as semidetached. The advantage of such an arrangement is in the savings of land, infrastructure, and wall construction. The lot area can be reduced by as much as 18 percent and the exterior wall perimeter costs reduced by a third (Canada Mortgage and Housing Corporation, 1981). In addition, each dwelling will enjoy the sense of privacy and independence apparent in a detached home. Greater privacy can be achieved by placing entrances to units in different locations. Side entrances will free more living and wall space for longer windows at the unit's front façade (Figure 3.6).

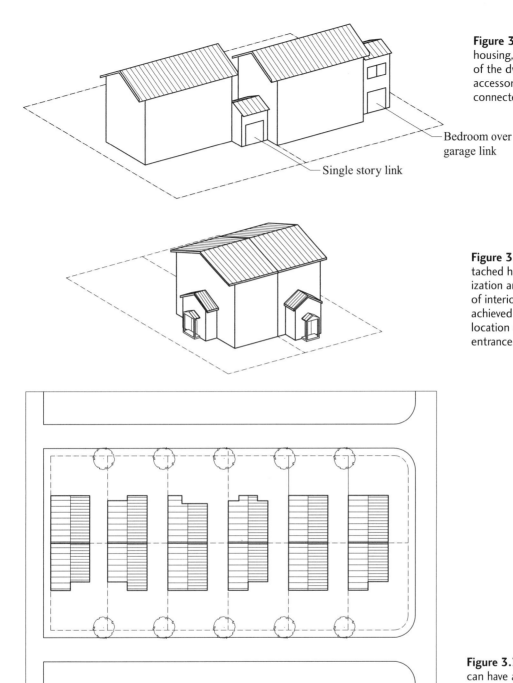

Figure 3.5 In linked housing, only a portion of the dwelling or an accessory structure is connected to the next.

— Bedroom over garage link

— Single story link

Figure 3.6 In a semidetached home, personalization and efficient use of interior space can be achieved by varying the location of the front entrance.

Figure 3.7 Dwellings can have a rear attachment.

Semidetached structures can be made of two single-family or multifamily homes of any type. In multifamily arrangements, the main concern will be the placement of entrances, stairs, and parking. In some prototypes, the basement or the ground floor can be the location of indoor parking for the occupants of the second and third floors. Units can also be joined at the rear. The advantage here is land savings, since the joint lot can be shallow as the traditional backyard no longer exists (Figure 3.7). Two units, therefore, can be placed on a single, narrow lot with streets on either side.

To further reduce the lot's width, the two homes can be "zipped" into each other. The dwelling's interior will have an L-shape. Entrances to the two structures, which can be any type of housing, may be at the front or one can be from the front and the second from the rear. Due to the dwelling's narrow width, front indoor parking is difficult to accommodate. It can be provided outdoors next to the unit or preferably at the rear when a lane is planned (Figure 3.8).

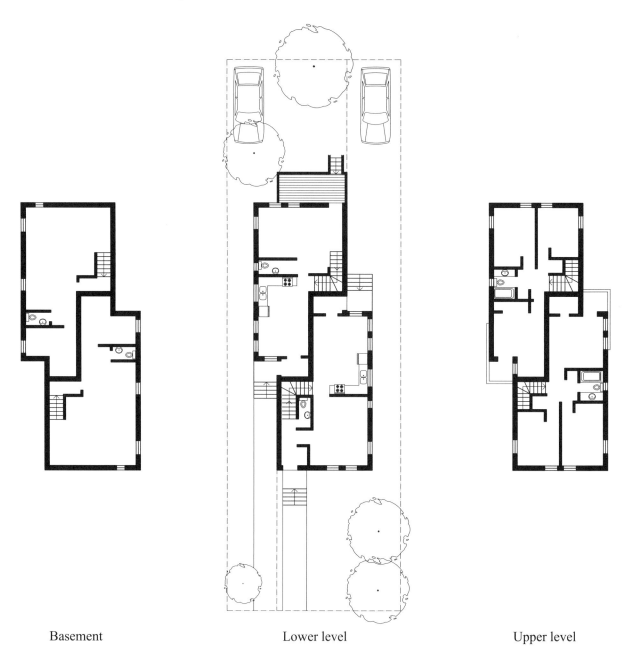

| Basement | Lower level | Upper level |

Figure 3.8 Floor plans of a single-family dwelling in a zipper-lot configuration.

Row

When more than two dwelling units are attached, the resulting building is known as *row housing*. Building residences in rows can be traced back to ancient settlements. Highly valued land within walled cities mandated high-density dwellings. Since property taxes were often charged according to the structure's width, row housing traditionally was designed with narrow frontages. The "compact" qualities of row-house arrangements give them an economic advantage. Yet they constitute a design challenge when parking and privacy solutions are sought.

The main advantage of row housing is how it saves on land and infrastructure costs. Simply put, the more joined-together units, the greater the savings will be. Joining the units results in a 33 percent savings in lot area and street length, and 70 percent savings in the exterior wall perimeter (CMHC, 1981) (Figure 3.9). When designing row housing, a question arises as to the preferred number of attached units. Some European and North American cities have block-long rows of homes. However, residential developments with very long rows often present a poor streetscape. The monotonous repetition of façades and cars parked in front have stigmatized row housing in the past. Experience shows that joining between 4 and 8 units no wider than 20 feet (6 meters) each will be a recommended number in a row. The decision about how many units to join will also depend on the number of stories, the type of roof, and the street width.

When the façades of aligned units are identical, the effect on the street can be highly monotonous. Options are available to break this monotony by varying the façades or staggering the units. Staggering units can also contribute to greater front or rear privacy. When the units are staggered, however, it is likely that the foundation will be more complex to construct and thus more costly. Each dwelling will have more corners, and the roof is also bound to be more elaborate to build (Figure 3.10).

No. of attached units		Land	Infrastructure	Construction
(4)		1.00	1.00	1.000
(6)		1.07	1.07	1.009
(8)		1.11	1.11	1.014

Figure 3.9 Joining more units will lower land, infrastructure, and construction costs for each dwelling.

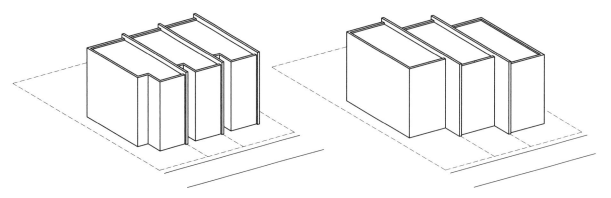

Figure 3.10 To avoid monotony and to increase privacy when joining dwellings, a variety of siting arrangements can be chosen.

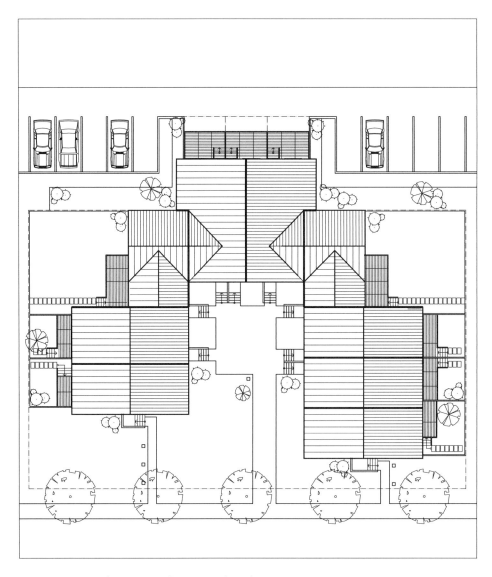

Figure 3.11 Row housing can be arranged as clusters.

Placing units in a row can be done in a variety of compositions. The objective of the varied arrangements is to use costly land and infrastructure efficiently, increase livability, and provide opportunities for personalization. One such arrangement creates a row of interlocked homes. As noted above, parking can become a challenge in such an arrangement.

In considering the length and composition of the row, a possibility exists to mix housing types. The end units in a row of six or eight buildings, for example, can be multifamily structures, whereas the middle units can be single-family homes. It will allow the offering of a range of units and, as a result, the targeting of households with a variety of affordability levels. Another type of row housing is the *cluster*, which is suitable for a PUD. Clusters will likely be built as condominiums, since nonconventional-size plots will be needed and parking must be arranged in common for several clusters (Figure 3.11).

In *checkerboard-housing* arrangements, the dwellings are grouped in a checkered form. They are linked to each other at one end and have open spaces in between them. In addition to the savings gain on land costs, such a plan can provide each dwelling with private outdoor space (Figure 3.12).

One of the most effective ways of reducing energy consumption is by joining units into semidetached or row-housing configurations, since heat losses are limited to fewer exterior walls and a small roof area. Joining four detached units into semidetached units, for instance, reduces the exposed wall area by 36 percent. Grouping all four units as row houses provides an additional 50 percent savings. Heat-loss reductions of approximately 21 percent can be achieved when two dwellings are attached, and a further 26 percent savings for the middle unit

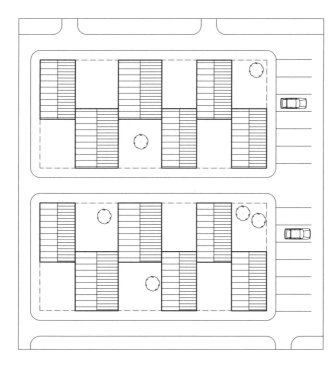

Figure 3.12 The checkerboard residential planning pattern is suitable for higher-density, low-cost housing.

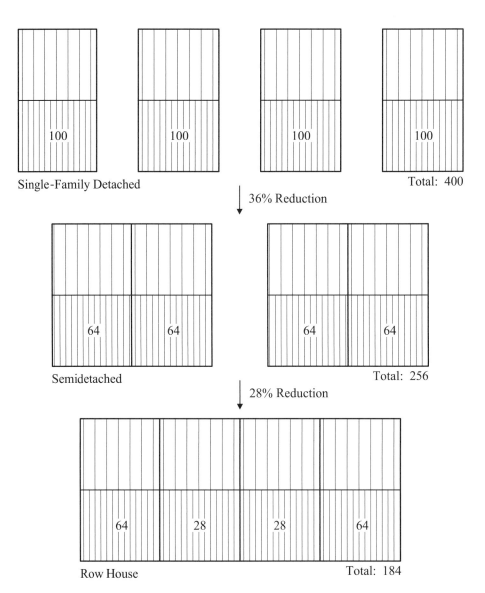

Single-Family Detached

100   100   100   100

Total: 400

↓ 36% Reduction

Semidetached

64   64   64   64

Total: 256

↓ 28% Reduction

Row House

64   28   28   64

Total: 184

Figure 3.13 Energy savings is obtained by joining units. As the exposed façades get smaller, there will be less opportunity for heat to escape.

when three or more dwellings are joined as row houses (Figure 3.13). Grouping units is also an effective way to improve construction efficiency. The repetition usually results in a shorter building period per dwelling. The reduction in perimeter area can have a significant effect on the delivery time, since construction of the envelope is a labor-intensive and costly undertaking.

GROUND AND ROOF

The architectural style of some homes is rooted in local culture and building tradition. Other architectural features have to do with the climatic conditions of a site. Two of these building components are the home's foundation and its roof. Whereas the construction of foundation and roof will be discussed in this chapter, the following section deals with the use of these features.

Ground

Construction of foundations has evolved over the decades. Early-century builders placed rocks on top of each other around the perimeter of the house on which they rested heavy timbers to form the lower floor. Wooden piles formed the foundation in other buildings. The lower floor was slightly raised above ground, creating a crawl space. Building foundations of rocks or timbers often resulted in building failures and settlements, primarily when floods occurred. These problems were solved with the use of concrete, which was rediscovered by Joseph Aspdin in England in 1824 and named *Portland Cement* after the local Portland Lime Stone. The material went on to revolutionize the way buildings were constructed, particularly with the development of reinforced concrete that enabled construction of concrete columns and beams. At the turn of the twentieth century, homebuilders began to use concrete in constructing residential foundations (Allen, 1990).

Because it is an artificial stone, concrete has a disadvantage as a building material: it cracked in below-freezing temperatures under the pressure of expanding frozen soil. As a result, foundation walls had to be extended further below grade to where the soil's temperature is warmer. The depth of the footing on which the foundation wall rests depends on the altitude and location of the building site. In a Nordic climate, where more days with deep freeze temperature are expected, the foundation will be excavated deeper. In warmer southern regions, a shallow foundation will be constructed or the lower floor will be built on grade.

With the evolution of home construction, builders in northern regions realized that when the soil within the perimeter of the foundation is removed, a gain of an entire floor, the basement, can be achieved. The 1940s and 1950s, therefore, saw the proliferation of basements in North American residences and the rise of construction costs. When designing a low-cost home, builders and homeowners should consider avoiding a basement altogether whenever possible. Elimination of the basement could also be beneficial when there is sufficient living space on the main and upper floors of a unit or where accessible dwellings for people with reduced mobility are designed. Slabs on grade, crawl spaces, and pier foundations use less concrete, are less expensive to build, and require less energy to heat.

When basements are designed, careful planning can result in lowering construction cost and providing a better, livable space. A key question will be how to use a basement. A large home will permit the fitting of both living and service functions on upper levels. In a small, affordable home, choices will be limited. Recent improvements in construction technology contributed to improving the basement's livability. Better damp-proofing techniques reduce the humidity often associated with the space, and advanced heating and ventilation technologies have ameliorated the air quality of the basement. Construction methods have also been developed to keep the footings down, raise the lower floor, and insert larger windows, letting in more light to rooms, such as a kitchen or bedroom, that not so long ago were placed above ground.

Several options are available to a designer. One of the most common uses of a basement is as an indoor parking garage. In an affordable home, this is a costly choice, since valuable space will have to be devoted to a service function rather than living space. Another option is to leave the basement unfinished for future expansion. It may suit the need of a young household with toddlers. The children's bedroom can be on the upper level after occupancy, and as means become available, the owners can finish the space. Completion of the basement at a later stage may coincide with the family's life cycle. As children get older, they are likely to seek more privacy, and bedrooms can be built for them at a lower level.

Planning for future, indoor expansion was the focus of the Grow Home, which was designed and built as a demonstration unit by the author and his colleagues (Friedman, 2001). The basement was left unfinished for the occupants to complete themselves or by a hired contractor at a later date. The dwelling's footprint, which measured 14 feet (4.3 meters) by 36 feet (11 meters), provided approximately 500 square feet (46 square meters) at the basement level, permitting a variety of interior configurations in the narrow, unpartitioned space. When the Grow Home was later built by developers for affordable housing projects, most of the buyers purchased the home with an unfinished basement and completed it progressively. They created a variety of layouts that suited their household needs and budget (Figure 3.14). A postoccupancy study of 200 dwellings showed that 25 percent of all the occupants built family rooms, 23 percent chose to create a laundry space, 21 percent used the area for more storage, 13 percent built bedrooms, and the remaining households chose to build for other functions.

Using the basement as a livable space provides an opportunity to create an independent accessory unit. The unit may have its own entrance and may be used as a source of supplementary income for the household that might reside in the space above. Such a solution will be possible in neighborhoods where multifamily units are permitted. A similar objective can be achieved when the basement becomes a home office. It may have an independent entrance or access through an upper floor. Turning a dwelling into a source of income is a monetary strategy for affordability. Rental income can offset mortgage payments, and a portion of the mortgage can be deducted when the space is used as a home office.

Roof

Similar to a basement, the design of a roof may also be affected by regional factors. The style and articulation are often influenced by architectural traditions and climatic conditions. Regions with heavy snowfall or rain will likely have pitched or flat roofs, with a superior drainage system. The roof will determine the dwelling costs in several ways. Complex designs will require more time and material. When poorly constructed, the roof can also be a source of heat loss. Proper attention to roof design can benefit the space management of a small dwelling and provide room for expansion. It will be worthwhile for affordable housing project initiators to consider some of the fundamentals of roof design.

Until the middle of the twentieth century, roof construction was a labor-intensive process. Carpenters constructed the roof on-site, using solid-sawn lumber. With ample low-cost labor, the homeowners who could afford to favored

Figure 3.14 Unfinished basement levels have been completed by their occupants in Grow Home units.

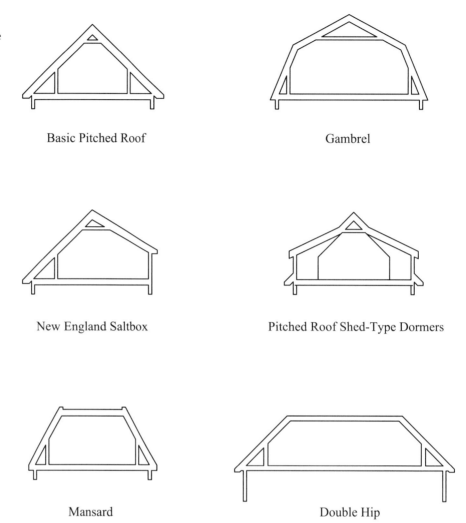

Figure 3.15 Traditional roof types with habitable attic space.

Basic Pitched Roof

Gambrel

New England Saltbox

Pitched Roof Shed-Type Dormers

Mansard

Double Hip

habitable roof styles (Figure 3.15). It was also an efficient way to manage the area of a small home. The attic space, however, was an area of secondary value. In more expensive homes, the space was used for storage or as sleeping quarters for the people employed by the household (CMHC, 1991).

Along with other innovations in home construction, the method of building a roof has changed as well. The invention of prefabricated wood trusses has contributed significantly to the reduction of labor and material costs. Prefabricated trusses are constructed in a plant and shipped to a building site for quick assembly.

The attic space was also reintroduced as an essential part of the space management of a small home. One of the best-known examples of such a design is the Cape Cod cottage, where—with the absence of a basement—the attic became an auxiliary yet useful family space.

Among the roof designs commonly used in North America, the flat roof is fairly easy to construct. It is built much like another floor in the dwelling. Joists are placed across the space and covered with plywood and other roofing material. When joists are used in roofs with large footprints, bearing walls will have to support them from below. The development of space trusses and I-joists eliminated the need to construct bearing walls, and the joist could now rest on the perimeter walls.

In a lower-cost dwelling, a flat roof can provide an area for future expansion. The design must ensure that the existing structure will support another floor, a space that could be easily accessed. When pitched roofs are designed, attention should be given to their complexity. Intricate roofs not only will take more time to assemble but, when poorly constructed, can become a source of heat loss. To reach affordability, simplicity of roof form should be an essential design criterion. Also, since heat rises, a well-insulated roof will keep the heat indoors.

When an attic is designed to be habitable, similar to a basement, it can be finished or left unfinished. Regardless of the state of completion, some key features need to be provided to accommodate livability. Windows should be installed in advance, based on the preplanned floor layout. They can be regular windows placed on the roof's gable ends or a dormer in the front or the rear of the dwelling, or both. A fixed or operable skylight can also be installed to let in light and fresh air. Both dormers and skylights are expensive to construct and install. Special attention should be paid to construction details since poor installation will be a source of heat loss in both. Prefabricated dormers are now being manufactured and sold along with special trusses, saving on labor costs (Figure 3.16). When energy efficiency is a chief consideration, it is best to avoid installation of skylights and dormers, since they are likely to be a main source of heat loss.

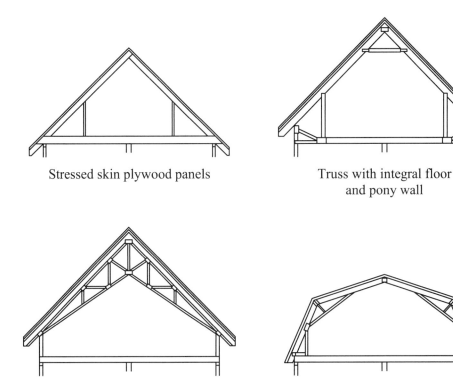

Figure 3.16
Prefabricated roof trusses designed and manufactured for attic space use and cost reduction.

Stressed skin plywood panels

Truss with integral floor and pony wall

Scissor's truss

Gambel truss

TYPOLOGY

The area that the footprint of a home occupies is fundamental to determining its cost. A larger footprint will require a bigger, more expensive plot of land. Infrastructure costs will also rise as more utilities are placed in front. The complexity of the home's design will also influence the cost. A dwelling with intricate elevations and many corners will take more time to construct. A taller building will have a larger exterior wall area to insulate and clad and have a greater number of windows. Aspects specific to some of the more common dwelling prototypes and their effect on cost are listed here. The cross-sections of the chosen prototypes are illustrated in Figure 3.17.

The Bungalow

The *bungalow* is one of the most recognizable house types in North America, primarily in northern latitudes where basements are common. The home has two levels. The upper level houses the livable spaces, including the bedrooms. The lower level contains services and leisure functions, like mechanical or laundry rooms, the garage, and the den, family, and study rooms (Figure 3.18).

Figure 3.17 Cross-section of key dwelling prototypes.

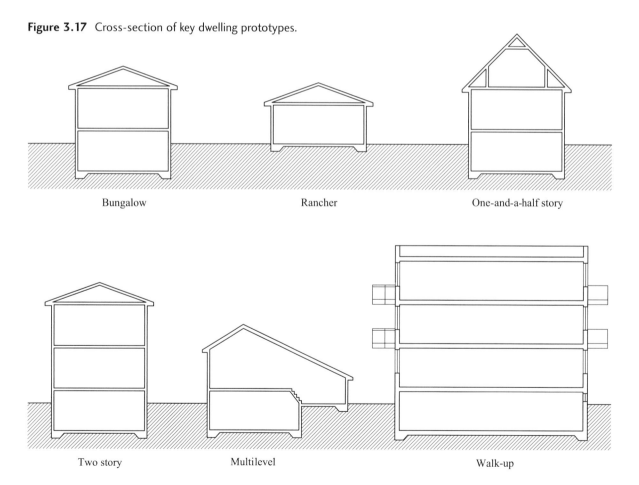

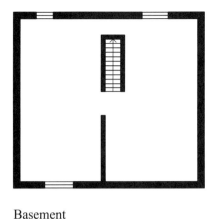
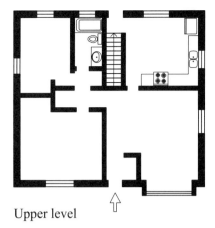

Basement   Upper level

Figure 3.18 In the Bungalow, most of the home's livable functions are concentrated on the upper level.

Bungalows can be of various sizes, yet to accommodate all the functions of a contemporary home, the footprint of the dwelling will be large. A big footprint also implies a large roof area, which is often costly to construct. The wide surface of both the roof and the walls can also be sources of heat loss. Bungalows, therefore, will not be a prime choice when it comes to the building of an affordable home.

The Rancher

The *rancher*, or the ranch home, which is also known as the single-story home, is primarily built in warm regions where a deep foundation is not required. The dwelling is constructed on grade or with a shallow perimeter foundation. The most notable advantage of this dwelling type as far as cost savings is concerned is the lack of a foundation. The disadvantage of a rancher-type home lies, similarly to a bungalow, in the need to concentrate all of its functions on one level, which can potentially increase the home's footprint and perimeter walls (Figure 3.19). The roof is also bound to be large and a source of heat loss. Savings gained by not having a deep foundation and a basement level can potentially be offset by the need to spread out, which implies higher land and infrastructure costs.

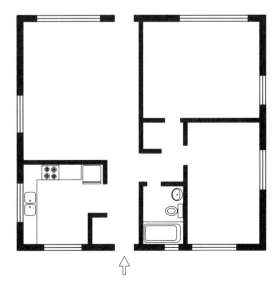

Figure 3.19 In the Rancher, all the functions are located on one level, and the home is built without a basement.

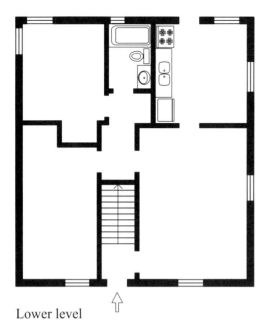

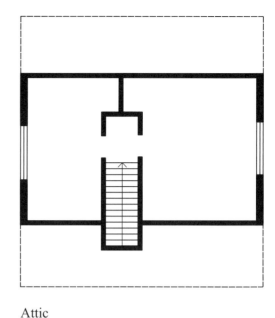

Lower level   ⇧   Attic

Figure 3.20 In the One-and-a-Half Story home, the unit's attic can become the family grow space.

The One-and-a-Half Story

This house type was very popular with builders and buyers in the post–World War II era due to its cost-saving advantages. Building firms like the Levitt Corporation used this prototype in many developments in several states, known as Levittowns. The most noticeable features of the *one-and-a-half story* were its small footprint and its use of the attic. It was offered with or without a basement, which provided additional cost savings. The home's lower floor plan, which measured 400–500 square feet (37–45 square meters), was compact and efficiently designed. The attic, left unfinished for the buyers to complete at their own convenience, could provide room for two additional bedrooms. Another advantage of the one-and-a-half story had to do with energy efficiency, since a lower level's warm air kept the upper level comfortable. Use of open plan at the lower level facilitated the upward travel of air (Figure 3.20).

The popularity of this dwelling type began to decline when postwar prosperity enabled builders to offer and buyers to purchase larger homes. There was no longer a need to take drastic cost-reduction measures. In addition, many municipalities enacted zoning bylaws that effectively made this type of home unwelcome by decreeing a large mandatory footprint.

The Two Story

The *two story* represents many of the strategies that contribute to lowering house cost. The design is also known as *cottage* or *townhouse,* when built in a row. Its key cost-saving principles rest with building two floors on top of the very same foundation (Figure 3.21). Depending, of course, on how large or small is the dwelling footprint, the design can potentially save on land and infrastructure. However, expenses may be associated with having an additional floor and more exterior wall to clad. The basement in this design can be made livable when it

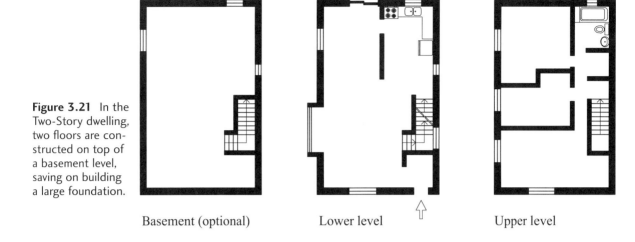

Figure 3.21 In the Two-Story dwelling, two floors are constructed on top of a basement level, saving on building a large foundation.

Basement (optional)   Lower level   Upper level

can be raised sufficiently above ground and windows included in it. The roof can either be habitable or not, depending on the chosen trusses. Similar to the one-and-a-half story, the attic can potentially become the "grow space" when left unfinished.

The structure can also be made of two two-story dwellings placed on top of each other, which is known as a *stuck townhouse*. The advantage in such an arrangement is savings in the cost of constructing a foundation for each and, of course, having both use the same land and services.

The Multilevel

The homes presented above can be regarded as archetypes from which additional forms can be created. One such design is the *multilevel*, also known as the *split-level*, home. The most common of these designs are hybrids between the one-and-a-half or the two-story home and the rancher (Figure 3.22). Costs often mount when such a combination occurs, since the foundation and the building envelope are not simple to construct, and the roof may have a complex form. Multilevel dwellings are also known to have large footprints. The on-grade part

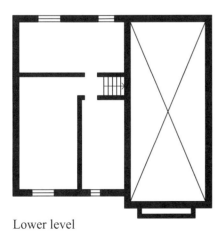

Figure 3.22 The Split-Level design is a hybrid of the one-and-a-half and two-story types.

Lower level   Upper level

of the dwelling is often used as an indoor parking garage. The cost of constructing such a house may also be higher because space needs to be allocated to the construction of stairs connecting the different levels.

The Multifamily Plex

As the number of units on a site mounts, each dwelling's share in the cost of land and infrastructure declines. A similar principle applies to a single structure. When several units share the cost of the common features, such as services, foundation, parking, stairs, utilities, and roof, the costs of these items per unit declines. The multifamily structure is an attempt to lower the cost of housing by increasing density (Figure 3.23).

The plex's design is based on the same principle. A multilevel structure is divided into several units in a variety of volumetric arrangements. The units may neither share the same entrance and stair nor have the same interior layout. The legal title of each unit, when unrelated occupants are using different floors, is that of a cooperative or a condominium. Occupants will own their dwelling and jointly own common elements, such as the land and roof. The multifamily plex can be built as a free standing structure or an attached dwelling, which most are.

One of the most notable plex types is the *duplex,* which houses two households in a vertical arrangement. The style will result in a 50 percent savings in the roof and foundation areas. The structure can be built on grade or have a base-

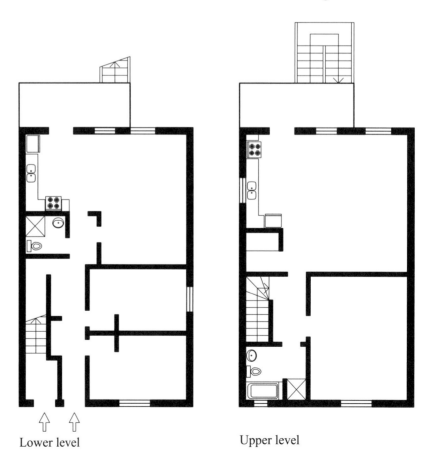

Figure 3.23 In Multifamily Plex (or multiplex), several households share the same structure.

Lower level   Upper level

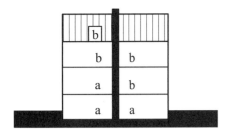

Semidetached duplex

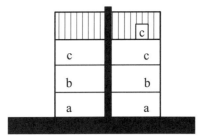

Semidetached triplex

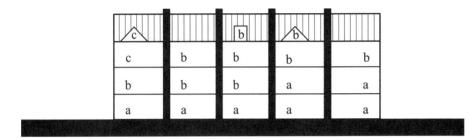

Row with variety of plex types

Figure 3.24 By joining Duplexes or Triplexes, other forms of high-density dwellings can be created to lower costs further. The letters in this diagram represent different households.

ment. When a basement is built, the lower level's occupant will have two stories and the upper a single story. At times, the lower level can become a parking place for one or both occupants.

When three households share a building, the structure is known as a *triplex*. The triplex results in a 66 percent savings in roof and foundation area. Each household can own a floor or two, depending on whether a basement has been constructed. The design challenge in a narrow building is to facilitate access to each dwelling without encroaching on the living area of each unit. Parking often poses another challenge, primarily when cars need to be parked indoors. It is, therefore, common to see such a building built with shared parking space inside or outside the main structure. When the building is a condominium, the outdoor space will be either shared by all users or purchased and used by the lower level's occupant (National Association of Home Builders, 1986).

When two duplexes are joined to make a single structure, the building is called a *fourplex* or *quadplex*. Each unit may have its own separate entrance. Similarly, when two triplexes share a common wall, they will be called a *sixplex*, each dwelling having its own entrance (Figure 3.24). When the density increases, more parking will have to be accommodated indoors or outdoors, which tends to increase the amount of land the dwellings require. For safety reasons, building codes mandate that each dwelling unit have an additional means of egress. Therefore, a common staircase must be built at the rear to allow each unit's occupants to exit in case of emergency.

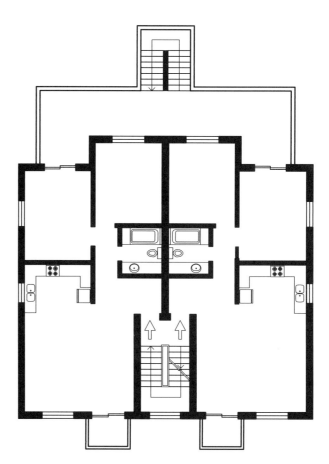

Figure 3.25 In typical Walk-ups, the units' plumbing is often stacked on top of each other, leading to further cost savings.

The Walk-Up

Walk-up apartments are considered low-rise multifamily dwellings and have a number of advantages that contribute to cost reduction. The units are stacked on top of each other, which simplifies structural and utility arrangements (Figure 3.25). Unlike the multifamily plex, they have a single stair system that serves all units, and in most jurisdictions they need to have another exit at the rear. Walk-ups can have any number of stories. Low-rise buildings commonly have up to four levels, primarily if the building is a wood-frame construction. Walk-ups can be built with or without an elevator, and parking for the apartments can be in common, at the structure's lower level or outdoors.

TRANSFORMATION

Transformation of the home's typology or form can be a strategy in achieving affordable housing. The process of transformation alters the original structure by conversion or addition. *Addition* can be a monetary approach whereby a structure will be added to and spending will occur progressively rather than at the outset upon purchase. *Conversion* will see an increase or decrease of density by placing more or fewer households than were initially planned for in the same structure. Resources can be shared among more users, lowering the cost for each if the density is increased.

Domestic transformation has been part of dwelling culture for centuries. Villages and cities expanded over time, enabling extended families to live in close proximity. Building an expansion to a dwelling was, in some regions, a family undertaking. Members gathered to construct an addition or alter the configuration of an existing home. Urban environments were in constant flux as more dwelling units were built and expanded upon. The industrial revolution marked a turning point in society and urbanity. Mass migration to cities necessitated the establishment of a new paradigm for urban management and growth. The emergence of building regulations was meant to ensure that a process that for centuries had evolved spontaneously and naturally would be controlled and that occupants' safety and orderly conduct would be respected.

Progressive building occurs today as well. Statistics show that renovation activities have grown several-fold in recent decades—as witnessed by bustling renovation centers—and that they are likely to continue to grow. Known as do-it-yourself (DIY) or self-help, these processes see a transformation of residences either on a small scale, such as replacing kitchen cabinets, or a large scale, like building an addition. The work is done by the occupants themselves or a hired contractor.

Progressive building was also used as a strategy for affordability. Homebuyers will begin their lives in a small dwelling, and as family needs dictate and budget permits, they will add on more space. The practice was common in postwar homes. Constructed on large plots, small homes were added to over the years. Renovating first indoors and then outdoors, transforming a dwelling unit was a common practice. Building regulations have since changed, and most municipalities set building volume limits and do not always permit major additions.

The practice of transforming one house type into another was also common over the past decades. The owner of a large structure would turn a portion of it into an independent dwelling with its own access and utilities. Such processes that created illegal suites were also prohibited. Those opposed to such additions argued that increasing the density of a community overloaded existing infrastructure, aggravated the parking situation, and reduced communal safety.

Economic restructuring, lifestyle changes, and demographic makeup brought housing affordability to the forefront in many communities. The need to provide smaller units is not only of present concern but a solution to many ongoing necessities. Realization that the elderly cannot all be housed in institutions requires reexamination of bigeneration dwellings. Part of a dwelling can be converted to accommodate an aging parent. Large homes that have been constructed for households with children can be subdivided to house a single person or a young couple. Revenue generated from sale or rental of such dwellings can supplement an aging household's income.

A designer converting or transforming a residence needs to consider several issues prior to and during the design process. The first step is to ensure that local zoning bylaws permit this kind of addition. Finding out what is the permissible area for an addition and whether such a transformation makes economic sense is another step. Ensuring that a new addition will not obstruct a neighbor's view is also a concern. Often a design is objected to when a permit is sought on the grounds that someone's view will be blocked. Before planning begins, one also needs to verify that the project can logistically be executed. In a dense, urban

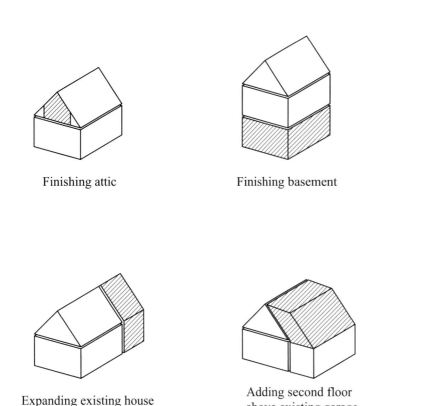

Finishing attic

Finishing basement

Adding floor

Expanding existing house

Adding second floor
above existing garage

Converting garage
to dwelling unit

Dividing existing house
into two dwelling units

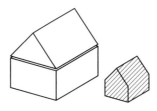

Constructing ancillary unit

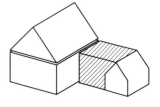

Connecting ancillary
unit to main house

Figure 3.26 Alternative ways of adding space to, and transforming, a dwelling unit.

area, it may be impossible to excavate, for example, due to the inability to negotiate access of heavy machinery to the site.

Design considerations in transformation may also deal with the chosen structural solution. Constructing a new foundation or cantilevering the addition from an existing structure may be two possible options. A thorough inspection of the existing structure must be made. Interior design aspects between the existing structure and the addition may also be looked at. Accessibility and circulation, for example, will have to be figured out to make sure that uninterrupted passage takes place between both sections. The designer will have to make sure that natural light to the rooms in the old structure are not blocked.

In general, it is easier to transform and add to a detached home. Rear, front, or even side extensions, when space permits, will be easier to construct on detached rather than semidetached homes. In a semidetached home, the directions are more limited. In addition, aesthetic issues will have to be considered as a result of the need to respect the architectural proportions and style of the adjoining unit. It is even more difficult to expand a row-house unit. Unless prepared and designed for by staggering the row homes, adding to the back of a dwelling will require attention to the entire assembly.

Transformation and addition can also be done by expanding a preprepared area. Expanding a dwelling onto an existing, attached parking garage, for example, is very common. The garage's structure will need to be reinforced to support the addition's weight. Expansion can be made when a space exists between the main structure and an auxiliary one at the rear or the side. The space can be filled to create a monolithic structure (Figure 3.26).

Transformation can take place when a house is designed to be converted by turning a part of it into an independent dwelling unit (Figure 3.27). As discussed above, a basement level can become an accessory unit when an entrance is con-

Before transformation

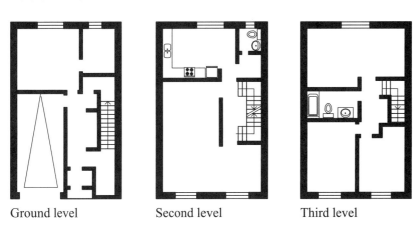

Ground level   Second level   Third level

After transformation

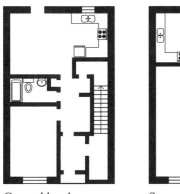   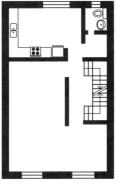   

Ground level   Second level   Third level

Figure 3.27 A house can be designed to have part of it transformed into an independent dwelling unit.

structed to allow direct street access. A parking space underground or on street level may also become an independent rental unit or a dwelling for an aging parent. The designer may anticipate future conversion by placing the utilities in a convenient place so future connections will be inexpensive.

Transformation can also occur when a multifamily building can change internally from one type to another. A duplex can become a triplex and vice versa. Offering choices to buyers in the preoccupancy stage and the ability to transform easily each dwelling's interior and the structure's internal arrangement in later years was a key feature of the *Next Home* design. The three-story structure was designed to demonstrate how flexibility and transformation can be used to achieve affordability (Friedman, 2002b).

One of the fundamental distinguishing features of the Next Home was the option extended to buyers of purchasing the type and "quantity" of house that they need and can afford. This option was made possible by designing a three-story structure, which can be built, sold, and inhabited as a single-family house, a duplex, or a triplex (Figure 3.28). If three separate households buy one floor each in the Next Home, the structure becomes a triplex as easily as it becomes a single-family home when a couple with children, for example, decides to purchase all three floors. Alternatively, if a household buys two floors while a single person buys the third floor, the Next Home becomes a duplex. In a row of such structures, therefore, triplex residents could be neighbors to single-family homeowners, who in turn live next door to people in duplexes.

The Next Home was designed as volumes to be subdivided and rearranged both pre- and postoccupancy and to accommodate transformation from one house type to another with minimal inconvenience and cost. A hallmark of the Next Home design is its nonstatic allocation of units by floor. A structure originally built as a duplex can at a later date be changed to either a triplex or a single-family home, according to the dictates of future owners. This built-in capacity for transformation is an inherent element of the design, which considered such aspects as the location of entrance and stairs and the placement of building systems.

The front entrance to the Next Home was recessed and positioned along the side lengthwise wall. This particular location, and configuration, was chosen for two primary reasons. The first reason is that such an entrance enables the grouping of the houses into rows; an entrance directly off the middle of the side wall, for instance, would not accommodate row houses. The second reason is that a recessed entrance resulted in the most efficient access and circulation pattern of all entrance options. Entering the Next Home units at the chosen location — whether at ground level or via the stairwell for the upper units — allows the residents to access the various spaces of the unit directly rather than pass through other spaces, as they would be obliged to do if the entrance were in the front.

To facilitate future transformation of the dwelling units within the Next Home structure and to maximize the impression of open space, special attention was paid to the location of the stairs. Flexibility and openness were achieved with the placement of the stairs along the side, longitudinal wall, in the middle of the units, and adjacent to the front entrance. Due to the modular nature of the stairs in the Next Home, the floor plates have standard shapes that allow the stair modules to be positioned in the same stairwell location for each floor plate. Within this location, a number of individual stair and landing components—

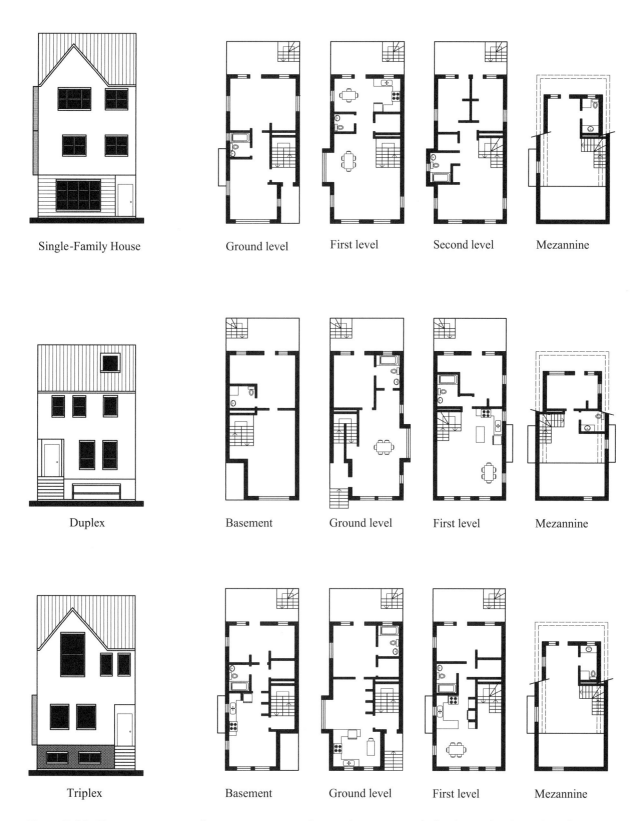

Single-Family House   Ground level   First level   Second level   Mezannine

Duplex   Basement   Ground level   First level   Mezannine

Triplex   Basement   Ground level   First level   Mezannine

Figure 3.28 The Next Home is a three-story structure that can become a single-family, two-family, or three-family dwelling. It also permits transformation from one configuration to another in later years.

including straight runs, landings, and winders—form the basis for the completed stair modules. The dimensions of these components and modules correspond with the wide range of prefabricated stairs that have been developed and are currently available commercially. The ultimate configuration of stair modules and stair enclosure walls was decided according to the individual floor arrangements of the different units. In the event of a postoccupancy modification—for example, from a triplex to a duplex—the introduction of a secondary stair within the new two-floor, lower unit will be necessary.

The mechanical systems of the Next Home were designed for simple adjustment at the preoccupancy stage to the chosen volumetric arrangement of the structure by incorporating a vertical shaft throughout the entire building height. This vertical shaft encloses the water supply, drainage, venting, electrical, telephone, and cable TV lines. In conjunction with a horizontal channel, which can be installed optionally by the builder to run the length of each floor and which would facilitate future relocation of rooms, issues of postoccupancy flexibility have also been addressed. Such an arrangement of channels permits access to utilities through the floor—not the ceilings or walls—therefore facilitating all changes for each occupant, making them as unobtrusive as possible to neighboring units.

Transformation as a strategy for affordability can also take place when originally conceived uses for the space are changed. Changing from commercial or industrial land use to housing is one of the most common forms of building conversion. Careful assessment is needed, however, when such a method is chosen, since high cost can render the process unaffordable. Industrial buildings, however, are often located in urban cores on valuable land, making investment in their conversion worthwhile. Such a process will be demonstrated in the following section.

ACCESSORY STRUCTURE

The planning and design thrust of affordable housing is to make efficient use of a small plot and dwelling space. "Fitting it all" while ensuring comfort and livability is a key objective. Building an accessory structure on site will, therefore, reduce cost and raise affordability by increasing the density and the site's usage.

One such structure is a parking garage or a carport. When a parking solution is sought for a dwelling, the choice will be between parking indoors or outdoors. Outdoor parking can be on a large lot in common or made of private stalls at the front or the rear of each unit. Indoor parking can be in the structure's basement or in a freestanding building attached to the main dwelling. When an independent structure is built and located in the front, it may be attached to one of the dwelling sides, thereby increasing the plot's size. It can also be placed in front of the structure or constructed as a part of it, thereby blocking the view and reducing curb appeal. A suitable location that helps keep the cost down for an accessory structure can, therefore, be at the rear.

Accommodating the car at the rear requires a comprehensive approach to community planning. Designing a lane system is part of such a solution and is outlined below. The garage can be independent or connected in different ways to the dwelling itself. The rear parking garage can be constructed at the same

One story accessory structures

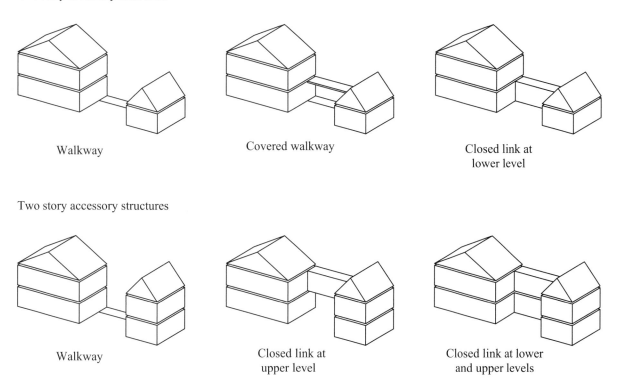

Walkway   Covered walkway   Closed link at
                                          lower level

Two story accessory structures

Walkway   Closed link at   Closed link at lower
                 upper level   and upper levels

time as the main structure, or it can be built at a later date (Figure 3.29). When a parking structure is attached to the house at the side or close enough to the main building at the rear, its roof can become a place for a vertical addition.

Another type of accessory structure that contributes to affordability by increasing density is a livable one. The structure can be constructed along with the main dwelling or added later, and it can have different uses. It can be a home for an aging family member and is known as a *granny flat*. Placement of such a unit, which is common and encouraged in several Australian towns, is often prohibited in North America. Cities fear that such structures may cause parking problems and load utilities. Where such structures have been constructed, these fears have proven unfounded.

Granny flats can be constructed via conventional methods or prefabricated in a plant and brought to a site (Figure 3.30). Avoidance of a basement makes such a dwelling accessible to a person with reduced mobility. It can be independent from or connected to the main structure. Years later, where permitted, the main dwelling can be expanded to the granny flat. Alternatively, the flat can be rented to another person when an entryway from the lane is introduced.

The rear additional structure can also become a home office. Investment made in such a building will be justified as the space can generate income and make the entire initiative affordable. Here, too, the main structure and the additional structure can be connected in a variety of ways. The structure may, for example, have a connection to and an entry from the main house. It may also have an entry from the lane. In recent years, in an effort to densify existing neigh-

Figure 3.29 Rear accessory structures can be connected to dwellings initially or at a later stage. The area in between the principal home and the accessory structure can provide a space for a later expansion.

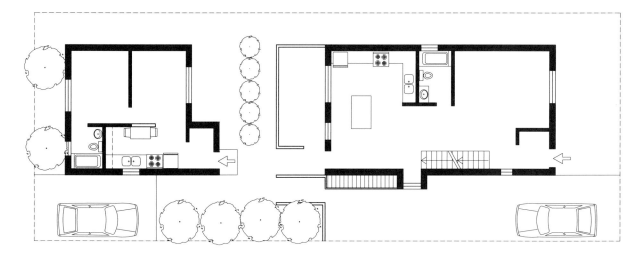

Figure 3.30 The ground level of a home with a rear accessory structure.

borhoods, some municipalities are permitting construction of family structures next to a lane at the rear of large ones. The new structure has its own street address, but it is connected to utilities either from the front or the back.

KEY CONSIDERATIONS

- The footprint dimensions of a home will be the outcome of the number of functions that are placed next to each other. A dwelling with a square footprint will commonly require a wider lot than a house with a rectangular footprint and, therefore, will be more expensive.
- Designing with standard dimensions for structural framing members, such as studs, joists, and plywood, can result in substantial savings. Designing for 4-foot (2.2-meter) modules and 24-inch (610-millimeter) stud spacing alone can reduce lumber use by 8 percent.
- Vertical designs make most efficient use of space, since more stacking results in the need for less construction material. The cost of a two-story square house, for instance, is lower than a one-story house with equivalent area since it has half the foundation and roof area.
- When a building has a number of projections, when the upper floor extends beyond the lower for example, costs are bound to rise. Projections therefore need to be introduced where they are most needed.
- When two dwellings are joined as a semidetached, the lot area can be reduced by as much as 18 percent and the exterior wall perimeter costs are reduced by a third (CMHC, 1981).
- Joining units in a row will result in a 33 percent savings in lot area and street length, and 70 percent savings in the exterior wall perimeter for a middle unit (CMHC, 1981).
- Heat-loss reduction of approximately 21 percent can be achieved when two dwellings are attached and a further 26 percent savings for the middle unit when three or more dwellings are joined as a row house.
- Dwelling types can be mixed in row housing. The end units in a row of six or eight buildings, for example, can be multifamily structures, whereas the middle units can be single-family.

- When designing a low-cost home, builders and homeowners should consider avoiding having a basement altogether as a cost-saving measure.
- The basement, when considered, offers an opportunity to create an independent accessory unit. The basement's unit may have its own entrance and can be used as a source of supplementary income for the household that might reside above.
- Roof with an intricate form will not only take more time and material to assemble but can become a source of heat loss.
- When a proper angle is chosen and special trusses selected, the roof can become an attic and offer lower cost options for future expansion.
- When energy efficiency is a key consideration, skylights and dormers should be avoided as they are known to be sources of heat loss.
- Design of a single-story dwelling is likely to require a larger lot as all the functions are congregated on a single level.
- As the number of units who use the same footprint mount, each dwelling's share in the cost of land, infrastructure, and foundation declines.
- When three households share a building, the structure is known as a triplex. The triplex results in 66 percent savings in roof and foundation area.
- When the wet functions are stacked in a walk-up apartment, further savings can be expected.
- In general, it is easier to transform and add to a detached home. Rear, front or even side extensions, when space permits, will be easier to construct.
- A rear accessory structure can house an older member of an extended family and, later, can be rented out to supplement household income.

4

Interiors

The easiest and most logical way to reduce housing costs is to make houses smaller. In reducing size, construction, heating and cooling, and general maintenance costs also go down. Additionally, smaller dwellings require smaller lots and, therefore, less infrastructure per unit. By understanding how different areas of a home are used and how interior design and finishes can increase efficiency and create a feeling of spaciousness, small dwellings can also be made comfortable and functional. Whereas macro issues related to choice of prototype and construction of dwellings were discussed in the previous chapter, this chapter walks the reader through the home's interior. Strategies ranging from conceptual approaches to space design, access, circulation, and finishes are discussed here.

DEFINING SMALL SPACE

Interpretation of what constitutes a small space varies from place to place and culture to culture. An average-sized apartment in New York City, for example, would most likely be considered small by Dallas standards. Also, a typical North American suburban home easily dwarfs the average Japanese dwelling. It is, therefore, worthwhile to understand the concept of "size" and "small" prior to investigating how to design small spaces.

The quest for small, efficient, and affordable space is a result of gradual expansion in the size of North American dwellings. It would be difficult to find, in most North American urban centers, a recently constructed single-family detached home that is smaller than 1,500 square feet (140 square meters) in area. Increases in personal wealth, periods of national prosperity, and the idea of the home as investment or savings portfolio are some of the socioeconomic factors behind the rise in dwelling sizes. This rise, which paralleled the decline in the size of the North American household, also has architectural reasons, many of which have to do with the home's interior.

Dependency on cars by several family members and the requirement or the desire to park indoors saw garages triple in size, to an average of 600 square feet (60 square meters). Other interior functions expanded as well. Half a century ago, sharing bedrooms was common; housing each child in a separate room has become the norm. The master bedroom has become a suite with its own walk-in closet and bathroom. From a utilitarian design, measuring 50 square feet (5 square meters) bathrooms on each floor doubled in size to accommodate more luxury features.

When one considers buying or moving into a small, affordable dwelling, trade-offs need to be paramount in decision making. The comfort that comes with having a large space will have to be traded for homeownership. It is a process that involves the household's budget, value system, and adoption of an appropriate design strategy.

Small Space Design Principles

When designing a small dwelling, functionality, and perception of the space must be addressed. Without this combination, a small house design will not be successful. A boat, for example, is a small space that is extremely efficient and functional, but few people would want to reside on a boat for a long period of time. The huge, two-story entry in many newer suburban homes, on the other hand, inspires a sense of spaciousness; but it serves no real function and is frequently described as wasted space.

In marrying efficiency and a sense of space, one can design small homes that feel comfortable and personal rather than cramped and suffocating. Designers of compact economy cars, for example, found a way to combine spaciousness and functionality. By carefully considering the driver ergonomics and maneuverability, they were able to inspire a sense of space despite the economy car's small dimensions. Attention to details and treating space as a precious commodity can, therefore, bring about a good design.

When focusing on efficiency, it is important to study lifestyles and how people use homes. By reviewing what spaces are important and most used, some less-used areas can be eliminated altogether. Formal dining or living rooms, for example, are seldom used in contemporary society's informal lifestyle. Creating multifunctional spaces can greatly reduce the floor area of a dwelling while still fulfilling the occupants' functional needs. By reducing or eliminating standard interior walls, practical and alternative means of dividing spaces can be achieved, such as shelving units, freeing up space and creating more opportunities for storage. Optimizing the storage potential of a small space can also help to reduce unnecessary floor space, eliminating the need for a basement or excessive closets.

Creating a sense of spaciousness is also essential to the success and appeal of small areas. Careful selection of floor material, wall color, window size and placement, ceiling height, and floor plan orientation can help produce the desired spatial effect in a home. Before discussing specific space-saving and perception-enhancing strategies for small dwellings, it will be worthwhile to examine the home and identify ways of increasing functionality on a macro level.

THE ZONING OF A HOME

Efficient space management in a small dwelling will be the outcome of the distribution of functions throughout the home. Those functions are commonly arranged in zones, for which there are several categories (Figure 4.1). Placing those zones within the dwelling's perimeter is a first interior design step. One distinction is between *public, semiprivate,* and *private* zones.

Public zones, which include the dining and the living area, as well as the powder room, are used by household members and their guests. Semiprivate areas include the kitchen and the bathroom, which at times can be used by visitors. The bedroom areas constitute the private spaces. In a two-story dwelling, public spaces are usually located on the ground floor, while the private areas—bedrooms and bathrooms—are placed on the upper floor. Public zones also tend to require more natural light, as they are mostly used during the day. They will preferably be situated along the southern exposure of a dwelling, to capitalize on sunlight.

Figure 4.1 A dwelling's area is commonly divided into zones that fall under a variety of categories.

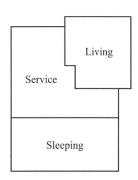
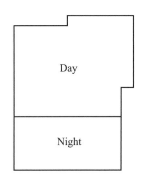
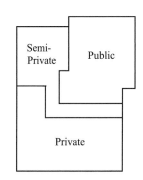

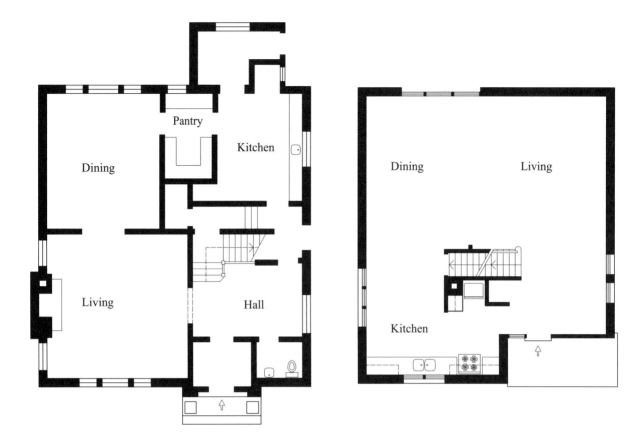

Figure 4.2 The lower floors of a turn-of-the-century home and a contemporary residence. Over the years, enclosed individual functions were combined to form a single space.

Zones can also be distinguished according to their functions, for example, sleeping, including the bedroom; living, including the living and dining room areas; and services, including the kitchen and the bathrooms. Other subdividing categories are the *day* and *night* zones. Here, too, day activities will be associated with public areas, while night activities will be associated with the private zone and will include bedrooms and bathrooms. Space can also be divided into areas in which activities take place and those areas devoted to circulation and passages. Distinguishing between indoor and outdoor spaces in the home is another way to categorize domestic areas.

Once the general zones have been established, division into functional uses within those zones must be addressed. Although the ways in which people use different rooms has changed greatly over the years, the manner in which they are noted on floor plans has not. A century ago, the kitchen was considered a private room to be kept separate from the living areas. The living and dining rooms were formal, used to entertain and to impress. Every room served a single function and was kept separate from other rooms with walls. This arrangement, however, does not accurately reflect current patterns of use of spaces in homes. Today, it is common to find a parent cooking a meal and having a conversation with a child doing homework on the kitchen table, while another child watches television in the adjoining space. Within an informal lifestyle, the kitchen often becomes the most-used area in the house, functioning as the place to make and eat meals or snacks, do homework, pay bills, entertain, and converse with family members (Figure 4.2).

Fortunately, this transformation in society's cultural attitudes also helps better manage a small space and reduce cost. It is achieved by considering a dwelling as a series of areas for various activities, rather than a sequence of enclosed rooms, and by eliminating unnecessary spaces. For example, eating and dining are activities that can be served by a single space. A kitchen table that can seat all members of a family and expand to accommodate a few guests eliminates the need for a formal dining room. By placing an informal and comfortable living room closer to the kitchen, the need for a separate family room is also reduced. Because activities in these areas are related and often occur simultaneously, creating a public open-plan zone for the kitchen and dining and living area is a practical and effective cost-reduction strategy (Figure 4.3). Through changes in floor or ceiling height, storage-providing partitions, and alcoves, various spaces for specific functions can be defined within this larger area (Susanka, 1998).

Other mixes of functions that require few or no partitions at all can take place in a small dwelling. A home office can be part of the living room. A small study might even be part of a bedroom. Service functions can also be combined. The laundry function can be placed anywhere near a plumbing stack, either in a bathroom or in the kitchen. In general, the smaller the space, the more compartmentalizing and merging of functions needs to take place. Small homes can have the same number and type of functions as large dwellings, yet the size of these functions is reduced and their location different.

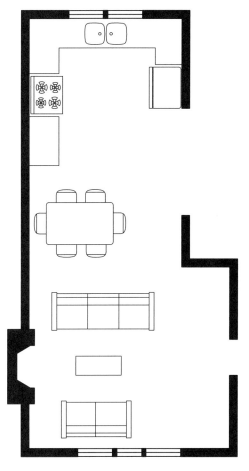

Figure 4.3 By combining a number of public-zone functions, space is saved in a small home.

Another method of ensuring that the home's interior lends itself to efficiency and affordability is to zone the spaces to permit physical transformation along changes in the occupant's life cycle. The approach regards the home as a flexible entity where ongoing alterations are initiated by the initial or subsequent occupants as new space needs emerge and means become available. As families change, so too does the amount of living space they require. A young couple, for example, needs less space than a household with two teenagers. As children grow up and leave the house, however, parents again require a smaller amount of living space. As the couple ages, decreased mobility may necessitate adaptation again. To accommodate these different requirements, a house can be designed to be flexible enough to provide varying amounts of space at different times. Portions of the home might even be segmented and become an independent dwelling unit for rental and supplemental income purposes (Figure 4.4).

Occupancy

(30) (30) (8)

The family moved in.

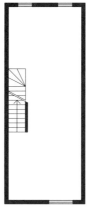

Basement

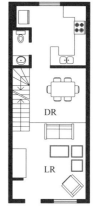

Ground Floor

Upper Floor

One year after occupancy

(31) (31) (9)

The powder room was converted into two closets. A newborn baby lived in his parent's bedroom and later the two sons shared one bedroom.

Basement

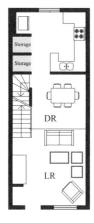

Ground Floor

Upper Floor

Two years after occupancy

(32) (32) (10) (1)

The front part of the basement was finished as a family room. A wall was added to separate the family room and the laundry area.

Figures 4.4 By not using bearing partitions or creating an unpartitioned shell, the household can complete and adapt the dwelling to their changing needs progressively.

Basement

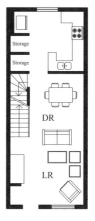

Ground Floor

Upper Floor

Five years after occupancy

(35) (35) (13) (4)

A closet was added on the upper floor. An opening direction of an existing closet was changed.

Basement

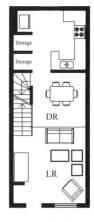

Ground Floor

Upper Floor

Six years after occupancy

(36) (36) (14) (5)

The family room was converted into a bedroom; the basement was finished into a laundry room equipped with a shower and sink and a storage room.

Basement

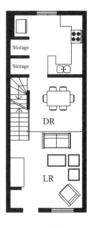

Ground Floor

Upper Floor

Eleven years after occupancy

(41) (41) (10)

The bedroom in the basement was converted into a family room.

Basement

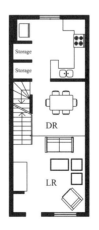

Ground Floor

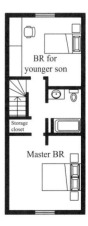

Upper Floor

The approach can be regarded as an economic strategy where money is spent only when needed. The young couple may leave a portion of the dwelling unfinished—the basement, for example—and complete it years after occupancy. By creating a home that can be better adapted to the changing needs of a family, expenses associated with mobility can be reduced. Transaction costs, legal fees, expenses for a moving company, and the cost of refitting the new home can all be saved.

When designing a home for future adaptation, steps need to be taken to facilitate such changes. By locating the wet elements—the kitchen or bathroom—between functional zones, future modifications in the zone's layout can be carried out without a need for demolition or costly installation of new plumbing. Similarly, in two-story dwellings, flexibility can be increased by providing conduits for a future kitchen on the upper floor. This facilitates the possibility of dividing the dwelling into two if so desired in the future. If a basement exists, rough plumbing can be installed for a washroom or a laundry room. There can also be simpler considerations, such as building a kitchen that can be rapidly modified for use by a disabled person or not building closets on common walls between bedrooms to allow for easy demolition.

ACCESS AND CIRCULATION

Once the zones in the home have been determined, thought should be given to the experience of moving through them. The quality of circulation spaces within a house can greatly affect its comfort and efficiency. In small homes, the amount of circulation space should be minimized and viewed as a multipurpose area, allowing both movement and other functions, such as storage, to take place. It can be achieved through good design without incurring significant, additional construction costs. The home's passageways need to be regarded as a comprehensive system and carefully designed to include outdoor and indoor areas.

The Porch

For many, the process of entering a home begins with a front porch and the path or stairs leading up to it. Porches or covered stoops give visitors a sense of arrival and designate a specific point of entry for the house. They also provide shelter from the rain as homeowners unlock the door or visitors wait to be received. Additionally, the front porch or stoop provides an intermediary zone between the street and the home, creating an outdoor room that eases the transition.

In a small home, a covered porch can become an outdoor entranceway and serve as a storage space. Shoes can be left there, and in summertime, toys and bicycles stored. Porches can be designed to be easily enclosed, insulated, heated, and turned into year-round rooms. They can also serve an important communal function by allowing neighbors to view each other as well as the street in front (Figure 4.5).

Figure 4.5 In small homes, porches can serve as an outdoor room or be enclosed, if the resident wishes, for year-round use.

Entry and the Entryway

The location of the entry influences the overall circulation patterns within the home. A home's condition of attachment will often determine the location of access to a unit. For a detached home, the main entry can be placed along any of the four perimeter walls; whereas in semidetached homes, the placement is restricted to three walls and to two walls for row houses. Although main entrances are often located in the center of a home's front façade, moving the entrance closer to one side of a house will increase the space's efficiency and facilitate addition of a separate entrance in the opposite side. In smaller homes, a centered entrance is less functional, as it forces the division of the area along the front façade into three separate small spaces rather than a larger, single space.

Once inside the house, the entryway becomes a homeowner's and a visitor's first impression of the home. Although in affordable housing, spaces such as entryways are often considered unnecessary and eliminated; however, they can serve a variety of functions that greatly increase a home's efficiency with a minimal investment. An entryway must be large enough to permit at least two or three people to stand and talk comfortably. Locating a closet nearby for coats and shoes helps increase its functionality. In cold regions, where a second indoor entry door is provided, the closet can be placed in between the two doors to save interior area. If space for a closet is not available, wall-mounted hooks can work just as well, and shoes can be stored on a mat. Ideally, an entryway will offer interesting views of the home as well. In general, having an entryway that opens to a washroom or other service spaces should be avoided. In small, long homes, such as row houses, this view should extend the length of the interior, creating an immediate sense of spaciousness upon entering. Preferably, an opening

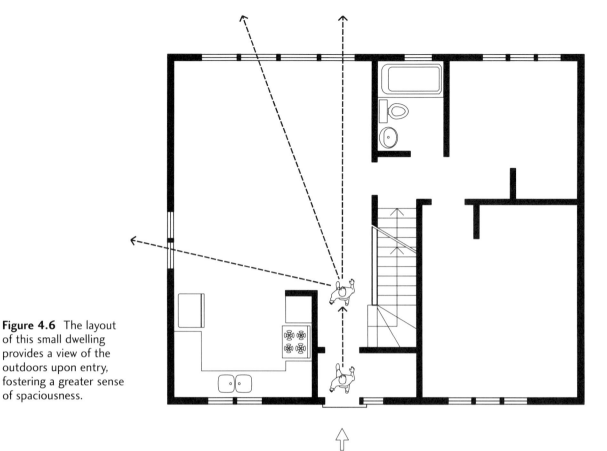

Figure 4.6 The layout of this small dwelling provides a view of the outdoors upon entry, fostering a greater sense of spaciousness.

placed at the end wall will extend this view further. In small homes with a square footprint, a view to the exterior or to a more open living space achieves the same effect (Figure 4.6).

Efficient Circulation

Efficient circulation allows for necessary and comfortable movement between zones of a home while occupying a minimum amount of space. Circulation should not force the crossing of one zone to get to another (Figure 4.7). The bedroom area, for example, should not be accessed through the living room. Within a zone, however, using the spaces themselves for circulation is a practical method for eliminating unnecessary passageways. A living room can provide access to the kitchen, yet it must be designed so that the passageway will consume as little living space as possible. In a semidetached or row house, the main circulatory artery can be placed along the longitudinal wall, providing a larger area for the functions themselves. Given the fact that circulation space can account for up to 30 percent of a home's floor space, using these spaces for circulation only could be considered a waste. When properly designed, hallways and corridors can serve as storage space as well. By allocating 48 inches (120 centimeters) to a corridor width, 12 inches (30 centimeters) of that width can be dedicated to shallow closets or shelves for books or other small-item storage.

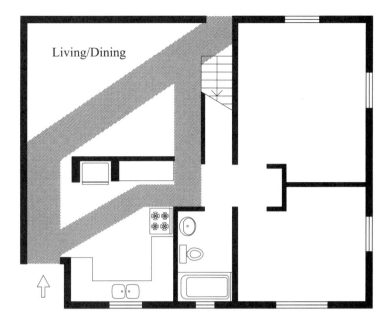

Inefficient Circulation

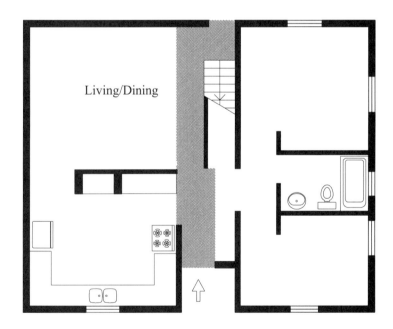

Efficient Circulation

Figure 4.7 Circulation in a dwelling should not force the crossing of one zone to get to another.

In addition to freeing up floor area through efficient circulation patterns in a home, careful design can allow for it to make a house feel bigger. By planning movement through rooms so that smaller ones are entered at an angle, one views the room along its diagonal. In a square or rectangular room, the diagonal line is longer than the sides, and this creates the illusion of a larger space.

Stairs

In multilevel dwellings, to reduce the length of corridors and prevent unnecessary circulation space, stairs should be located close to a home's entrance (Figure 4.8). The remaining interior space can then be left for the various functions. Placing the stairs along or close to the front façade should be avoided, as such an arrangement occupies valuable window space, preventing exterior views, natural light, and ventilation. In houses with a long and narrow configuration, the longitudinal wall is the best location for stairs. This configuration provides a structural support for the stairs, frees the main spaces, and prevents the obstruction of light penetration from both front and rear façades.

For homes with wider footprints, several locations for stairs are recommended as a cost reduction measure. Placing the stairs centrally, as a wedge between interior areas, limits restrictions to modification within these areas. Another option is to place the stairs in a long narrow run close to the entrance between two zones. If the home has a basement, the same stair shaft will lead to that level. To maximize use and free interior space, locating the shaft outside the structure will free up the entire floor.

In addition to location, the chosen type and configuration of stairs will also have a significant bearing on the circulation patterns and affordability of a house. Stair systems include straight runs, landings, and winders that can be combined and arranged according to the desired composition of the units in the structure. The exact configuration of a set of stairs should take into consideration local building codes, cost, and effect on circulation. Additionally, in small spaces, where all areas count, attention should be given to the residual space created under the stairs.

Because on-site stair construction is labor-intensive and therefore costly, prefabricated adjustable steel- or wood-framing systems can be a more affordable option. To further reduce costs, stairs should remain open, as this will eliminate additional finishing expenses and increase the sense of spaciousness. When enclosures are built to facilitate adaptability, placing utility conduits in these walls should be avoided, as they may be demolished in the future.

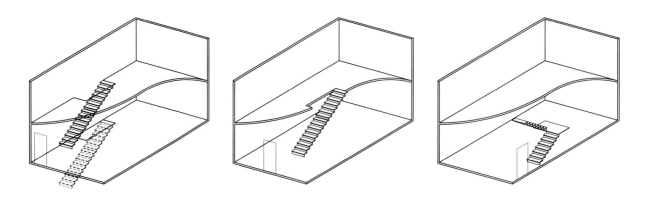

Figure 4.8 In a multilevel dwelling, stairs should be placed as close as possible to the entrance for maximum efficiency of space.

SPATIAL CONFIGURATIONS

Thoughtful interior design can contribute to cost reduction by creating a dwelling with a layout that maximizes the efficiency of small spaces. Additionally, designing with flexibility in mind can allow a home to grow and change with its inhabitant's life. Although the building's form was treated above, for the purpose of clarity, some aspects related to the envelope will be looked at again.

Aside from a circle, a square encloses the most area for a given perimeter. In housing, the construction of exterior walls tends to be among the most costly components, as framing, insulating, and weatherproofing combine to demand high investments in both materials and labor. By starting with a rectangular footprint, envelope building expenses can be lowered (Figure 4.9).

A variety of design strategies can be used to add space and appeal to square or rectangular footprints. Bays can break up the mass of a home's façade and create intimate alcoves or designate a separate, functional space in the interior. To keep costs down, these bays can be cantilevered so that the foundation below will not have projections. Additional exterior functions that do not require a foundation, such as porches, can further add interest and disguise the otherwise plain envelope. Several traditional housing styles, such as colonial, embrace and emphasize the simplicity of the rectangular plan through symmetrical façades. A square plan, therefore, works well when these styles are chosen.

Due to ample envelope surface, the square plan also allows more natural light to penetrate to the interior and to increase the sense of spaciousness. Additionally, the placement of the functional zones within the home is also

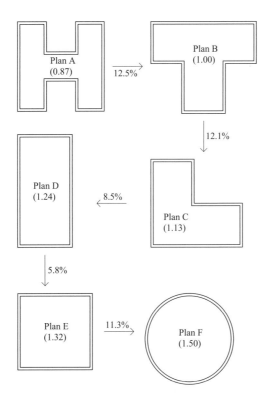

Figure 4.9 Different footprint forms for the same floor area will also affect the length and area of the dwelling's enclosure walls. (Numbers in parentheses show ratio of floor area to perimeter walls. Arrows indicate reduction.)

made more flexible by a square plan, as more than one room can occupy a given side of the home. A drawback to the square plan, however, is that a wider footprint will require a larger lot and increase land costs. A compromise between a square and a more rectangular form can maximize interior square footage and flexibility and can also lower land and infrastructure costs.

Within the building envelope, several distinct design approaches can be used to create a layout for a small home's interior, each with its own cost implications. The most traditional approach to creating spatial demarcations in a house is through interior partition walls, through which every room is enclosed and separated from other areas of the home. The construction of partition walls, however, adds costs to a home; and for small interiors, permanent walls can make spaces feel cramped and uncomfortable. The area that the walls themselves occupy is large, and they contain plumbing, electrical receptacles, doors, and molding that further contribute to the cost of building them.

A more efficient and affordable alternative to wall partitions is the open floor plan. The open plan uses furniture, shelving, ceiling heights, and other means to define spaces without the use of walls. Certain rooms, of course, require walls, such as bathrooms; in dwellings with children, walls separating individual bedrooms are also usually considered necessary. The juxtaposition of an open plan for the more public living spaces, with enclosed rooms for more private functions, reinforces the separation of these functional zones. Since in small homes these zones are often close together, such arrangements allow for an area that feels spacious and inviting next to more private spaces.

Another strategy for laying out the interior effectively and affordably is to use add-ins. This method allows homes to be occupied with minimal interior finishing, thereby reducing construction costs. The homeowners can then create interior partitions progressively, when and where they wish. Much of the success of this strategy depends on the envelope design. Care must be taken to ensure that components such as stairs, plumbing, and windows are located with cost savings in mind. Where the side of a home is large enough to accommodate more than one room, multiple windows should be provided to facilitate such changes, especially for spaces that may be converted into bedrooms.

Making Small Spaces Feel Bigger

Once the envelope and the zones have been settled upon, individual spaces and rooms are designed to create functional, comfortable, and affordable homes. For smaller interiors, a variety of strategies can be employed to make spaces feel larger. Although not commonly thought of, a careful manipulation of ceiling heights can help to designate different spaces for different activities and make certain areas look wider than they really are. In open plan designs, varying floor and ceiling heights is an effective method for dividing spaces without building walls and sacrificing valuable floor area. Low-ceiling heights foster a sense of warmth and privacy and work well for bedrooms and alcoves. Having a small space, such as a hallway or kitchen, with a lower ceiling open into an area with a relatively higher ceiling enhances the sense of spaciousness in that area. An entrance foyer, with a low ceiling, for example, that looks onto a living room with a higher ceiling will foster a sense of openness to the house upon entering (Figure 4.10).

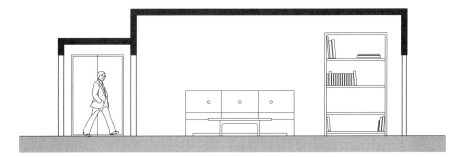

Figure 4.10 An entrance foyer with a low ceiling that looks into a living room with a higher ceiling will give a sense of openness to the house upon entering.

One way to create the illusion of a tall ceiling without incurring additional construction costs is to leave the ceiling joists exposed. The void between the joists creates the illusion of a taller space, while adding depth and character. Sound transmission can be a problem with exposed joists, however, as less material exists between floors to absorb noise. For single-family homes, this situation is less problematic, but for multiunit dwellings, sound insulation means, such as carpeting, will have to be provided.

For very small rooms, a high ceiling can help foster a sense of openness. To avoid wasting too much volume, a *mezzanine* can be introduced over the kitchen or living room areas, providing additional space and defining the spaces below it through changes in ceiling height (Figure 4.11). In a very small dwelling, the addition of a mezzanine sleeping loft allows a person to live comfortably in a home with a 240 square foot (22 square meter) footprint (Bradford, 1991). A space with a 16-foot (4.9-meter) ceiling is necessary for a mezzanine, and a skylight will let in natural light. In many North American jurisdictions, mezzanines are permitted to occupy up to 40 percent of the area below. Mezzanines also help to increase the versatility of a home, as they are suitable for everything from an extra sleeping area, home office, or simple storage space, and their function can be changed with minimal effort. To make the most of a limited space, an attic can function similarly to a mezzanine. The addition of a skylight or dormer to the roof will help improve the quality of this space. Like a mezzanine, the attic can be a family room, adolescent's bedroom, or storage area, as needs change.

Varying floor levels within a home can help a small space feel larger as well as define separate functions when partition walls are minimized. In open plans where kitchen, living, and dining areas occupy a single space, a simple step down from the kitchen and dining area to the living space can create a separation between spaces while maintaining a sense of openness. A level change from public to private zones is common in single-family detached homes. A single level, however, is more cost-efficient and provides an accessible dwelling for

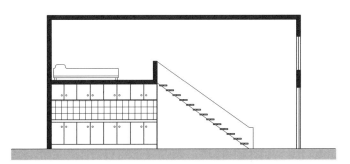

Figure 4.11 A mezzanine can provide additional space and define the function below through changes in ceiling height.

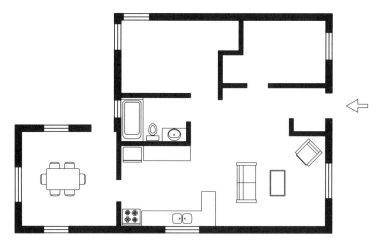

Figure 4.12 A rear porch was enclosed to become the dining area of this small home.

people with reduced mobility. It also enhances the home's flexibility, as it is easier to switch functions around.

In addition to optimizing spaciousness, creating a dynamic relationship between a home's interior and exterior can further compensate for a small indoor footprint. Windows and glass doors that offer views of the exterior open up interiors, making them feel larger. Corner windows break up the enclosed feeling of a space and facilitate the placement of furniture in small rooms by freeing more wall area.

Outdoor rooms—such as balconies and patios—can also compensate for a lack of indoor space, to varying degrees. In milder climates, where outdoor spaces can be used more often, exterior areas can become outdoor rooms without increasing construction costs. To ensure that these areas feel like and are treated as an integral part of the home itself, the distinction between interior and exterior should be blurred. This can be achieved in a variety of ways. Glass doors to the exterior space are the most common means of connecting the interior to the exterior. Using the same floor treatment on the outdoor space and the abutting interior room or continuing ceiling elements from the interior room to the outside also work well. For example, joists that form an interior ceiling can be extended to the exterior to create a pergola for the outdoor room. The location of outdoor spaces will also greatly affect their effectiveness as an extension of the interior. Outdoor eating spaces should be located off or close to the kitchen to facilitate taking food and tableware outside. Screened porches can also be used to augment interior space (Figure 4.12). Porches and decks are suited for small affordable homes, as they are typically much less expensive to construct than finished interior rooms, because they do not require a foundation. They can also be added on years after occupancy.

Residual Spaces

Residual spaces are leftover areas after allocation of all others to rooms and to circulation. These spaces in large homes are less important, but in small homes—where space is at a premium—they can be exploited and used. In addition, creative use of such space can help with everyday domestic chores and even give a home its unique character.

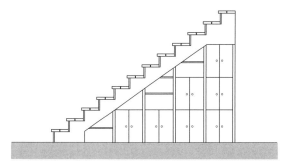 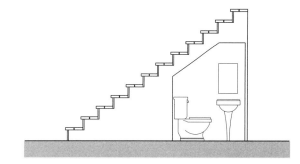

In multistory dwellings, the area under the stairs can be considered a residual space and used in a variety of ways (Figure 4.13). A drawer, for example, can provide storage for everyday items (Govan, 2003). For stairs next to a living room, the lowered ceiling area under the stairs can define a work space and create the impression of a distinct place for a specific activity. Shelves can be mounted on the wall to make use of awkward triangular spaces. For stairs beside a kitchen, the space under the stairs can be enclosed to serve as a pantry.

Figure 4.13 Residual spaces like those under stairs can be used in a variety of ways.

An *alcove* is a pocket of space attached to a larger room or area, and it is often used to separate one activity from the main room (Susanka, 2004). It can be created by suspending a bay over the side of the home. Alcoves increase the functionality of a room. While alcoves work best for creating a cozy and inviting space, they can be expensive to construct and are often not possible in a small budget, affordable housing project. Other less expensive methods can be used to create an effect similar to that of an alcove. For a rectangular living space, bookshelves can be built into the wall to frame a space.

Moreover, the design strategy in using these residual spaces needs to be the creative use of spaces that are not commonly thought of as valuable areas. One such approach can be the multiple use of the very same space. A counter, for example, can unfold from the wall to become a desk and can then be folded back to add more space to the living room. *Window seats* are another type of alcove that consist of a bench area along a view of the exterior. To optimize their use, the area under the bench's seat can provide extra storage.

Basements can also be considered a type of residual space. In large homes with ample space above ground, basements are considered uninhabitable due to lack of natural light; they are regarded as habitable in small homes. When designing new housing, measures should be taken to ensure that basements allow for a variety of functions. By raising the ceiling of the basement above grade, windows can introduce natural light, making the space suitable for a bedroom or a family room (Figure 4.14). For some sites, the grade can be manipulat-

Figure 4.14 By raising the ceiling of the basement above grade, windows can let in natural light and fresh air, making it suitable for habitable functions.

ed to allow for larger windows or even doors to the outside. Proper insulation and ventilation systems will ensure that a basement does not become damp. When properly finished, basements can serve several functions and provide a space that can be adapted to a family's changing needs.

SPACE-MAKING DEVICES

In addition to utilizing a home's residual spaces, various materials and products can also increase the efficient use of small areas and add to an overall sense of spaciousness without adding to construction costs. Such strategies also lend themselves to adaptability, as they can be easily altered without the need for demolition or construction. *Pocket doors* provide desired privacy to an area and take up less space than traditional swinging doors. While a traditional swinging door requires clearance that restricts the placement of furniture, pocket doors, once opened, hide completely within the wall cavity. Pocket doors are best suited for areas that often remain connected but where occasional separation is desirable, such as between kitchens and dining rooms or bedrooms and studies. Although their installation is more expensive than conventional swing doors, their space-saving advantage makes the investment worthwhile.

To keep costs low, homes can be constructed and sold with only a few enclosed rooms. As a family grows and changes, however, additional partitioning may become necessary. With the current method of constructing partition walls, such changes are expensive and will cause great disruption to a homeowner's daily life. Walls developed for use in office buildings, however, offer easy installation and relocation. At present, the prefabricated walls are code-approved for commercial use and permitted for residential use only in certain jurisdictions.

There are three basic types of *demountable wall systems*. The first is a *mobile* or *operable system,* which has a sliding mechanism that allows a wall panel to move along ceiling tracks. The second type is a *demountable system,* which is similar in concept to the traditional drywall system. Walls are constructed with metal studs that are placed at specific intervals. Prefinished gypsum wallboards are then affixed with special slips to the metal frame. The third type is the *portable partition system,* made of prefabricated panels, which are brought to a desired location and held in place by channels in the ceiling and floor (Friedman, 2002b).

Another option for creating interior partitions is through the use of *sliding screens.* This space-dividing method is common in Japan, where large screens made from wooden frames and paper are moved along tracks affixed to the floor and ceiling. In Western homes where floor tracks are uncommon, similar screens can be developed to run along the ceiling. Sliding screens can be thought of as large doors that help to create spaces without taking up large amounts of floor area. While such screens provide useful visual dividers, sound is still transmitted through them, and so they should not be used for areas that require acoustic isolation.

Furniture partitions work in several ways to increase the efficiency and comfort of small homes. Using shelving and furniture to divide spaces reduces the need for interior partition walls. Additionally, furniture partitions help to make

small spaces feel larger by blurring boundaries between rooms, allowing the eye to see beyond them, preventing small spaces from feeling boxed in. When shelves, cabinets, or other storage units are used to create partitions, small areas are provided with much-needed storage space. Furniture partitions also make spaces versatile, as they can be moved easily to change the size and function of spaces (Figure 4.15).

Figure 4.15 Using shelving and furniture to divide spaces reduces the need for interior partition walls.

Terence Conrad (2001) argues that the primary problem faced by people living in a small space can be summed up with one word—stuff. Because of rampant consumerism and the popularity and accessibility of new affordable goods, the need for storage space in every room has grown. When a space, regardless of its size, is clean and uncluttered, it will seem larger. This problem is particularly pronounced in small homes. The most obvious solution is to eliminate any unnecessary or unused items. This responsibility, however, falls on the homeowners themselves. As for the designer, by considering storage needs in the design of an interior space, homeowners can avoid facing the clutter and lack of openness that makes a small space feel cramped and uncomfortable.

Built-in storage is best suited for small spaces, since it fits the house design to create a seamless and clutter-free look (Conrad, 2001). Freestanding storage, such as armoires, dressers, and chests of drawers, tend to eat into floor space and can make room layouts and circulation routes awkward. Custom-made, built-in furniture is expensive to construct and can inhibit the adaptability of rooms to different activities. To maximize storage possibilities and minimize costs, a compromise between the last two forms of storage should be reached, which can be built-in storage.

Several options for increasing storage without decreasing free floor space exist for homeowners. A key strategy for providing storage is to add upward. Shelves and closets can be cantilevered out from the wall using concealed shelf supports. This arrangement allows floor space to be preserved and the circulation uninhibited. Suspended storage also helps to eliminate clutter and increase efficiency. In kitchens, pots and pans can be hung above islands where headroom is not needed. Utensils can be hung along walls on racks or hooks. This provides storage that is less expensive and easier to use than cabinets. In entryways and living areas, hooks can provide easy storage for coats, hats, and umbrellas; this solution is less expensive and easier to use than a coat closet, and it frees up the space that a coat stand would occupy. Clothing can be double-hung in closets or alcoves with doors, screens, or blinds to protect clothing from dust and remove them from view.

Within closets, storage systems can be added to maximize its storage potential. Shelves, drawers, baskets, and rods can be used to allow closets to accommodate an entire wardrobe, often eliminating the need for a separate armoire or chest of drawers, saving homeowners space and money (Figure 4.16). Additionally, by removing such furniture, the extra bedroom space can be used for a small office or as a sitting area to provide each family member with a private space of their own during the day as well as at night. To further liberate bedroom space, beds can be elevated to accommodate storage underneath. The most creative example of this strategy is the loft bed, under which a desk or shelving system is often placed. While it is true that the more elevated the bed is the greater the storage possibilities, even raising the bed a foot or two can provide enough storage to eliminate the need for a chest of drawers.

FINISHES

Once the interior spaces of a home are created, finishing materials, furniture, and lighting can further contribute to its comfort, efficiency, and affordability. Changes in construction practices and the introduction of new products have led to new opportunities in interior finishes. Builders and homeowners are offered a huge variety of finishing options that also vary greatly in quality and cost. Many of these products advertise easy installation and removal, further reducing costs.

Colors

Finishing a home will begin by selecting colors and textures for the various spaces. Color preferences vary from person to person, but certain colors tend to evoke particular spatial and emotional responses, regardless of individual preferences. Dark colors absorb more light than they reflect, and so they seem heavy in one's peripheral vision (Susanka, 2004). When people look at dark walls, most feel that the wall must be closer to them than it actually is. The opposite is true of lighter walls. Because of this effect, dark colors connote contraction, while light colors connote expansion. Similarly, rough textures, such as unfinished wood or brick, absorb more light and create shadows while smooth surfaces

reflect light off of them. As a result, smooth surfaces should be used in small spaces, and darker, textured surfaces should be avoided. Employing a carefully selected variety of colors in a small space can create an environment that feels spacious but also possesses visual interest and character (Susanka, 2004).

When selecting interior finishes for a small home, it is important to conceive each zone as parts of a whole rather than a series of separate areas. When space is limited, keeping colors, textures, and detailing to a minimum will help create spaces that avoid feeling cluttered or congested (Conrad, 2001). One particularly effective strategy is to use one floor material for the entire interior or, at least, materials within the same tonal family. Doing so will help spaces blend into one another, creating the illusion of one larger area.

Figure 4.16 Within closets, shelves, drawers, baskets, and rods can be used to eliminate the need for a separate armoire or chest of drawers.

When selecting a color, several qualities of that color should be examined. A color's *hue* refers to the wavelength the color reflects, for example, red, blue, or green. *Brightness* is a measure of how strong is a color. For example, yellow and white are typically bright, while blue and black are darker. Finally, a color's *saturation* measures how pure it is. Chocolate syrup, for example, is a very saturated brown; but when milk is added to it, the brown becomes less saturated and imposing (Conrad, 2001).

The human eye is very sensitive to changes in hue. This helps to explain why so many different varieties of white are available for interior paint. While each "white" may contain a very low saturation of color and all appear relatively bright, the small amounts of a particular hue can completely change the effect of a white in a room. For example, whites with a low saturation of blue are often described as "cool" while whites with a yellow or red hue are described as "warm." The more saturated the color, the greater its visual weight. In small spaces, highly saturated colors can be used effectively as accents on selected walls.

For a small dwelling, however, lighter and brighter colors are necessary to create a sense of openness. This openness is especially true of ceilings, which are often left white regardless of wall color. It is also true that light ceilings will look taller while dark ceilings will feel lower; yet darker, more saturated ceilings can also be effective in creating a sense of intimacy and warmth. When ceiling joists are exposed, they can create a pattern whose shadows can make a ceiling feel darker and lower. Joists in small spaces should, therefore, be light, made of bright wood, or painted a light color to ensure that a space feels comfortable (Susanka, 2004).

Floor Covering

The way to find cost savings on wall and floor finishings is to reduce the costly labor and material involved in their installation. Therefore, new surface coverings are designed to cover more areas using fewer items. A labor-intensive area is tiling. Innovative products made of polyvinyl chloride (PVC) can be applied to the area around the bathtub. The product is made of large waterproof sheets that can be installed much faster than tiles.

The choice of floor finish can greatly enhance the appearance and comfort of a home, but it can also increase costs. Ideally, quality floor materials, such as ceramic tile and hardwood, should be used since they add to the beauty and value of a home. For affordable housing, however, such materials are not always within a homebuyer's price range. Buyers with limited budgets can choose less expensive products, with the possibility of upgrading them later.

Floating floors have become a popular alternative to traditional wood floor options. They differ from conventional wood floors in that they are not attached to the subfloor. The floor is held in place by tongue-and-groove connections, which make installation quick and cost-effective. The panels are made of high-density, moisture-resistant fiberboard panels composed of wood residues such as sawdust, woodchips, and shavings from processing factories. The ligneous material is ground to a pulp and then resin is added, which makes the final product highly durable. Floating floors are not only easy to install, but, because they "float" above the subfloor, they are very easy to remove and lend themselves to adaptability.

If wood floors are too expensive, carpet is often an affordable alternative. For many buyers, especially those with young children, carpet is preferred over wood as it provides a safe play surface. While carpet can be less expensive initially, there are added maintenance costs. Carpets will need to be cleaned periodically and tend to deteriorate with wear more rapidly than hardwood. New carpeting products can be purchased in squares that have padding attached and can be joined together seamlessly, piece by piece. This method reduces labor and also allows for easy installation and repairs by the homeowner to damaged areas, as the entire carpet does not have to be replaced.

Vinyl or linoleum flooring is typically less expensive than either wood or carpet. While often confused for one another, linoleum and vinyl are not the same material. *Linoleum* is derived from the flax plant and is a highly durable, ecologically friendly substance that can last for 50 years or more. *Vinyl* flooring, on the other hand, is an artificial product that has become more popular than linoleum, especially in new housing projects, because it is less expensive and easier to install. Although vinyl is often viewed as an undesirable material, new innovations and designs have created durable flooring that can complement a variety of decors and budgets. When ceramic tile is too expensive, designers or homeowners can use vinyl sheets for bathroom flooring, bearing in mind the possibility of upgrading to tile at a later time.

Lighting

Lighting can be a useful tool in dictating the atmosphere and the feel of a space. There are two types of light that can be used in a home: *natural daylight* and *artificial lighting*. The quality of natural light within a home largely depends on a dwelling's orientation and the quantity and positioning of windows within the building envelope. An abundance of natural light within a home helps make small spaces feel larger and reduces the need for artificial lighting. Because of their location or type, however, many dwellings allow for little flexibility in the location of windows and skylights; row houses, for example, can have windows on only two façades. For homes with limited natural light penetration, several strategies can be employed to optimize the effect of existing natural light sources.

Mirrors are perhaps the most simple, common, and affordable means to enhance daylight in a home. When light hits a mirror, it is reflected back into a space. Additionally, mirrors help small spaces seem larger by creating false perspectives. When cleverly located, mirrors can not only compensate for insufficient daylight from windows but also provide interior spaces with exterior views. This effect can be achieved by placing a mirror opposite a window or glass door.

In long, narrow homes, such as row houses, bringing natural light into the center of the dwelling can be a difficult task. Skylights are a good option, but they can be expensive and only work for the top floor in apartment buildings or multifamily plexes. They are also known to be a source of heat loss. Minimizing solid interior partitions allows light from front and back windows to spill throughout a home. Furniture partitions such as shelving units can be left open to allow light to pass through them. In bathrooms, where privacy is essential, natural light can penetrate through translucent interior semiwindows of sand-blasted or block glass.

Natural light within a dwelling must be supplemented with artificial light sources. Interior lighting can be broken down into several categories based on its function. *General* or *background lighting* provides an overall level of illumination when natural light levels are low (Conrad, 2001). This sort of lighting often takes the form of a single overhead light fixture in the middle of a room, but it can also be supplied in the form of table or floor lamps, spotlights, and hanging lights. Including an overhead light for each room in a home reduces the burden on homeowners to purchase lighting themselves, but it also increases construction costs and reduces the flexibility of the interior. Additionally, high ceiling lights have a tendency to draw in the walls, which can make rooms feel smaller.

Task lighting, on the other hand, provides bright, focused light for specific working areas. Popular task lighting includes the gooseneck and smaller desk lamps. This method of lighting provides light when and where it is needed, which can help reduce energy costs by eliminating unnecessary lighting. Task lighting works best in rooms equipped with plenty of outlets. In dwellings with an open floor plan, this can be difficult, as permanent partition walls, where codes dictate that outlets be located, are minimized. One possible solution is to install electrical sockets on the floor, as practiced by commercial building, when permitted by code. Another alternative is to install suspended ceiling track lighting to which light fixtures can be plugged.

The interior design and finishing strategies that have been listed above need to be regarded as a menu of options for a designer, builder, and homeowner. They have to be selected and fitted according to a particular situation. Some designs will be more suitable to some ideas whereas other layouts will appropriately accommodate others.

KEY CONSIDERATIONS

- In marrying efficiency and sense of space, one can design small homes that feel comfortable and personal rather than cramped and suffocating.
- It is important to be familiar with lifestyles and, as a result, how people use homes. By reviewing what spaces are important and most used, some less-used areas can be eliminated altogether.
- Optimizing the storage potential of a small space can help reduce unnecessary areas, eliminating the need for a basement or excessive closets, for example.
- Creating a public, open-plan zone for the kitchen and dining and living area is a practical and effective cost-reduction strategy. This arrangement also reflects contemporary lifestyle patterns.
- In general, the smaller the space the more compartmentalizing and merging of functions needs to take place. Small homes can have the same number and type of functions as large dwellings, yet the size of these functions is reduced and their location different.

- Long-term efficiency and affordability can be ensured by zoning spaces to permit physical transformation and flexibility along changes in the occupant's life cycle.

- In small homes, the amount of circulation space should be minimized and viewed as a multipurpose area, allowing both movement and other functions, such as storage, to take place.

- In a small house, a covered porch can become an outdoor entryway and serve as a storage space. Porches can be designed to be easily enclosed, insulated, heated, and turned into year-round rooms.

- Locating the entry along one of the lateral walls frees the front elevation for windows to take advantage of natural light.

- In small, long homes, such as row houses, an entryway should offer a view through the length of the interior. Preferably, an opening placed at the end wall will extend this view further.

- Circulation in a small house should not force the crossing of one zone to get to another.

- To further reduce cost, stairs should remain open, eliminating additional finishing expenses and increasing a sense of spaciousness.

- Where the side of a home is large enough to accommodate more than one room, multiple windows should be provided to facilitate such changes, especially when spaces are converted into bedrooms.

- Manipulating ceiling heights can help designate different spaces for different activities and make certain areas look wider than they really are. Having a small space such as a hallway or a kitchen with a lower ceiling open into an area with a relatively higher ceiling enhances the sense of spaciousness in that area.

- In a very small dwelling, the addition of a mezzanine-level sleeping loft allows a person to live comfortably in a 240 square foot (22 square meter) footprint (Bedford, 1991).

- Creating a dynamic relationship between a home's interior and exterior can further compensate for a small indoor footprint. Windows and glass doors will make small spaces feel larger. Corner windows will facilitate the placement of furniture in small rooms by freeing the wall area.

- Porches and decks are suited for small affordable homes, because they are less expensive to construct than interior areas and provide useful functional uses.

- When properly designed, an inexpensive, suspended alcove can add space to a room and increase its functionality.

- Residual space under interior stairs can become a useful storage area or accommodate a powder room.

- Pocket doors provide desired privacy to an area and take up less space than a traditional swinging door.

- The use of demountable partitions, sliding screens, and furniture partitions should be considered as affordable space-making devices.

- A useful strategy for providing storage is to add upward. Shelves and closets can be cantilevered from the wall using concealed shelf supports.

- For a small dwelling, lighter, brighter colors are necessary to create a sense of openness. Light-colored ceilings will appear taller than darker ones.
- Flooring materials such as floating floors, vinyl flooring, and carpets can offer low-cost alternatives to conventional floor finishings when their patterns are well-chosen and well-integrated into the design.
- Task lighting can help reduce energy costs by eliminating unnecessary lighting. They work best in rooms equipped with plenty of outlets, which can prove difficult in dwellings with open floor plans.

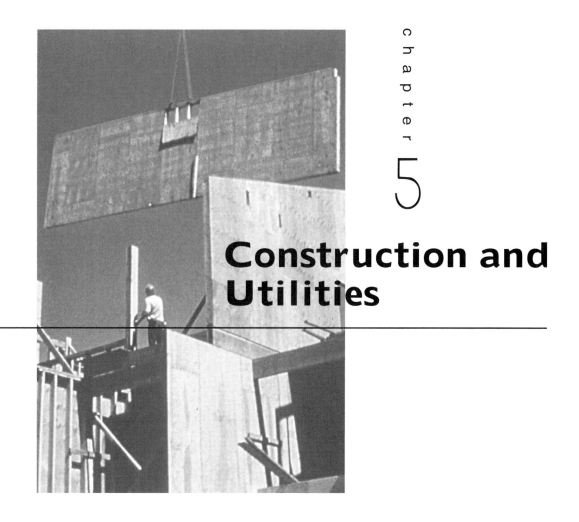

5

Construction and Utilities

A popular saying suggests that people of lesser means should not buy poorly built products, since they cannot afford to replace them. The same goes for buyers of affordable housing, which must be inexpensive yet well built. Since labor and materials account for 53 percent of the dwelling cost, savings can be significant when attention is paid to these two items. As some low-income families may spend over 15 percent of their income on heating and cooling, good construction practices also contribute to a lower energy bill and to the occupants' comfort. The need to find a balance between lowering cost and maintaining quality construction is the thrust of this chapter, which looks into cost-reduction strategies related to the construction of a home and its utilities. Following a description of general preconstruction steps, various key building components, such as the foundation, framing, roof, interior, and, finally, home utilities, will be described.

PRECONSTRUCTION CONSIDERATIONS

The life cycle of a home's construction is made of a number of phases and includes many participants. Once the construction documents have been prepared and permits issued, the building process begins. The construction of a home needs to be a continuous, short as possible sequence of steps that will see drawings turn into a habitable structure. Cost-saving strategies, therefore, must be planned prior to construction. The two chief elements that make up the larger share of construction costs are labor and materials, and it is on these two that reduction efforts must be focused. Prior to elaborating on specific methods, it would be of value to outline background aspects that contribute to cost savings and increase the process's efficiency.

The planning stage is an instrumental part of cost savings. The initiator, whether a builder of a mass housing project or persons building for themselves, needs to make sure that they are well prepared and did not leave portions of the process unplanned. The process begins by having a well-drafted set of drawings, which need to be regarded as a tool of communication with the trades. Poor communication may result in additional costs. Altering old plans or hiring an inexperienced designer is the wrong approach. Designing lower cost housing requires more attention to details and evaluation of appropriate strategies to make construction simple.

When, during construction, on-site improvised decisions are made, they might not be well thought out, and they might prolong the process and as well add expenses. When the design strays from conventional forms, materials, or details, a premium will also have to be paid. The engagement of a specialized trade or the ordering of uncommon equipment or products may be required. The desire to design a nontraditional structure will have to be carefully studied for its effect on cost. This does not mean to suggest that innovation should not be attempted, rather, that it must be studied and prepared for.

Reducing the number of tasks and people involved in the building process can be a useful cost-reduction strategy. Preferably, the same tradespeople will perform several tasks. It will lead to better time management and an advantageous contract. A contract can be made for labor only or labor and materials. At times, it is better to have the latter and enjoy the savings that professional tradespeople will get from their suppliers. On the other hand, when initiators purchase materials, they might have more time to spend looking for and finding the best deal.

Another preconstruction necessity is coordination among the trades for the purpose of creating a flawless process. It can be achieved by inviting the key trades, such as the framer, electrician, and plumber, to a preconstruction meeting. There, a discussion between the trades on how the design can be made more cost efficient and time saved by altering the sequence of tasks can take place. Since the construction of a home is made of a number of steps, total savings will be achieved by compiling increments of each task. Some may be of large items and lead to substantial savings while others will lead to small ones. Therefore, it makes more sense to focus on savings in large tasks first.

Labor cost can also be reduced by designing for self-help. Once moved in, the occupants will invest their own manual labor, a process known as "sweat equity." Construction details can be simplified and drawings prepared to illustrate future phases and methods of completion in greater detail and given to the new owners. The proliferation and the convenience of renovation centers and the vast range of products that they offer, coupled with the many "how-to" knowledge sources, have made self-help a very popular cost-saving approach. Construction can also be done by volunteer labor. Organizations such as Habitat for Humanity have demonstrated that the entire labor segment of a home can be eliminated. As a result, the home can be designed to be "volunteer friendly," as if it were to be constructed by laypeople.

When the design has too many deviations from standard procedures and conventions and when each building component is to be different, premiums will be incurred. Savings can be obtained through volume building. Whether several structures of the same kind or repetition of a single component in the very same building, cost reduction will be achieved through time saved or volume discount.

When designing a home, a life-cycle return decision-making approach can be adopted for the choice of construction methods and products. Investment in the dwelling can be made in better workmanship and more expensive, higher quality products. Alternatively, savings can be obtained by using less expensive products and poorer construction quality. *Optimal value engineering* (OVE) is a method that helps balance short- and long-term economic benefits and obtain the utmost return on an investment. In general, the preferred approach will be to opt for a better-built home. Yet, at times, funding makes it impossible. A recommended strategy, therefore, is to invest in quality where the fundamentals of house building are concerned. Building a poorly insulated house, for example, will result in higher energy costs and occupants' discomfort. It will be very costly to upgrade the dwelling's insulation later. It would make more economic sense to use less costly finishes—linoleum rather than tile as a floor covering material, for example—and assume that the occupants will upgrade them later. It is, therefore, recommended that the designer look into getting the best product value, one that will not require ongoing repair and maintenance.

The construction process of a home sees the rough structure built in the first phase and the finishes as a second phase. A cost-saving approach will be to overlap these two phases. Well-chosen structural materials can also become the finished product. Better-grade plywood can be varnished to become the finished floor, or the joists can remain exposed, adding space and saving the need to clad them with drywall.

Planning with modular dimensions in mind or designing for inclusion of certain mass-produced prefabricated products that are known to be less expensive is another preconstruction saving strategy. The chosen dimensions will reduce the amount of on-site waste and, as a result, expenditure. Cost can also be brought down by using salvaged materials. Yards do exist in numbers of cities where such products are available. Recycled timber-framing, for example, can be less expensive and pleasing to look at.

FOUNDATIONS

Foundation design is one of the first stages in preparing construction documents for a building. Since the foundation supports the entire structure, aspects related to its type and method of construction must be considered carefully. Site selection and soil testing, which have been described above, are critical in ensuring that a proper foundation is chosen. It is a process of verifying the weight of the proposed structure and fitting it to the type of soil below. Some soils, such as rock, are known to be favorable places to site a house, while other soils, like clay, pose risks as they tend to expand when saturated with moisture. Wet soil, a result of poor grading or underground water, will require careful attention to avoid excess humidity. When given a choice, the foundation should be built on a higher elevation where soil grading directs the water away from the foundation itself.

There are a variety of construction methods and materials in building foundations. Each has its own advantages and disadvantages and will largely depend on the project's budget, location, the builder's familiarity with the technique, the type of home, and building codes and regulations, to name a few. In general, foundations can be segmented into the following categories: *concrete slab, crawl space,* and *basement.* A variety of building products can be used in constructing these types. They also offer challenges and opportunities as far as cost is concerned.

Concrete Slab

In general, it costs less to build above ground than under it. When deep foundations can be avoided, *slab foundations,* which are also known as *slab-on-grade,* are recommended. A U.S. Housing and Urban Development (HUD) report (1994) lists two types of slab foundation (Figure 5.1). The first, *monolithic slab-on-grade,* is designed to reduce cost by having the entire foundation constructed in a single pour. In this design, the foundation's edge and the floor will be constructed at the same time. It is a type that works best for mild climates, where winter freezing is not a concern. The additional cost-saving

Figure 5.1 Slab foundations are considered to be the least expensive to construct since excavation and formwork are minimized.

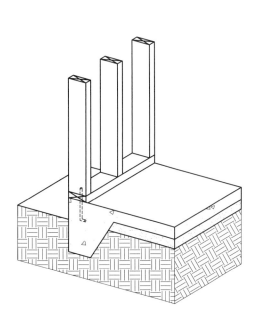

Monolithic Slab-on-Grade Foundation

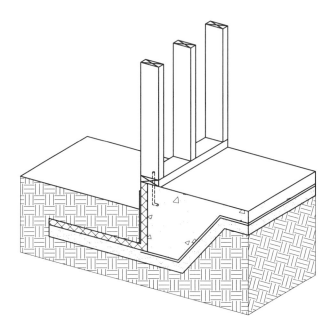

Frost-Protected Shallow Foundation

advantage with such a method lies in the fact that the slab serves as a rough lower floor. As a result, plumbing drainage lines or radiant floor heating is typically installed in the slab.

A *frost-protected shallow foundation* is a variation of slab-on-grade. It is suited for construction in cold-based regions and was designed to protect the foundation against freezing. The method is used primarily where excavating deep foundations is impossible. A shallow foundation can be constructed of poured concrete or concrete blocks. The challenge in laying foundations in cold regions is preventing *heaving*, which is caused by the freeze-thaw cycle. Several methods are used to protect the foundation in such a climate. Placing a rigid foam insulation around the facing edges of the foundation is the most common. The same product is also placed around the perimeter of the structure below grade to a distance of 1 to 2 feet (0.3 to 0.6 meters). When budget permits, to increase the occupant's comfort, insulation is placed above the crushed stone on top of which the concrete is poured. Constructing an insulated wooden subfloor above the concrete will further lower energy bills.

Crawl Space

The *crawl-space foundation* is another cost-saving method of building a lower structural support for a home (Figure 5.2). It can be built using concrete blocks or poured-in-place concrete. The structure can also be suspended on piers made either of wood or concrete. It adapts the monolithic slab-on-grade approach by "distributing the building load directly from a concrete wall to the soil without the need for separate spread-footing" (HUD, 1994).

It is common to see such foundations in high-moisture areas. The lower floor is raised above ground, providing easy access to plumbing. The space between grade and the lower floor must be ventilated to prevent moisture damage to the wood structure and to lower the floor temperature. Crawl spaces also require attention to insulation since the plumbing may be exposed. The method commonly used in lower-cost housing is to place insulation between the joists of the lower floor. Space, then, needs to be left between ground and the floor to allow easy maneuvering. In such a case, vapor barriers will be installed under the subfloor to prevent moisture leakage to the outside. Another method is to insulate the perimeter wall by affixing rigid insulation to the exterior or by installing batt insulation on the inside. The method is recommended for an unvented crawl space and requires proper attention to installation methods to prevent detachment. Perimeter drainage pipes should also be installed around the wall.

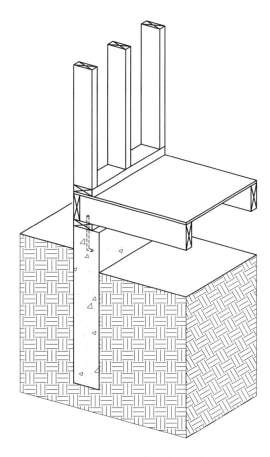

Figure 5.2 Crawl space foundation has cost-saving advantages, since excavation is reduced and footing eliminated.

Basement Foundation

The most elaborate foundation is the *poured, concrete basement*. A trade-off is made in its construction; more money is spent in return for getting functional and habitable space. The high cost of the basement is a result of the tasks involved in its construction, which include excavation, setting forms and pouring footings, preparing additional forms and pouring walls, construction of a lower concrete floor, drainage, insulation, damp-proofing, and backfill.

Insulation is a prime consideration in basement foundations. To prevent damage to the foundation in cold climate regions, the footing has to be constructed to an average depth of 4 feet 6 inches (1.4 meters). Therefore, the exterior side of the wall must be insulated as well. To lower cost, when the basement is left unfinished, exterior insulation provides the only protection for the foundation wall. Some regional building codes require that the interior upper portion of the foundation, the one above grade, be insulated. The most common cost-effective exterior type of insulating product is rigid foam. It can be affixed to both concrete and concrete blocks and can have tongue-and-groove edges that help with alignment and water protection. When the basement is designed as fully habitable space, the space's interior must be insulated.

Preventing moisture penetration is one of the key challenges in basement construction. The common prevention methods are *damp-proofing* and *waterproofing*. According to Johnson (1990), "dampproofing regards dampness or water penetration under non-hydrostatic pressure due to capillary action in a construction material." Waterproofing, on the other hand, prevents water penetration under hydrostatic pressure from entering the basement. The most common material used in damp-proofing is a bituminous coating over the cement. It is highly popular due to its low cost. The layer needs to be at least 20 millimeters thick to provide the covering with a much-needed elasticity. A watertight membrane is also used for waterproofing. It can be made from a variety of products that loosely or tightly affix to the wall. The cementitious coating to the foundation wall, which is commonly referred to as *purging,* can also be effective as a moisture prevention measure when mixed with acrylic-based products.

Additional Foundation Construction Methods

Several alternative methods of constructing a foundation are also available. Each has advantages and disadvantages that ought to be carefully studied in low-cost building.

Insulated Concrete Forms

Insulated concrete forms (ICF) combine two functions (Figure 5.3). Made of polystyrene, the forms are placed on top of each other to form a hollow wall. When rebar reinforcement is inserted and cement poured into the cavity, a concrete wall insulated on both sides is ready. It saves the need to construct traditional wooden forms, pour concrete, remove the forms, and insulate the wall. The product does not require specialized installation skills, and in most regions, it is offered with a choice of buying either materials only or labor and materials. The disadvantage of such a product lies in the fact that it breaks and dents easily and can offer a hidden pathway for subterranean termites (Haun, 2002). A product

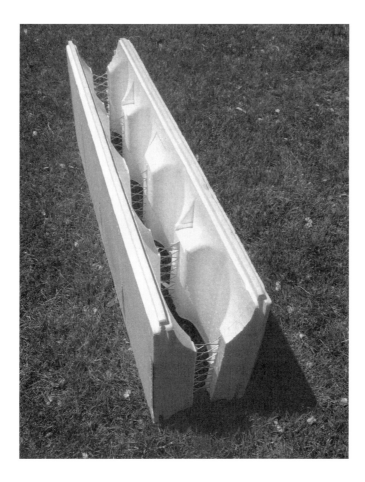

Figure 5.3 Insulated Concrete Forms (ICF) combine two functions: they serve as a form for the poured concrete and insulate the wall after its construction.

similar in nature to ICF are blocks that "sandwich" foam insulation in between two layers of concrete. The blocks are placed on top of one another, like common cinder blocks, to form a wall.

Permanent Wood Foundation Systems

Permanent wood foundation systems offer another alternative when planning foundations. The system is commonly produced as prefabricated sections from pressure-treated wood. The product can rest on crushed stone or on footing. The advantage of such a system is that it can be installed in cold weather without heavy machinery. Reluctance to use them may rest with their assumed relatively limited longevity compared with concrete or blocks and issues related to termite infestation. This system may also include *structural insulated panels* (SIP). The panel is made of engineered, stressed skin panels, and they have an injected insulation in the cavity in between. A similar concept product includes a precast concrete-panel system. Installation of such a product requires heavy lifting equipment and is more suitable for a large, mass-housing project.

Framing

Stick-built, wood-frame construction has been the main method of constructing low-rise residences in North America for decades. The method, notable for its simplicity, has precut materials sent to the site where they are assembled to form floors, walls, and roofs. A similar process was used in the interior finishing of a home and included premanufactured doors and cabinets. The system provided a relatively inexpensive home that could withstand cold, northern weather, and southern heat. It was a highly effective method in an era of low material and labor costs. As a result, millions of such homes have been constructed across the continent.

Things have changed in recent decades. Increased pressure on dwindling natural resources, primarily solid, sawn lumber, has caused a sharp price hike. Labor costs have also increased, often in regions and times of high demand. Unfortunately, there were not many substitutes to replace the stick-built method as predominantly conservative attitudes stood in the way of innovation. The result was a sharp rise in the cost of housing compared to its price a half a century ago.

Here, too, lowering the construction cost of housing requires close evaluation of two main aspects: materials and labor. Under the material category, study how products can be saved or replaced by lower-cost substitutes need to take place. The labor component looks into how the tasks involved in assembling a structure can be simplified, shortened, or eliminated altogether by incorporating a new application method or technology. The main thrust of all the cost reduction methods in wood-frame construction is common sense. Optimizing wood framing by making sure that materials will provide the greatest effect and avoiding unnecessary design complexity are the foundations of these principles. This section examines the main components and products required for affordable framing. Current tasks are analyzed and alternatives proposed.

Floors

Wood-frame floor design is guided by several principles and includes a few key components. First, the floor has to be designed to sustain building and occupant loads. It also has to accommodate the greatest desired span possible to permit flexibility in altering the interior in the future. Finally, it has to take advantage of new floor trusses, sheeting material, and fastening techniques. These objectives are highly compatible with small-size affordable homes. A 1987 HUD report suggests several cost-saving methods that can bring down the cost of a home even further.

In recent years, the use of floor trusses have gained widespread use. The product—either open web, which is also known as a space truss, or I-joist—is often purchased with dimensions beyond the required load-bearing capacity. Ensuring that the appropriate size is used can lead to savings. Among the two types of trusses, open web is recommended, as it eliminates the need to punch holes in the web for passing utilities through. According to the report, the use of built-up wood girders is usually more cost effective than using steel girders. At times, the installation of heavy steel girders will also require a lifting device, the cost of which can be saved when a wood beam is used instead.

The choice of an appropriate thickness of *floor sheeting* will also contribute to the stiffness of the floor and result in reducing the size and increasing the joist's spacing. When the sheeting is screwed and glued, it will help achieve a greater strength and span. Sheeting made of aspenite has also become popular

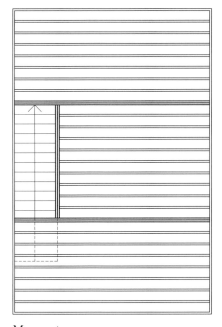

More cuts

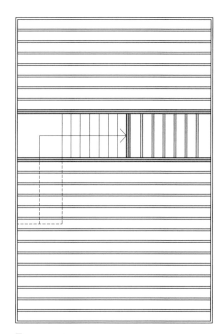

Fewer cuts

and is a known cost saver. The use of bridging or blocking between floor joists has proven to be ineffective for strengthening purposes in most cases and can be avoided altogether. When the span requires the use of blocking, a 1 inch by 2 inch (25 millimeter by 50 millimeter) strip is preferred as both a material and labor cost-saving method.

When anchoring wood-frame floors to the foundation to sustain wind forces, a sill plate is used. Another possible floor anchoring method is to use metal anchor straps and to eliminate the sill plate if the top of the foundation is sufficiently levelled. When the floor is built on a pressure-treated wood foundation, a sill plate is not required. The joist can then be nailed directly to the foundation's top plate.

In a multistory building, when stairs are designed, placing them parallel to the joist will lead to lower labor expenses as fewer joists will have to be cut (Figure 5.4). Also, doubling the joists on each side of the opening is not necessary when the stairs are close to the end of the joists' span (HUD, 1987). Another recommended practice that can save lumber is to reduce the size of the header joist, which is also known as a bond joist. The joist can be made of less expensive 1-inch (25 millimeters) plywood to keep the floor joist aligned.

Figure 5.4 In a multistory building, placing stairs parallel to the joists will contribute to material and labor savings.

Exterior Walls and Partitions

Cost savings in building walls and partitions can be achieved through proper planning and challenging the conventional practice of wood-frame residential construction. The choice of a modular dimension for the width and the length of the house will not only reduce the floor's sheeting offcuts and waste but also help place the studs properly. Whenever possible, preparing an enlarged floor plan that shows every stud will help manage and control their quality (National Association of Home Builders, 1971).

The main point of framing is the transference of loads from the upper floor members to the foundation. Lining up components is, therefore, highly important. When the vertical members are non-load-bearing, they need not be of a large size. A 1994 HUD report notes that "over the years, residential framing methods have evolved based largely on tradition. As a result, unneeded framing members have found their way into conventional practice." In an earlier publication, HUD lists several methods all aimed at cutting waste and simplifying home assembly (HUD, 1987). According to the report, many of these techniques, based on "optimal value engineering" (OVE), have been tested and used in a variety of projects.

The building of a 7 foot 6 inch (2.3 meters) wall rather than an 8-foot (2.4 meters) wall will save on exterior cladding as well as wall insulation. When a room has large enough windows that let in natural light, they will offset the effect of the height reduction on the space. Building such a low wall also permits the use of a single top plate rather than two top plates, as commonly done. Lumber used in wall framing can be further reduced by over 12 percent by spacing the studs at 24 inches (610 millimeters) on center rather than 16 inches (405 millimeters). Similar savings can result from aligning floor joists with wall studs within an average sized home; this can eliminate 200 feet (61 meters) of wall studs (Friedman et al., 1993). In addition, since the maximum load on a corner stud of an exterior wall is one-and-a-half (or less than) the load on a regular stud, two-stud corners are more than adequate structurally (HUD, 1987) (Figure 5.5).

The spacing of the studs 24 inches (610 millimeters) on center rather than 16 inches (410 millimeters) is the result of the adoption of 2 inches by 6 inches (50 millimeters by 150 millimeters) as a standard wall stud. Several advantages have resulted from this change. More space in the wall cavity was made available for insulation, gaining a higher R-value. Thermal bridging, a result of having fewer studs, was also reduced. There was more space to insulate around pipes and ducts to reduce energy loss and prevent freezing. Perhaps most importantly, there were fewer studs to nail, resulting in lower labor costs. The disadvantages of this method—studding at 24 inches on center rather than 16 inches on center—is the bowing of exterior siding due to the wider spacing. Also, the window and door jambs must be wider, which can increase the cost of each opening.

When the construction of interior partitions is planned, the traditional 2 inches by 4 inches (50 millimeters by 100 millimeters) can be replaced by 2 inches by 3 inches (50 millimeters by 75 millimeters). The studs can even be placed at 24 inches (610 millimeters) center to center, leading to more savings.

Figure 5.5
Alternative practices can save material in framing a corner.

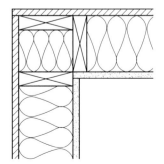
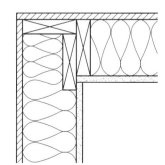
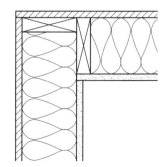

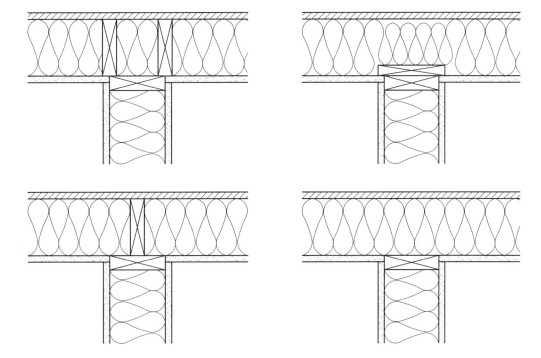

Another common practice that can be done away with is the use of interior partition posts built into the exterior wall. The partition can simply be nailed to the wall block rather than adding another stud (Figure 5.6). The use of headers or lintels can also be questioned. When there is no need to transfer load to the side of the window or the load is being carried by other vertical members, the headers can be eliminated or downsized. Openings in non-load-bearing walls can have a 2 inch by 4 inch (50 millimeters by 100 millimeters) lintel to which the windows or door will be affixed. New lintel materials such as plywood can also be used as headers. The space in between two layers of plywood can provide room for additional insulation. Also, the midheight fire blocking in the wall can be eliminated, as experience shows that it has little effect on the stability of the structure.

Alternative methods can be used in bracing a wall to sustain wind. Traditionally, exterior walls have been clad with plywood or 1 inch (25 millimeters) board sheeting, which provided bracing as well as some measure of insulation. Modification to codes in several jurisdictions is permitting the installation of metal bracing in corners of structures of up to three stories (Figure 5.7). HUD (1994) notes that "corner bracing can consist of a 4 foot (1.2 meter) section of structural sheeting (e.g., plywood) 1 inch by 4 inches (25 millimeters by 100 millimeters) diagonal let-in braces, or approved metal straps."

Innovation has brought to the construction forefront new building products that reduce consumption of natural resources as well as save builders and buyers money. Some of these products have gained acceptance and are widely used while others have encountered resistance. The two main products are engineered lumber and light-gauge steel. The manufactured products are used as joists, beams, and flooring materials. *Glue-laminated lumber* is stacked, fingerjointed layers of standard lumber. To reduce cost, varying grades of lumber are used and are placed in a way that will enhance performance. Another product is

Figure 5.6 Interior partitions can be nailed to the wall block rather than adding another stud.

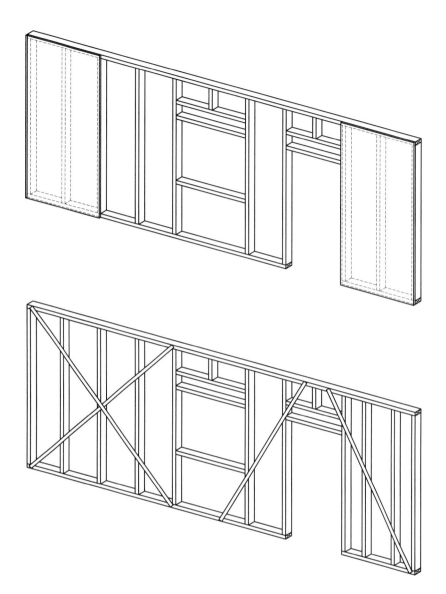

Figure 5.7 Codes in several jurisdictions are permitting the installation of metal bracing in corners of structures rather than using plywood as a brace.

laminated-veneer lumber, which is made from thin layers of wood glued together and run parallel to each other. *Parallel-strand lumber,* which is known as "parallam," is packed with long strips of wood fibers, which are glued parallel to each other. These products are more versatile than solid-sawn lumber, and their prices are becoming competitive and, in some instances, cheaper (Gibson, 2002).

Another product that shows promise but is not fully accepted by the industry is *light-gauge steel.* Steel studs offer several advantages—they have consistent quality; they do not rot, warp, or twist; they are fire-resistant, lightweight (so they don't crack the foundation), and, finally, are manufactured with recycled content. The disadvantage of the product lies in its unfamiliarity to most builders; subsequently, there is a need to train the labor force in their use, as well as engender consumer acceptance, which has yet to be developed. Light-gauge steel studs, however, offer a real alternative to wood and are likely to gain popularity in years to come (Builder, 1993).

Once the exterior has been constructed, its insulation begins. A wide range of products have been introduced over the years. Product choice needs to be guided by the greatest energy saving potential for the lowest investment. In general, *batt insulation* is the least expensive, yet it requires careful attention to proper installation procedures. *Cellulose insulation*, which is made of recycled newsprint, costs more than batt insulation and has labor-intensive application procedures as well, but it offers reduced air leakage and better sound insulation. Rigid foam sheets have higher R-values than other products, but they are known to be more expensive as well.

Roofs

The use of prefabricated roof trusses is an efficient and cost-effective way of constructing a roof. There are, however, several simple building methods that can further reduce cost. Carefully following a modular dimensioning system would be instrumental in saving plywood. By some accounts, the scrap and waste can be reduced by about two-thirds (Friedman et al., 1993). Particular attention should be given to the length of the roof slope from peak to overhang. The roof opening for chimneys should be between the modular truss spacing for the purpose of "allowing the roof sheathing's layout to be one module and preventing waste or an additional roof truss or roof framing" (NAHB, 1971). To save on lumber, it is also recommended that the truss web members, in certain designs, be 2 inches by 3 inches (50 millimeters by 75 millimeters) rather than the conventional 2 inches by 4 inches (50 millimeters by 100 millimeters). The use of metal fasteners is also considered an acceptable substitute for edge blocking. The thickness of plywood used to cover the trusses can also be questioned. At times, a thicker than necessary product is chosen, leading to waste.

Another avenue of cost savings in roof construction is through simplification of overhang and trim details. The overhang plays an important role in protecting the wall from falling rain and providing shade in summertime. Yet, the underside of an overhang can be altered by eliminating the trim details and leaving an open soffit.

WINDOWS

Heat losses through the building envelope can occur by any of the following three mechanisms: conduction, convection, and radiation. In all three cases, windows are the weakest link in the thermal performance of a building envelope and, as such, represent the most important investment in the construction or renovation of any dwelling. They are also highly variable in price, appearance, and performance, making their selection a sometimes difficult process. This section outlines the factors that affect a window unit's energy performance and provides guidelines for its selection, installation, and integration into the dwelling's general layout in a cost-effective manner.

Heating and cooling requirements are largely controlled by the envelope design, of which windows represent the single largest source of heat loss. The size, type, location, and orientation of windows in the unit play a critical role in the dwelling's energy efficiency. While high-performance windows are available, they are usually too expensive to be used in an affordable housing project. Considering that the window unit is the most significant investment as far as energy efficiency is concerned, their selection and installation should be carried out carefully.

It is best to begin by discussing window units in terms of their subcomponents. There are two basic parts that have to be considered: the frame and the glass, or glazing, unit. There are two types of frames within a window unit. The first is the outer frame, which is anchored to the wall, and the second is the interior frame, also known as the sash, which encloses the individual glazing units and can be opened in a variety of ways. The glazing unit consists of two or more layers of glass or plastic, separated by spacers and coated in various ways to control heat gains and losses.

Coupled with losses from the glazing unit, heat losses through the frame can account for up to 20 percent of the total heat losses from the window unit. The selection of an appropriate frame material is therefore not simply a question of appearance. Wood, for instance, is a good insulator, but it is easily damaged and has a high-maintenance requirement. Metal, aluminum for example, requires much less maintenance but is a very good conductor. The selection of an aluminum frame must ensure that it is designed with a thermal break, a separation that uses materials with a lower thermal conductivity, such as cellular foam, rigid polyvinyl chloride (PVC), polyurethane, or wood, to keep frost from entering.

Metal frames are also very susceptible to temperature changes, and they will expand and contract significantly on a seasonal, daily, or even hourly basis. The joint between the glazing unit and the sash must, therefore, be flexible enough to accommodate any movement without breaking the glass. Finally, some frames use a combination of materials, usually a wood core covered with either aluminum or vinyl. These are intended to take advantage of thermal qualities of wood while protecting it with either vinyl or aluminum and reducing the maintenance requirement. They are, therefore, very expensive and are not common choices for affordable housing.

Infiltration losses between the frame and the sash depend on the number and type of operable components and on the type of gasket selected. There are several types of windows categorized by the type of operation: fixed, awning, hopper, casement, sliding, single hung, double hung, and pivoted for cleaning and ventilation. It is also possible to have window units manufactured with combinations of these options.

Generally, windows with fewer operable parts are less costly and more energy efficient. The more linear feet of joint, the greater the potential for heat loss through leakage. Fixed windows are best in this regard. As far as the type of operation is concerned, pivotal components are more energy efficient, since they make use of compression seals. Sliding parts are least effective in terms of air leakage. The general quality and craftsmanship of the window are also critical. A poorly-assembled casement window from one manufacturer, for instance, can be susceptible to more air leakage than a well-crafted sliding unit from another manufacturer. A poor seal can overcome the advantages of using a casement or awning window.

Significant heat losses can occur across the glass. These losses are controlled by the type and number of layers in a glazing unit, the type of space that separates them, the type of coating, if any, applied to the surface, and the type of gas that fills the cavity between them. There are several possible alternatives for glazing units, along with their thermal resistance, that should be considered. The joint between the frame and the wall is the final but critical link in an energy-efficient envelope. The performance of this joint relies entirely on the installation procedure and sealing material used. Generally, the installation should provide an air-tight seal while allowing for differential thermal or structural movement between the frame and the wall.

The energy implication behind the use of various window types will vary depending on building type, size, and orientation. In an affordable row house, for example, windows occupy some 25 percent of the total exposed wall area and account for 45 percent of the total heat loss. The selection of energy-efficient windows is, therefore, an effective way of lowering energy costs and reducing maintenance and upkeep expenses in the long run.

PREFABRICATION

With the growing demand for affordable housing, increasing costs of materials and labor, and a heightened concern for energy-efficiency, large-volume builders and individuals planning to build a single home are naturally exploring alternative construction methods. This trend has resulted in a growing interest in prefabricated building systems. The main question, however, is what cost advantage prefabrication has over conventional construction. Prior to investigating the economic aspects, it would be worthwhile to review the main systems available to builders of affordable housing.

There are three main prefabricated methods:

- *Modular* refers to factory construction of sections that can be an entire house or part of one. The sections are sent to the site where they are hoisted into place by crane.
- A *kit of parts* is made of well-marked building products, such as studs or windows, that are shipped to the site for assembly.
- *Panelized* is the third method. Panels of different sizes, some with framing only and others with insulation and windows, are assembled according to plans.

This section focuses on panelized methods due to their similarity to on-site construction, which makes them more acceptable and more commonly used in an affordable housing project.

Panelized Prefabricated Systems

There are several types of prefabricated panel systems, subsystems, and components that can be combined at various levels to provide a complete system package. Nine types of panel systems are applicable to wood-frame residential construction. These nine can be divided into three categories: (1) open-sheathed panels, using conventional construction methods; (2) structural sandwich panels; and (3) unsheathed structural panels (Figure 5.8).

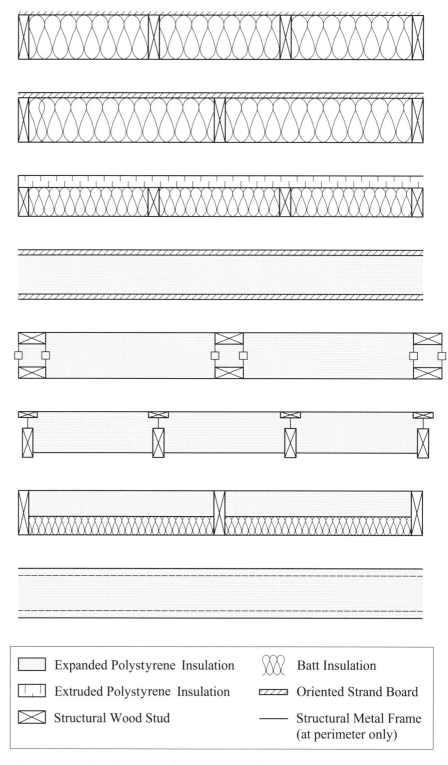

Figure 5.8 Horizontal section of prefabricated wall systems.

Open-Sheathed Panels

Open-sheathed panels (OSP) are available in almost as many different variations as conventional wall construction. The most common systems are built either with 2 inch by 6 inch (38 millimeters by 140 millimeters) studs with plywood or aspenite sheathing or with 2 inch by 4 inch (38 millimeters by 89 millimeters) studs and extruded polystyrene sheathing. In either case, the panels are delivered open to the interior to facilitate the installation of electrical or plumbing services. Batt insulation is usually installed on-site and is sometimes supplied by the manufacturer.

Structural Sandwich Panels

Structural sandwich panels (SSP), which are also known as *foam-core panels,* consist of a core of rigid foam insulation that is laminated between two facing materials. In its most basic form, the sheathing materials may be either plywood or aspenite. More complete options offer exterior or interior finishes that replace the basic facing material and become an integral structural part of the panel. The core material contains precut electrical chases, and may be any one of four different types of insulation: molded bead expanded polystyrene, extruded polystyrene, polyurethane, or polyisocyanurate. A variety of details and options are available for the joints between the panels for better structural stability and reduced air leakage.

Unsheathed Structural Panels

Unsheathed structural panels (USP), or *composite panels,* are built using a combination of wood or metal structural elements combined with rigid-foam insulation infill, usually expanded polystyrene. There are four basic variations of these systems available with different configurations for their structural elements, which provide a continuous thermal break or an air space on the interior of the panel. Horizontal chases are often cut into the insulation to accommodate electrical wiring and pipes. Each system accommodates integration of a larger portion of the building envelope during fabrication, which contributes to lowering on-site labor costs. Added components vary from exterior air barriers to interior finishes. The extent to which the panels are finished has different implications for the builder and the installer.

Other Costs Associated with Prefabricated Wall Systems

As is the case with any manufactured component, waste generation from prefabrication of panel systems is less than what could be expected from site construction. Assembly of the wall system in closed, controlled environments ensures that materials are used efficiently, and offcut pieces of materials are more easily recovered and reused. Furthermore, the fact that the home is erected and closed to the elements within a short period of time reduces delays due to bad weather. Since there is less material waste, the cost of clearing and removing debris is lower. Considering that the construction of an average house produces some 2.4 tons (2.5 tonnes) of waste, 25 percent of which is dimensional lumber and an additional 15 percent manufactured wood products, the cost savings could be substantial, particularly in large developments (Canada Mortgage and Housing Corporation, 1991).

The cost per unit of floor area of prefabricated systems will vary significantly depending on the type, size, and configuration of the dwelling units. Designs that lend themselves to simplicity and repetition are more likely to result in attractive savings, since they optimize the prefabrication process. A comparison of construction costs for single-family detached units using modular prefabrication to those using conventional construction found that there were no significant savings to be gained through prefabrication (Friedman, 1992).

When considering, however, the time saved by either using modular or panelized prefabricated systems, there is an economic advantage. Due to the quick and efficient assembly that takes place on-site, the effect of poor weather conditions, particularly in cold climates, is reduced, as is the potential for damage due to inadequate material storage and vandalism. Cleanup time and material costs are also reduced because there is less waste; construction management and trade coordination can be simplified with these types of products, and the need for large teams of skilled on-site labor for multiple-unit construction is substantially lowered.

Transportation and lifting costs associated with the delivery of prefabricated systems, however, can be significant and, in some cases, capable of reversing potential savings to cost increases. These costs will vary depending on both the manufacturer and the product. In addition to the actual transportation distance, costs will depend on the equipment used, number of trips required, number of homes built, as well as on the party assuming the delivery.

Most manufacturers deliver the panels on specially equipped trucks. The panels are normally transported and lifted into position in two separate trips— the first at completion of the first floor platform and the second upon completion of the second floor. This approach has the advantage of eliminating the need to store the product on site. It also eliminates the cost of hiring an independent crane. For a small project consisting of one or two homes, however, the delivery in two trips may not be cost-effective, particularly when longer distances are involved. Alternatively, the components may be delivered by an independent party, who will deposit the panels on site, leaving the responsibility for storage and lifting to the builder. The use of larger trucks from independent transportation companies may reduce the number of trips required and be cost-effective for larger projects in remote locations.

UTILITIES

Utilities is an all-encompassing word that refers to the home's subsystems. These are the networks—mechanical, electrical, and natural gas, for example—that link a dwelling to the city's infrastructure. Utilities are an essential part of the home's functions and reflect the many necessities of modern life. Their quantity and quality increased severalfold in the last half century. In addition to electricity, fresh water supply and drainage, and gas, homes are now fed by and wired for telephone, cable TV, Internet, and security systems, among others. The cost of installing and maintaining these systems also mounted. Careful selection among these utility options needs, therefore, to be paramount in the design of affordable housing. Selection of systems and their installation will determine short- and long-term expenditure. Several key utility systems have been selected for discussion and review in this section. Their cost-savings attributes will be outlined along with descriptions of their functions.

Plumbing

Once the dwelling's rough structure has been constructed, installation of the home's plumbing begins. Three main components make up this system: water supply, water and waste removal, and fixtures through which the water is used. Historians attribute the invention of plumbing to ancient Romans, who constructed a network of lead pipes to bring fresh water into the house. The term *plumbing* is derived from the Latin word *plumbum*, meaning lead (Winter & Associates, 1999). Since the turn of the twentieth century, plumbing developments have accelerated. Nickel-plated, enameled iron pipes were installed outside the wall. A tin-lined pipe that combined the durability of lead with the purity of tin was used to prevent poisoning. The use of galvanized steel pipe was subsequently introduced and later abandoned, as it was subject to rust. Rigid copper pipes that were introduced at the same time were also expensive and hard to handle. New trends and practices led to the installation of plumbing in the walls themselves. The 1950s saw a proliferation of soft copper pipes for water supply and cast iron for drainage. Lightweight PVC pipe was introduced in the 1960s. This was ideal for drain and vent pipes, relatively inexpensive, and much easier to install and connect. Flexible pipes were introduced and became common in the 1990s. They were made possible by the invention of a unique, durable plastic called cross-linked polyethylene, formulated specifically to withstand high temperature and pressure (Ou, 1999).

Cost-saving considerations in plumbing begin in advance of the installation of the pipes themselves. The framing process needs to be done with the plumber in mind. Each time the plumber has to pose and alter the wood-frame structure, time is lost and, as a result, money. Hemp (1988) suggests several aspects that must be carefully considered in framing a house to facilitate plumbing. When designing a floor, special attention must be paid to ensure that the joist will not interfere with the toilet waste pipe and the bathtub drain. Space should be left for the passing of pipes and their installation. When the house's wet functions, such as the kitchen and the powder room, are designed back-to-back, the common wall should be wide enough to permit the passing of several drain and water pipes.

A number of innovations were introduced over the past few decades in plumbing installation, yet their implementation is often difficult as the industry is governed by codes. Updating these model codes is unfortunately a lengthy process. When attempting to find a cost-reduction alternative to current practice, one needs to bear in mind that any change will have to be approved by local code officials.

Water Supply System

The home's water supply system distributes the city's water to the dwelling's wet functions. After passing through the building's main pipe, the water branches into hot and cold water networks that often run in parallel. As a principle, since the water supply system is under pressure, the pipes can be laid in the shortest, most convenient way for cost-saving purposes. Another principle relates the sizes of the pipes to their load. There is, therefore, no need to use more than the diameter required to serve the planned function, as it will incur additional costs. In locating plumbing conduits, attention must be paid to climatic considerations. Placing pipes in exterior walls in a cold climate area may expose them to freezing and costly damage. Additionally, if water pipes are in exterior walls, the hot water temperature can drop several degrees in cold weather, requiring greater expenditure on heating.

An innovation that increased efficiency and changed water supply plumbing is the manifold distribution system. A HUD report from Winters & Associates (1999) noted that "the introduction of flexible plastic tubing like cross-linked polyethylene (PEX) allows easy distribution of small-diameter, joint-free branches to individual fixtures." A brass or copper manifold forms the supply point. The system's greatest advantage is that individual lines can be isolated and controlled. There are three methods for connecting pipes to the manifold. The first is the "home run" method, which uses one line to serve each fixture. The second method is called "branching," which uses large pipes to supply smaller ones. The third is the "hybrid" method, which combines the first two systems (Fine Homebuilding, 2003). The chosen method will depend on the house's layout and the project's budget. The advantages of the manifold distribution system lie in its quick installation, the need for fewer connections, the minimal noise, and the ease of repair.

Cost-saving options in water distribution systems depend on the type of pipes used and their method of installation. Most codes now approve of the cross-linked polyethylene (PEX) flexible, thin tubing, which has cost advantages over copper pipes, for example. Their use should, therefore, be explored. A HUD report (1987) questioned the need for individual fixture stops, which often tend to deteriorate and may require service or replacement. With regard to size, except for dishwashers and lavatories, ⅜ inch (9.5 millimeter) or ½ inch (12.5 millimeter) widths are sufficient. Clustering the plumbing conduits can save on labor and material as well. It was suggested that when buying fixtures, white had a cost advantage compared with other colors. Fiberglass bathtubs and shower stalls also cost less than conventional fixtures. Smaller-sized and insulated water heaters will save on energy bills and water consumption and will cost less.

Another source of cost savings for homeowners is water conservation. Water meters have become a reality in many North American communities. As water sources in arid areas are diminishing, rates have gone up. The rise in rates is also a result of constructing and maintaining costly infrastructure systems. Energy costs needed to purify fresh water and treat waste also have mounted, causing an increase in municipal taxes. Lastly, the environmental ramifications of overconsumption of water is also evident as waste water pollutes waterways. The best way to ensure reduction in water consumption is to use water-efficient technologies. Several such fixtures have been introduced in recent years (Friedman et al., 1993). As opposed to conventional toilets that use as much as 5.3 gallons (20 liters) or more per flush, low-flush water closets use only 3.4 gallons (13 liters). Newer models use only 1.8 gallons (7 liters). They also generate less noise.

In some states, a two-lever system is mandatory where smaller quantities of water are used for liquids and greater quantities for solid waste. There are also systems that direct the sink waste water into the toilet tank, reusing it as flush water. Showerheads that conserve water can reduce water consumption from 5.3 gallons (20 liters) to 2.6 gallons (10 liters) per minute. Similar conservation can be achieved in faucets. Installation of aerators can reduce excessive flow from the conventional 3.6 gallons (13.5 liters) per minute by more than 50 percent, depending on the faucet type and location (Friedman et al., 1993).

Recycling rainwater for garden use is another water- and cost-conserving strategy. Finally, when purchasing home appliances, how these appliances use water should be closely examined, as some consume more water than others in their operation. Dishwashers and clothes washers need to be studied before purchase, for not only energy efficiency but also water consumption. The most energy- and water-efficient appliance may have a high initial cost, but they will be cost savers in the long run.

Drainage Systems

Skaates (1985) suggests that a residential drainage system is like a watershed. Each domestic plumbing fixture is "like a small creek that drains into a larger stream." It is a gravity-based system with venting that assures proper performance. A variety of cost-saving techniques have found their way into a domain that is also largely governed by codes. Prior to discussing specific cost-saving strategies, it would be worthwhile to be familiar with the system's key components (Figure 5.9).

Unlike water supply systems that operate under pressure, drain systems must have sufficient capacity, proper slope, venting, and a place for clean out. Since waste generates gases with bad odors, venting these gasses must be an integral part of the system. The common approach to drainage design is to create a network in which smaller-sized pipes are linked to a larger, single main drain. This main pipe is connected to the city's drain or to a private septic tank.

Each component plays an important part in the system and has a name. The *soil stack* is a vertical pipe that collects waste from several fixtures. When a toilet drains into the pipe, it is known as a *main stack*. When the stack drains fixtures other than toilets, a sink, or a bathtub, for example, it is known as a *secondary stack*, which is smaller in diameter. The connecting component between the attributary and the main stack is known as the *branch main*. All the stacks eventually connect with the house drain in the lowest point, usually a crawl space or the basement. When the house drain extends beyond the home, it is known as the *house sewer*.

Since clearing out gasses is an important consideration of a drain system, each fixture has a built-in trap that contains water to block passage of gasses through the fixture drain into the house (Kicklighter et al., 2000). In addition, each stack is designed with a clean-out spot at its base to unclog the pipe in case of blockage. Each soil stack is extended above the roof to provide air to the system. A common practice of construction is to avoid penetrating the roof more than necessary. Therefore, many fixtures are connected to a principal vent.

The main products used for drainage systems are ABS plastics, PVC plastics, copper, and cast iron. ABS plastics are considered to be the least expensive and

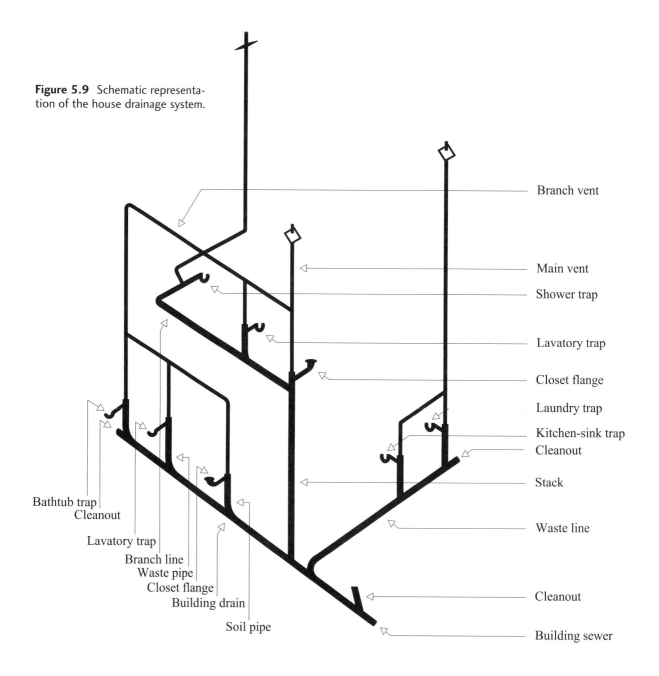

Figure 5.9 Schematic representation of the house drainage system.

Branch vent

Main vent

Shower trap

Lavatory trap

Closet flange

Laundry trap

Kitchen-sink trap

Cleanout

Stack

Waste line

Cleanout

Building sewer

Bathtub trap
Cleanout

Lavatory trap

Branch line

Waste pipe

Closet flange

Building drain

Soil pipe

the simplest to work with. The product's disadvantages are its vulnerability to weather changes, requiring a stronger support as a result of bonding, and its release of poisonous gasses in fires (Skaates, 1985). In addition to selecting inexpensive products, the system's layout will also determine its cost. When the plumbing fixtures are stacked, less labor and material will be required. Sizing the system properly and allocating appropriate pipes for their actual function will also lead to cost savings. Similar to the water supply system, clustering wet functions near the same core should lead to savings. Another cost-saving practice is to avoid penetration of roof by a vent pipe. Rather, as HUD notes, "the pipe can be extended through an exterior wall or roof overhang and terminate downwards" (HUD, 1987).

Heating and Cooling Systems

North American homebuilding underwent and incorporated many technological advancements since World War II. Today's houses are much more energy efficient as a result of innovative building science, products, and techniques. Because building envelopes are more airtight, concern for air quality has increased and, with it, the need for proper mechanical ventilation.

The selection of heating, ventilating, and air-conditioning equipment for homes is also made complex due to the variety of systems and technologies. The appropriate alternative will depend on the dwelling size, configuration, and cost of the system, among other factors. Several functions can be performed by a mechanical system, including heating, cooling, humidification, air purification, and ventilation. Two types of distribution systems are considered in this section: *convection* and *forced-air*. Figure 5.10 summarizes the air-conditioning functions performed by the different systems.

Central systems—that is, forced air—require limited space and have to be attached to a network of conduits to force the air through the house. They require pipe chases and wall sections to allow for the installation of ducts. The convection systems, such as ductless heat pumps, electric baseboard heaters, and fan-assisted room heaters are more flexibly located inside the house. For the two electric systems mentioned, it is recommended that they be placed under windows when possible. The ductless heat pump, on the other hand, is usually installed on an exterior wall close to the ceiling. Fortunately, it is not necessary to install the units on an exposed wall if the process is planned prior to construction, which allows the builder to pass the pipes through the walls. Finally, air heat pump systems require an outdoor heat exchanger.

Another factor to consider when selecting a mechanical system is the availability of energy. One must be aware of the cost of gas and electricity before

Figure 5.10 Air conditioning functions performed by different systems.

Category	Type	Functions				
		Heat	Cool	Humidification	Purification	Ventilation
A. Electrical						
1. Central	Forced air	X		X	X	X
2. Baseboard	Convection	X				
3. Fan-assisted	Convection	X				
B. Heat Pump						
1. Geothermal	Forced air	X	X	X	X	X
2. Air central	Forced air	X	X	X	X	X
3. Ductless	Convection	X	X	X		
C. Oil/Gas						
1. Central	Forced air	X		X	X	

Figure 5.11 Advantages and disadvantages of heating system alternatives.

Systems	Efficiency	Advantages	Disadvantages
Electrical			
Central	100%	High efficiency High air quality	High initial cost Central control Space requirements
Baseboard	100%	Very low initial cost Individual room control Silent Easy to install	Poor heat distribution Low effectiveness
Fan-assisted	100%	Low initial cost Good heat distribution Excellent thermostat control Individual room control Silent	Space restriction (furniture)
Heat Pumps			
In general		Very high efficiency Low operation cost Environmentally friendly Reversible (heat and cool)	High initial system cost Auxiliary system (cold climate) Outside heat exchanger
Geothermal	COP* 4	Highest efficiency (COP)	Land requirement (soil) Central control
Air central	COP* 3.5	High efficiency	Central control
Ductless	COP* 3.5	Excellent thermostat control Individual room control	
Oil/Gas			
Central	90%	High air quality High efficiency	High initial cost Fossil fuels Central control

*COP—Coefficient of Performance

deciding to install any system, as the energy rates can greatly affect the life-cycle cost of the system. While some of the functions described above are essential for a comfortable living environment, the costs associated with the selection of more sophisticated systems may be problematic in the context of affordable housing. An evaluation of the varied systems must, therefore, take into consideration cost, efficiency, and effectiveness (Figure 5.11).

Efficiency and effectiveness can help compare the available systems. *Efficiency* represents the ability of a system to transform a power source into usable energy. It is a measured value usually provided by manufacturers. *Effectiveness,* on the other hand, measures how much of the energy produced is actually used to condition the environment.

Systems that can be considered in affordable housing design are divided into three categories that are based on their main source of energy. Electrical systems use electricity as their source of power. Since all of the energy put into the system is transformed to heat, except energy used by fans and other such devices, their gross efficiency is commonly rated at 100 percent. In the electrical system, a current is passed through a resistor that, in turn, generates heat. There are three basic types of electrical systems: forced-air, baseboard, and fan-assisted units. The electrical furnace is a central unit that distributes hot air through a network of ducts. Such systems produce heat efficiently as heat is forced through the different rooms of the house. However, systems with a heating capacity of less than 10,000 watts, for use in small houses, are rarely available, making the initial cost for the system higher than it should be.

The permanently mounted baseboard heater is probably the most common type of room heater and ideally installed under windows. However, their effectiveness is significantly compromised, since only a portion of the heat delivered is actually used to heat the air. Thermostats in each room allow independent temperature control. However, the long time delay between temperature readings often leads to wasted energy and very warm temperature in the vicinity of the baseboard heater. The electric baseboard system also requires a lot of power to operate, but its very low initial cost probably explains its popularity in some parts of the continent.

The ceiling-mounted, fan-assisted units are also popular. In addition to circulating the air for better effectiveness and comfort, some systems include a pre-heat device to reduce energy consumption. The heating element is consistently kept at a "ready to heat" temperature to reduce the electrical load generated when initiating the heating of a resisting element. The fan-assisted units consume less energy than standard baseboards due to forced convection; the pre-heat device and the built-in electronic thermostat provide better temperature control. Like the baseboard units, the fan-assisted units are available in different sizes, shapes, and capacities.

A *heat pump* is a system designed to transfer energy from one place to another. These systems are increasingly popular due to the high level of comfort they provide and also because of their high efficiency. Another appealing characteristic of heat pump systems is their reversibility. Indeed, a heat pump cools or heats the home, depending on the season. Efficiency for the heat pumps is computed in terms of Coefficient of Performance (COP). It is a ratio of the overall energy output over the energy input; for example, the electrical systems described previously have a COP equal to 1, meaning 100 percent efficiency. The costly work input, which is the electricity necessary to run the pump, is less than the amount of energy delivered to the building (Wark, 1988). There are two main types of heat pumps that are categorized based upon the heat sink with which they are associated: *ground source* and *air source*.

The *geothermal heat pump*, also called a ground-source heat pump, is a device that uses ground water as a heat source or a heat sink. Looped pipes containing a liquid are installed in the ground, and the system transfers the energy available from the ground to the interior of the home or vice versa. A central heating unit, usually located in the basement of the house, forces conditioned air through the duct network into the home. The unit performs several tasks and can also be attached to the hot water distribution system to preheat the water and increase the overall efficiency. These systems, however, have certain limitations due to their energy transfer technology. When operating in cold climates, the ground-source heat pump supplies about 70 percent of the heating demand, and auxiliary heating systems have to be installed to compensate for the heat pump's limitation. The typical ground-source heat pump operates with a COP of approximately 3.5, varying with size and climate.

The *air-source heat pump* draws heat from the outside air during the heating season and dumps heat outside during the cooling season. There are two possibilities with this category of systems: the central unit and the ductless unit. The central unit is composed of an outside heat exchanger attached to an indoor central unit that forces air through a duct network. The air-air heat pump is also limited in terms of energy supply during cold periods, and auxiliary systems, including electrical resistors to heat the air within the duct networks, have to be considered (Energy, Mines and Resources, Canada, 1989). The ductless heat-pump system is composed of an outside heat exchanger and several wall-mounted units inside the house, and therefore no ductwork is required. The units are connected through pipes running inside the walls and ideally installed on exposed walls. The ductless heat pumps have a COP of about 3 and are cost-effective. The initial cost of the system for a small house, however, is high, and the need for auxiliary heating devices would increase the total cost.

The efficiency of *gas-* and *oil-fired furnaces* has significantly increased in recent decades. With new technologies, such as the condensing furnace, their efficiency can top 90 percent, whereas traditional systems have efficiencies around 65 percent (EMR, 1989). However, systems with a heating capacity of less than 10,000 watts are not yet available, and the initial cost associated with efficient systems, such as the condensing-gas furnace, is high.

A *ventilation system* is a device that replaces stale and humid air by allowing fresh air inside the building. Codes in many jurisdictions stipulate that every newly constructed home must be equipped with a mechanical ventilation system to provide air changes in different parts of the house. For example, according to the regulation, a small home may require a total airflow of 10 gallons per second (40 liters per second) combined with one-third of an air change every hour. A substantial amount of heat can be lost in the process. However, if the house is equipped with a *heat recovery ventilation system* (HRV), up to 80 percent of that heat can be recycled, and heating and cooling costs can be kept relatively low (EMR, 1989). A number of manufacturers provide such equipment in different sizes and shapes. Installation of the system requires minimal space, and a duct network is needed to distribute the air. It is also possible to add heating elements in the ductwork to preheat the fresh air that goes into the house. A financial comparison of the alternatives listed above reveals that systems with a central-heating unit require a much larger initial investment. In addition, considering the low heat-load requirement of a house, the payback period associated with the central heating systems would be very long. This makes it difficult to justify such alternatives on a purely economic basis, and one needs to consider the overall range of advantages and disadvantages.

KEY CONSIDERATIONS

- The construction of a home needs to be a continuous, short as possible, sequence of steps. On-site, improvised decisions, during construction, might not be well thought out, and they may prolong the process and add expenses.

- Reducing the number of tasks and people involved in the building process can be a useful cost-reduction strategy. Preferably, the same tradespeople will perform several tasks.

- Additional ideas for cost-reduction can be generated when better coordination takes place among the trades. Holding preconstruction meetings of key trades can be a forum for discussion of cost-reduction ideas.

- *Optimal value engineering* (OVE) helps balance short- and long-term economic benefits and obtain the utmost return on investment. It can help rationalize the construction cost of affordable housing.

- When a well-chosen structural item can also become the finished product, cost-savings can be obtained.

- Planning while following modular dimension guides and integrating mass-produced products will contribute to cost savings.

- When given a choice, the building's foundation should be built at a higher elevation on the property, where soil grading directs the water away from the dwelling.

- Monolithic slab-on-grade is one of the most inexpensive ways to construct a concrete foundation. The slab also serves as a rough lower floor.

- *Insulated concrete forms* (ICF) save the need to construct traditional wooden forms, pour concrete, remove the forms, and insulate the wall, and they therefore have cost-saving potential.

- The use of bridging or blocking between floor joists has proven to be ineffective in most cases and can be avoided altogether.

- Doubling the joists on each side of an opening is not necessary when the stairs are close to the end of the joists' span (HUD, 1987).

- The building of a 7 foot 6 inch (2.3 meter) exterior wall rather than an 8 foot (2.4 meter) wall will save on exterior cladding as well as wall insulation. Lumber used can be further reduced by over 12 percent by spacing the studs at 24 inches (610 millimeters) on center rather than 16 inches (405 millimeters) on center.

- When there is no need to transfer loads to the side of the window or the loads are being carried by other vertical members, the headers can be eliminated or downsized.

- Following a modular dimensioning system in roof design would help save on plywood costs. By some accounts, scrap and waste can be reduced by about two-thirds in a modular dimensioning system.

- Coupled with losses from the glazing unit, heat losses through the frame can account for up to 20 percent of the total heat loss from a window unit. The selection of an appropriate frame material is, therefore, not simply a question of appearance.

- Generally, windows with fewer operable parts are less costly and more energy efficient.

- The selection of energy-efficient windows for a narrow row house is an effective way of reducing maintenance and upkeep expenses, since they occupy 25 percent of the total exposed wall area.

- Waste generation from prefabrication of panel systems is less than what could be expected from site construction. Panel assembly in a closed, controlled environment ensures that materials are used efficiently and offcuts are recovered and reused.

- Housing designs that lend themselves to simplicity and repetition are more likely to result in attractive savings, as they optimize the prefabrication process.

- The framing process of a house needs to be done with the plumber in mind. Each time the plumber has to pose and alter the wooden structure, time and money are lost.

- Cross-linked polyethylene (PEX) flexible, thin tubing has cost advantages over copper pipes.

- Reducing water consumption is another source of cost savings to homeowners. Water conserving showerheads can reduce water consumption, for example, from 5.3 gallons (20 liters) per minute to 2.6 gallons (10 liters) per minute.

- Sizing a drainage system properly and allocating appropriate pipes for their actual function will lead to cost savings.

- Circulating the air using ceiling-mounted, fan-assisted units is a cost-effective method to reduce energy consumption and increase comfort.

- When the home is equipped with a "heat recovery ventilation system" (HRV), up to 80 percent of that heat can be recycled, and heating and cooling costs can be kept relatively low (EMR, 1989).

chapter

6

Lots

Lot sizes and types, placement of homes on them, and the urban configuration of a community will greatly influence the cost of each dwelling.
In the design of an affordable housing project, many conventional
design strategies must be altered to reduce costs. It is a complex process
wherein three aspects—lots, dwellings, and streets—are considered jointly.
This chapter focuses on lot subdivision. Following an introduction to useful
terminology, as well as measures of density, this chapter outlines a typology
of lots and their attributes and examines their relationship to homes and
streets.

Dwelling Type	1 Single detached	2 Semidetached	3 Joined court	4 Duplex	5 Row house	6 Triplex	7 Quadruplex	8 Back to back Semidetached
Isometric								
Plot Plan								
Dwelling units/acre (dwelling units/hectare)	8 (20)	14 (35)	16 (40)	17 (42)	19 (47)	21 (52)	23 (57)	24 (59)
Floor area ratio % open space	0.24 76%	0.38 81%	0.44 56%	0.48 88%	0.56 72%	0.60 80%	0.66 67%	0.66 67%
Unit area in square feet (unit area in square meters)	1200 (111.5)	1200 (111.5)	1200 (111.5)	1200 (111.5)	1200 (111.5)	1200 (111.5)	1200 (111.5)	1200 (111.5)
Number of floors/units	1 or 2	1 or 2	1 or 2	1	2	1	1	2
Lot size in feet (lot size in meters)	50 x 100 (15.2 x 30.5)	30 x 100 (9.1 x 30.5)	25 x 100 (7.6 x 30.5)	50 x 100 (15.2 x 30.5)	21 x 100 (6.4 x 30.5)	60 x 100 (18.3 x 30.5)	60 x 100 (18.3 x 30.5)	30 x 65 (9.1 x 19.8)
Unit relationship to grade	on grade	on grade	on grade	50% on grade 50% gr. related	on grade	33% on grade 66% gr. related	50% on grade 50% gr. related	on grade
Access to unit	private on grade	private on grade	private on grade	50% priv. on gr. 50% priv. stair	private on grade	33% priv. on gr. 66% common stair	50% priv. on gr. 50% priv. stair	private on grade
Unit aspect	quadruple	triple	triple	quadruple	double (opposite)	quadruple	triple	double (adjacent)
Private outdoor space	on grade	on grade	on grade	50% on grade 50% gr. related	on grade	33% on grade 66% gr. related	50% on grade 50% gr. related	on grade
Parking	private on grade	private on grade	private on grade	common on grade	private or com. on grade	common on grade	common on grade	private on grade

Figures 6.1 Relationship between type of units, their density, and the floor-area ratio (FAR).

DENSITY

A telling index of the affordability level of a project is its *density*, which is a measure of how many dwelling units per acre (hectare) are placed on the site, sharing its land and infrastructure costs. Knowing the density of a site plan also helps gauge the environmental impact of a housing project. Building more units will require allocation of additional land to roads and parking, a process that will affect the site's landscape, for example. Three measures are commonly used in expressing density: gross density of an entire neighborhood, gross density of a specific project, and net density.

Gross density of an entire neighborhood refers to the total number of built units divided by the total land area. This measure will provide designers of affordable housing projects with a sense of the urban character of the area in which they are about to propose a new project.

Gross density of a specific project refers to the amount of units proposed for a site divided by land allocated to residences, streets, and public open spaces. It serves as a proper index of the project's environmental quality.

Net density considers only the land allocated to the dwellings and leaves out

Dwelling Type	9 Stacked row house (1½ / bay)	10 Stacked row house (2 / bay)	11 Garden apartment	12 3-story walk-up apartment	13 Medium rise stacked units	14 Combined apartments & row houses	15 Slab block apartment	16 High rise point block apartment
Isometric								
Plot Plan								
Dwelling units/acre (dwelling units/hectare)	31 (77)	35 (86)	52 (128)	65 (160)	71 (175)	84 (207)	90 (222)	120 (296)
Floor area ratio % open space	0.86 72%	1.14 72%	1.06 62%	1.36 55%	1.95 68%	1.92 62%	1.78 62%	2.62 87%
Unit area in square feet (unit area in square meters)	1200 (111.5)	1200 (111.5)	800 (74.3)	800 (74.3)	800 (74.3)	800 & 1200 (74.3 & 111.5)	800 (74.3)	800 (74.3)
Number of floors/unit	1 and 2	2	1	1	2	1 and 2	1	1
Lot size in feet (lot size in meters)	consolidated	consolidated	consolidated	consolidated	consolidated	consolidated	consolidated	consolidated
Unit relationship to grade	33% on grade 66% gr. related	50% on grade 50% gr. unrelated	33% on grade 66% gr. unrelated	33% on grade 66% gr. unrelated	33% on grade 33% gr. related 50% gr. unrelated	25% on grade 75% gr. unrelated	small % on grade majority ground unrelated	small % on grade majority ground unrelated
Access to unit	33% priv. on gr. 66% priv. stair	50% priv. on gr. 50% com. stair	common stair	common stair	common elevator	33% priv. on gr. 66% com. elev.	common elevator	common elevator
Unit aspect	double (opposite)	double (opposite)	double (opposite)	single	double (opposite)	double (opposite)	single (and double adj.)	single (and double adj.)
Private outdoor space	33% on grade 66% gr. related	50% on grade 50% gr. unrelated	33% on grade 66% gr. unrelated	33% on grade 66% gr. unrelated	33% on grade 33% gr. related 50% gr. unrelated	25% on grade 75% gr. unrelated	small % on grade majority ground unrelated	small % on grade majority ground unrelated
Parking	common underground	common underground	common underground	common underground	common underground	common underground	common on grade or u/g	common on grade or u/g

the land taken by roads and public spaces. It regards the built area only divided by the entire residential area.

Floor area ratio (FAR) is another key index for measuring the potential affordability of a project. It is the habitable, enclosed floor area of a building, or buildings, divided by the area of the lot. Excluded from the definition are open porches, balconies and decks, parking garages, and carports. A project made of triplexes, for example, will have a higher FAR—more residences share the same lot and become more affordable (Figure 6.1).

These indexes reveal several principles that contribute to achieving housing affordability. The first is that when the net density increases, lot sizes as well as the area allocated to roads decrease. The homes cover much of the land. When the area allocated to residential lots decreases, more land can be allocated to the preservation of natural green areas (National Association of Home Builders, 1986). The measures can also indicate strategies that need to be employed to achieve cost reduction. Smaller lot sizes in areas zoned for high density will save on land costs. In addition, when more units are attached, the density increases and more land is saved. The leftover land can be used for additional dwellings or left as open space. A demonstration of gradually increased densities on a cul-de-sac configuration is shown in Figure 6.2.

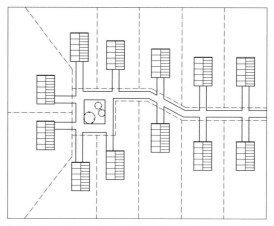

2 dwellings / acre (2 dwellings / 0.4 hectare net)
12 dwelling units
6 acres (2.4 developed hectares)

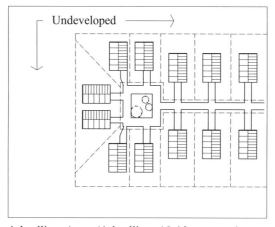

4 dwellings / acre (4 dwellings / 0.4 hectare net)
12 dwelling units
3 acres (1.2 developed hectares)

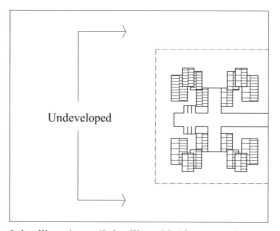

Figure 6.2 When the density increases, more land is left for additional units and the cost of land per dwelling unit drops.

8 dwellings / acre (8 dwellings / 0.4 hectare net)
12 dwelling units
1.5 acres (0.6 developed hectares)

LOT TYPES

Once the site has been selected, the planning process begins. Two distinct design approaches can be taken by the planner and the builder: *adhering to existing zoning ordinance* and *planned unit development* (PUD). In the first approach— working within existing zones—the designer closely follows predetermined municipal zoning bylaws. The size of the lots and the housing typology allowed will affect many design decisions. Achieving affordability will be harder to reach since key elements such as lot sizes, infrastructure, and road design are not under the planner's control. To provide affordable housing, the objective, through advocacy and consultation, will be to influence the process by legislating into the bylaws smaller lot sizes.

The second planning approach, PUD, provides the planner with greater flexibility. The site, usually a large plot, will be designed and submitted for approval with its own bylaws, guidelines, and standards. The plan may be approved in its entirety or partially modified. Yet the PUD approach has greater potential for achieving affordable design. The configuration of the selected lots can be based on those that contribute to increased density and to lowered land and infrastructure costs.

Another factor affecting design is whether the project will be titled and sold as a *freehold* or a *condominium*. A freehold project will limit the implementation of affordability strategies. Since each occupant will own the land and the home, there will be fewer sharing opportunities, which contribute to lowering cost. Each dwelling unit, for example, will have its own utilities connections rather than common ones. Those early decisions about the planning and marketing processes will be essential in determining the unit cost. Prior to listing the typologies of lots and their attributes, it is worthwhile to reflect on the historical evolution of land subdivision.

In 1820, fewer than 7 percent of the North American population resided in cities. In the United States, only 10 cities had populations greater than 100,000 inhabitants (Jackson, 1985). The continent's economy was agriculturally based, with many rural towns. The industrial revolution altered the urban landscape of many cities. People left farming communities to reside in and around cities. Suburban neighborhoods started to spring up near towns on previously cultivated farmland. The grid pattern of the streets in some developments often followed that of farms—unpaved roads become streets between two rows of homes. Land purchased by developers had set dimensions, which led to their subdivision to lot sizes, common nowadays. A 200 feet (60 meters) wide strip of land was divided into two strips of 100 feet (30 meters) each. Unlike urban land that was subdivided into narrow lots for economic reasons, suburban land was cheap. It was common to see 80 feet (24 meters) wide by 100-feet (30 meters) long lot subdivisions.

Converting agricultural land to residential use accelerated in the post–World War II era. The need to house young families saw the rapid emergence of many new subdivisions, and the proliferation of car ownership made it easy to reach them. Development standards also improved over the years with the introduction of elaborate infrastructure that included utilities such as storm drain, telephone, and cable TV. Near major urban centers, where land was expensive, the

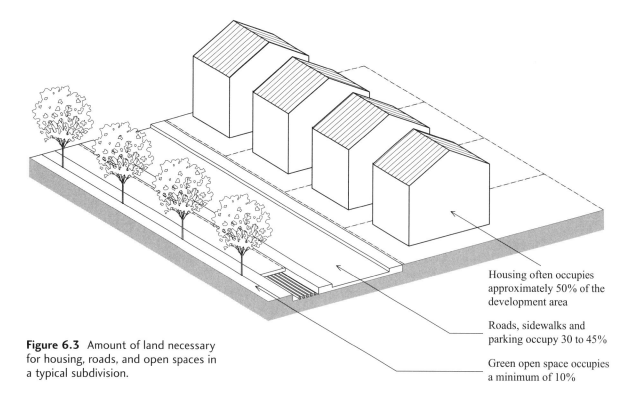

Housing often occupies approximately 50% of the development area

Roads, sidewalks and parking occupy 30 to 45%

Green open space occupies a minimum of 10%

Figure 6.3 Amount of land necessary for housing, roads, and open spaces in a typical subdivision.

width of lots was gradually reduced to 60 feet (18 meters), which, later, became the norm in North America.

Parallel to the rapid expansion of suburbia in the 1940s and 1950s, municipalities legislated Planning Acts to ensure public safety and regulatory standards. Many communities, for example, mandated that 10 percent of future neighborhoods' areas be devoted to public open space. To access each home by car, some 30 percent of the community area was commonly allocated to circulation and public parking. The rest of the land was subdivided for residential building purposes (Figure 6.3).

When the design of affordable homes is considered, subdividing into smaller lots will yield a significant economic benefit, as more units share the same infrastructure (Figure 6.4). The definition of smaller lots and what constitutes low or high density depends on the type of subdivision to which cities are accustomed. In some communities, small lots—primarily in urban areas—will measure 14 feet (4.3 meters) by 80 feet (24 meters) when a row of townhouses is proposed. In other cities, small lots will be twice as big, measuring 30 feet (9 meters) by 100 feet (30 meters). In suburban towns, lots narrower than 50 feet (15 meters) wide will be considered "small."

Some cities set a minimum lot size for a *freehold* home, which may be 18 feet (5.5 meters) in one municipality and 20 feet (6 meters) in another. A width of 40 feet (12 meters) is commonly required for a house with two side yards and an attached one-car garage. An Alberta (Canada) Housing report suggests that when the size of the lot is further reduced to anywhere from 25 feet (7.6 meters) to 35 feet (11 m), the lot will be called a *narrow, deep lot*. Parking, then, will have to be in front of the dwelling or at the rear where a lane is provided. The car can then be accommodated in a garage that is constructed on the lot (Figure 6.5).

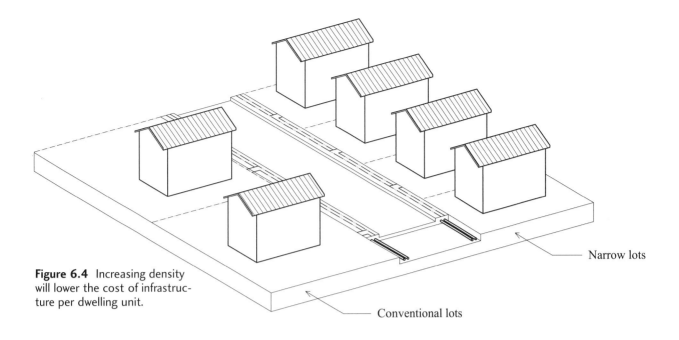

Figure 6.4 Increasing density will lower the cost of infrastructure per dwelling unit.

Narrow lots

Conventional lots

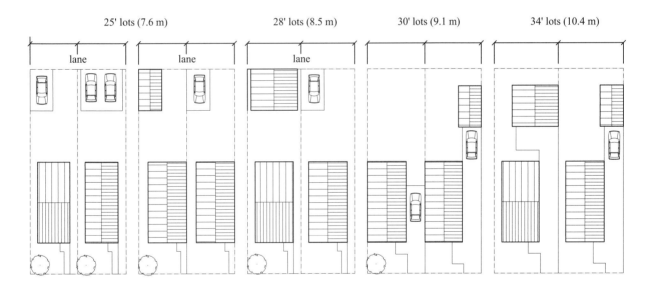

25' lots (7.6 m) 28' lots (8.5 m) 30' lots (9.1 m) 34' lots (10.4 m)

lane lane lane

Figure 6.5 Narrow lots with alternative parking options.

Choice of narrow lots will contribute to significant reduction in the cost of land and, as a result, infrastructure. The cost of a 50 foot (15 meter) by 100 foot (30 meter) lot with a price tag of $10 per square foot ($100 per square meter) would be $50,000. Infrastructure, which is usually charged by linear foot (linear meter) frontage, will add another $25,000 to the cost when the cost per unit is $500 per foot ($1,600 per meter). When the same figures are used for a 30-foot (9 meter) wide lot, the cost of land will drop to $15,000 for the land and $15,000 for the services, a savings of $40,000 per unit. Additionally, savings can be achieved when the density is further increased and the homes are attached.

The key difference between the planning process of an affordable housing development and that of any other residential project lies in the choice of lot sizes, housing prototypes, and their placement on the lot. There are common, and some less common, lot configurations which will be outlined below, that contribute to increased density. There can be *narrow center lots* with homes either detached or attached, which will determine a lot's width. *Corner lots* can be as wide as center lots or wider. A wider, corner lot will permit the placement of a multifamily unit, a duplex for example, with entrances at both the front and the side. There can also be an *angled lot* to fit into a site's corner. A dwelling placed at an angle should have a slightly wider front to provide comfortable access to the home (Figure 6.6).

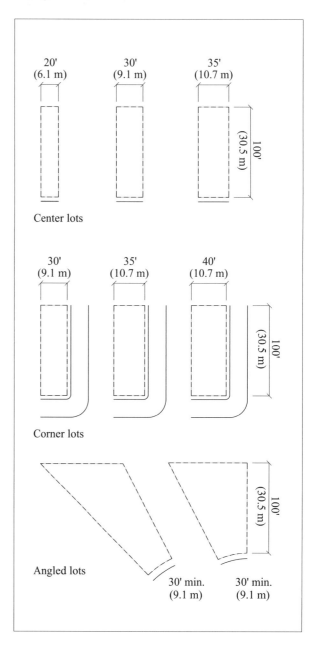

Figure 6.6 Variety of small size lots for center, corner, and angled configurations.

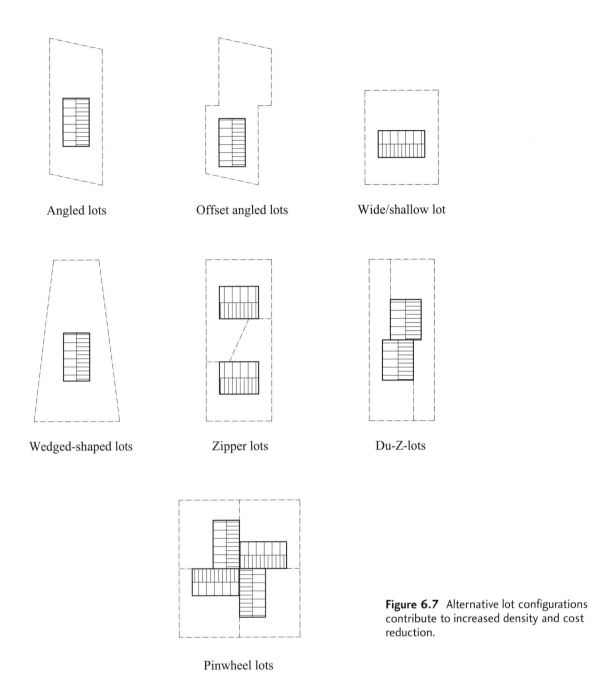

Angled lots   Offset angled lots   Wide/shallow lot

Wedged-shaped lots   Zipper lots   Du-Z-lots

Pinwheel lots

Figure 6.7 Alternative lot configurations contribute to increased density and cost reduction.

Angled lots can help reduce the amount of land needed for each unit. Angling the lots allows them to be shallower, and, as a result, the home is placed closer to the street, which can save on connection to infrastructure costs. Another type of angled lot is the *offset angled lot* where the homes will be sited not to block each other's side views and to maximize solar exposure (Figure 6.7).

In *wide, shallow lots,* the longitudinal dimension of the home is parallel to the street. Reduction in the depth of the lot will help increase density by permitting placement of additional similar lots on the site. According to Wentling (1991), lot proportions can be 70 feet by 70 feet (21 meters by 21 meters). The disadvantage of such an arrangement is that it may contribute to an increase in lot frontage and, as a result, to longer roads and utilities cost. Another disadvantage to wide, shallow lots is the nearness of the dwellings to one another, compromising privacy.

Wedge-shaped lots are those used at the end of a cul-de-sac and with curved streets. The lots can be used for attached or semidetached homes. Despite the fact that the arrangement of the lots is highly compact, more land is required for each dwelling than in a single, orthogonal arrangement. The economic advantage of these lots lies in their short frontage, which helps reduce infrastructure costs.

Zipper lots are a variation of wide, shallow lots. The front, in such an arrangement, will appear to be similar to wide, shallow lots, yet the rear of each lot is "zipped" into one another, thereby reducing land allocated to backyards. In high-density designs, the placement of entry doors, garages, and, in particular, rear windows is of critical importance. Functions that require privacy, such as bedrooms, should face the street and public ones, like family rooms, are profitably placed at the rear. Such arrangements help detached homes achieve densities of 15 units per acre (37 per hectare).

The *Du-Z-Lot* arrangement combines the attributes of zipper lots, semidetached dwellings, and *zero-lot-lines* (which are discussed in the next section). By attaching the dwellings to each other, savings are achieved through reducing land consumption and lowering construction costs. The challenge in such an arrangement lies in the need to accommodate parking. Since one dwelling unit will have a larger front yard and the other a larger rear yard, such a configuration works well when a lane exists at the rear to provide access to the back unit's on-lot parking. Privacy issues will also need to be carefully considered in such a design because of the units' proximity to one another.

The configuration of *pinwheel lots* takes place when several dwelling units are grouped together. In the plan, four dwellings are attached to each other to permit three façade exposures. The challenge in such design lies in the need to find parking solutions for all four dwellings. Often, the parking will be on surface and in common, which requires the legal title of the project to be condominium rather than freehold to allow joint ownership of land.

An entire development, or even a row, can be made of a mix of lot sizes, allowing the introduction of a range of dwelling types. The mix can include detached homes with different widths or multifamily as well as single-family dwellings.

LOTS AND HOMES

Decisions about where to place the home on the lot will affect a range of factors, including the occupant's comfort and community appearance. It will also have a direct affect on the dwelling cost. Prior to the beginning of the project's design, planners should familiarize themselves with *setback* regulations that decree the distance between the lot line and the home. The purpose of these mandatory distances is to ensure a minimum level of privacy and safety in case, for example, a fire breaks out. Bigger setbacks will likely require larger lots. In the interest of land savings, it is therefore preferable to reduce these distances as much as possible.

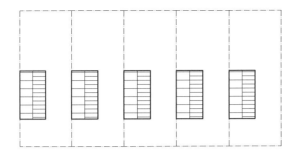

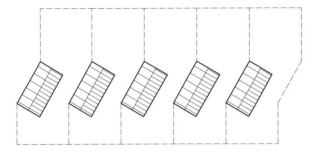

Figure 6.8 Homes placed on lot line with a single side setback.

The *zero-lot line* is another land-saving strategy. It emerged on the West Coast (of the U.S.) in response to high land prices and the need for more affordable detached, single-family housing. The advantage of this arrangement is that the usability of side yards on smaller lots is enhanced by shifting the siting position of the house against one side of the property lines. Narrow-lot frontages and the reduced setbacks associated with smaller lots help to minimize development costs. Savings can be derived from lower land and infrastructure improvement costs per unit. Narrower frontages and reduced front-yard setbacks allow for reductions in length of road pavement per unit, shorter utility runs, along with reduced ongoing road and infrastructure maintenance costs. The proximity of the dwelling to adjacent units will require careful attention to privacy. It is, therefore, common to see an unfenestrated wall on the lot line. Preferably, this wall will face north for energy savings. The home's stairs and service functions can be placed along this wall, since they require less natural light (Figure 6.8).

Land can be saved in the front and rear of the dwelling as well. Most municipalities mandate a minimum front setback of 20 feet (6 meters). This mandatory distance was set after World War II when land and infrastructure were inexpensive. By setting the home back, not only was more land required but streets lost a human scale. A regulated footprint coverage also determined the area and distance left at the rear. In an affordable housing project, these standards must be revisited. Reducing the front setback to 10 feet (3 meters) will contribute to reducing infrastructure distance from the street to the dwelling, thereby saving expenses. In an urban area, the distance can even be reduced to zero, placing the home on the front-lot line, as was the case in old towns.

Another aspect of affordable housing planning affected by the placement of the dwelling on the lot is parking. It is common to see shared outdoor parking in

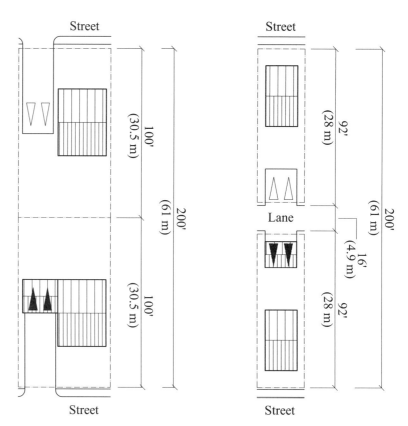

Figure 6.9 Parking at the lot's rear, with access from a lane, can help reduce both the width and the length of the lot.

small-lot projects. Private parking, however, can be arranged if certain considerations are adhered to. For basement parking to work, the home needs to be recessed well enough to permit the necessary entry slope. Street level indoor parking will consume valuable livable space and is, therefore, not recommended. A side on-lot parking either in a built garage, wall-less carport or simply in the open will be a possible solution. Yet, on a street made of small-lot homes, having a row of attached garages or carports will lend the street an unwelcome image (Figure 6.9). Parking at the lot's rear with access from a lane either on the lot outdoors or in a parking structure can lead to valuable savings, even with the cost of constructing a lane.

A consideration in placing a home on a lot is access to the dwelling. Most people tend to associate a main entry door with the front façade. When homes on small lots or zero-lot lines are proposed, an alternative placement for the entrance needs to be found. Relocating the main entrance from the front to the side will require changing the dwelling layout. A designer, therefore, needs to see dwelling design in a flexible light to permit a variety of layouts, configurations, and entrances.

When residential density increases, privacy may be compromised. The need to consider views and to enhance the residents' sense of comfort in a high-density community becomes important. The placement of the dwelling on the lot and the design of window locations, therefore, needs to be carefully considered. When the home is placed on the lot line, more lot area will be freed. If the lot-line wall remains unfenestrated, it will increase privacy. Placing the dwelling closer to

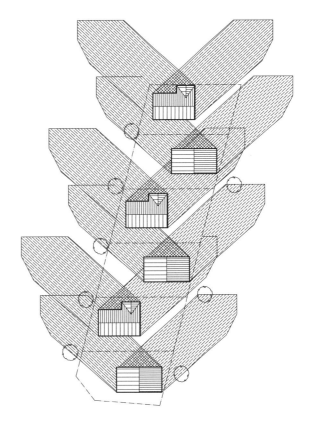

the front will leave more area at the rear of the house. Orienting the units toward common amenity spaces, like parks or play areas, will foster a greater sense of distance and elevate the residents' feelings of privacy. The situation might be more critical in row housing where proximity can compromise privacy. The row, then, must be configured to prevent residents from seeing each other's yards. Staggering the units may prevent undesirable views by creating private outdoor spaces at the rear of the houses (Figure 6.10).

Climatic conditions are another valuable design consideration affecting the placement of units on lots. Passive solar energy can be achieved if fenestrated façades face south and southeast. In a higher-density project, where homes are in close proximity, the dwellings can cast shadows on each other. Staggering detached units can resolve this problem (Figure 6.11). When the community has mixed types of dwellings, some of the homes can act as wind barriers. Tall row housing, for example, can assume that role.

LOTS AND STREETS

The origins of current urban configurations can be traced to ancient pedestrian cities. In more recent times, ideas that were proposed at the birth of suburbia generated forms that influenced the design of contemporary developments. Ebenezer Howard's 1898 book, *Tomorrow: A Peaceful Path to Real Reform,* is considered by some to be the ideological catalyst to current suburban planning. Howard proposed that people withdraw from overcrowded industrial cities to communities that combined the social and public convenience of towns with the healthy and serene aspects of rural life. He called his plan Garden City and foresaw homes with attached gardens surrounded by rings of parkland. There was also a centrally located building in which community commerce was located. The first implementation of Howard's concept was in the design of the town of Letchworth, England, by Raymond Unwin and Barry Parker in 1903 (Macfadyen, 1933). In their scheme, there was a central commercial area and housing that radiated from the center (Figure 6.12).

Garden City and Letchworth concepts went on to inspire a small group of North American planners, architects, and historians, to unite as the Regional Planning Association (RPA). The association became prominent in the planning and execution of these new concepts. Two of the group's leaders were Clarence Stein and Henry Wright, who produced some of America's most progressive planned communities of the time and remained influential thinkers and writers in the following years (Stein, 1957).

Radburn, New Jersey, is the most renowned product of the Stein-Wright partnership. It is essentially a realistic translation of several of the principles espoused by Howard and put into practice by Unwin and Parker. Though some elements were sacrificed in this implementation—the greenbelt surrounding the town, for example, was never purchased because of financial difficulties, and the proposed industrial areas were abandoned due to the Depression—the overall result was a safe, healthy community for young families. A variety of housing types were used in Radburn, and neighborhoods were serviced by small retail centers and defined by cul-de-sacs and scenic, curving streets.

Part of Radburn's success was in its accommodation of cars, whereby the pedestrian and the automobile were completely separated via interior paths and overpasses (Parsons, 1992). This phenomenon stimulated many new development patterns. Housing was arranged in large blocks with interior greens; the innovative use of the cul-de-sac created "superblocks," each one 35 to 50 acres (14 to 20 hectares) in size (Lynch, 1981). Although most dwellings in Radburn were single-family, there were some rental units in garden apartments. Individual unit planning was oriented toward the internal open areas rather than to the streets (Figure 6.13).

A development that looked to Radburn, at least superficially, as a model and in whose likeness most of the late twentieth century's suburbs have been built was Levittown, Pennsylvania. Laid out by a private development corporation on a flat site, the town was designed for a homogeneous population—the young, white, middle-class, car-dependent, mom-dad-and-the-kids family. It lacked the Garden City's ideological roots and did not separate pedestrian and vehicular traffic, and the curving streets are arbitrary as there is very little topography to

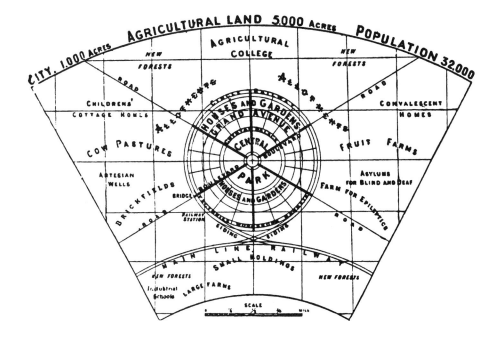

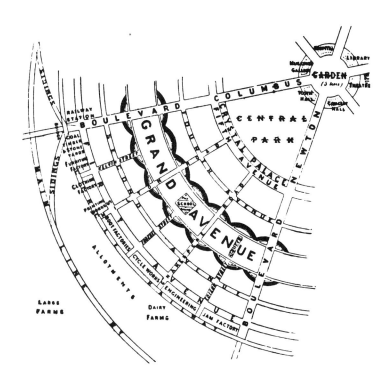

Figure 6.12 Ebenezer Howard's Garden City concept was one of the sparks of modern planning and suburban design.

Figure 6.13 Clarence Stein and Henry Wright's design of Radburn, New Jersey, with its cul-de-sacs, had a significant influence on suburban planning in the twentieth century.

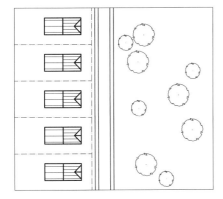

Single-loaded street

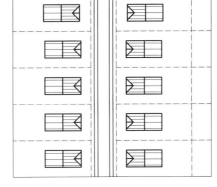

Double-loaded street

Figure 6.14 By double-loading a street with residences, the cost of infrastructure is shared between two rows of homes.

respond to. Also, there was no localized industry or business—Levittown was intended to house those workers commuting to Philadelphia or to the nearby Fairless works of United States Steel. The 17,300 homes that comprise Levittown were poorly built, had no regard for solar orientation, and were spread over 5,750 acres (2,300 hectares) and 1,300 streets (Grans, 1967). Nearly unlimited cheap land resources and standardization made such towns popular with developers throughout the North America, giving rise to some well-recognized urban configurations.

Another objective, in addition to achieving efficient land use in affordable housing design, will be to increase density without compromising livability and occupant's comfort. Common amenities, such as parks, need to be integrated into the design, and the parking arrangements need not stigmatize the appearance of the neighborhood. A fundamental principle in land use efficiency is double-loading versus single-loading of a road with homes. Building on both sides of a street will be preferable since the cost of building the road and placing infrastructure will be shared between two rows of homes. In a single-loading development, only one side of the street carries the economic burden (Figure 6.14).

Another principle has to do with the road's pattern. Avoiding monotony is preferable in high-density developments. Planning streets with detached homes close to each other, row housing or zero-lot-line dwellings may create undesired repetition and a wall-like effect. When conceiving an urban configuration, therefore, several measures can be taken to avoid such a situation. The street network can be curvilinear. The disadvantage of such a pattern is that some of the lots will not have an orthogonal shape, and the layout and construction of the infrastructure may be more complex and costly. Using a variety of urban configurations rather than repeating the same ones is another strategy. Adopting an agreed-upon system for one type of dwelling and creating courts or cul-de-sacs for another type can ensure a greater variety and visual interest.

Designing streets with an appropriate human scale also needs to be a consideration. Reaching proper scale by reducing setbacks, for example, works in favor of affordable housing, because placing taller, multifamily dwellings next to wider roads or large open spaces can foster intimacy. Landscape is another tool available to the designer in achieving human scale. Rows of trees can help

Figure 6.15 Reducing the front setback and placing taller buildings next to a street can shorten the lot's length and foster a better human scale.

diminish the effect of a wide road and create a comfortable microclimate (Figure 6.15).

A known configuration for roads and building sites is the *gridiron*, which is recognized as an urban archetype. It also has higher-density advantages, as both land and street designs are efficiently divided. A grid system can easily form long or short blocks. A block made of high-density narrow lots can be as much as 1,000 feet (300 meters) long. When proposing a long block, the planner runs the risk of a monotonous appearance, especially when the units are identical. It is common, in grid configurations, to see wider corner lots for larger units. Proposing a short block will foster more variety, yet it will increase the number of intersections a neighborhood will have and, as a result, will increase costs. An economic analysis, therefore, needs to study the expenses associated with long- and short-block alternatives (Figure 6.16).

A block can have a simple back-to-back lot arrangement, typical of suburban planning, or it can have a middle lane in between (Figure 6.17). The introduction of a lane provides access to rear parking, which helps reduce the lot's width. The benefits of constructing a fully paved lane needs to be economically studied in each location as it holds risk of further increasing the cost of the project's circulation.

The use of *cul-de-sacs* in North America accelerated following its introduction in Stein and Wright's Radburn scheme. The point of the design was a dead-end street, an extension from a local road. It is a highly popular planning form, as it prevents through traffic. The common paved area in such a design often functions

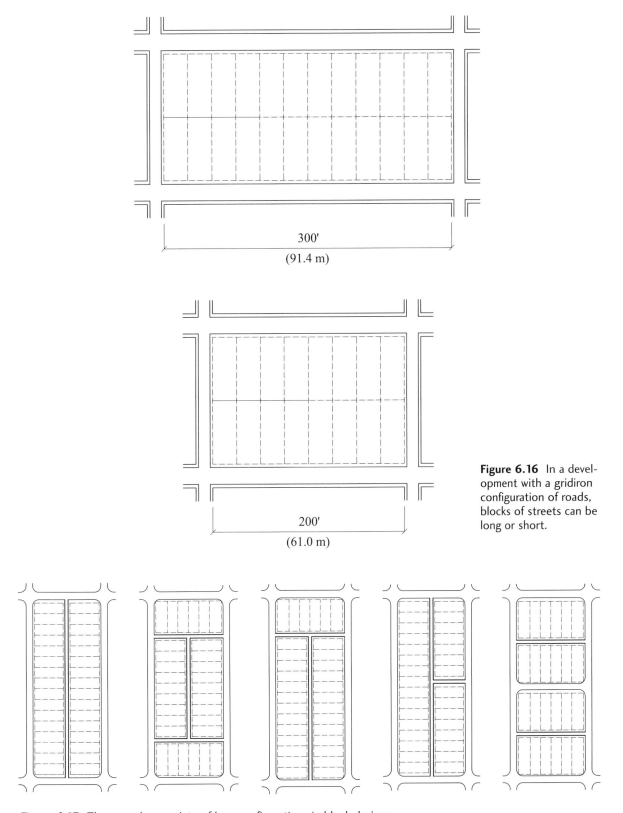

Figure 6.16 In a development with a gridiron configuration of roads, blocks of streets can be long or short.

300'
(91.4 m)

200'
(61.0 m)

Figure 6.17 There can be a variety of lane configurations in block designs.

as open space or even a children's play area. A cul-de-sac is regarded as a safer arrangement than the grid, because cars cannot speed up and residents can watch the street and one another's homes. The disadvantage of cul-de-sac lies in having some angled lots that reduce the land compactness and density.

Parking is also a valuable consideration, because the homes are concentrated in a relatively small area, and lot parking or parking garages may render a poor curb appeal to the community. Cul-de-sac streets can be either public or private. In a public arrangement, the often wider streets will be cared for by the municipality. When the street is private, it will be narrower and a likely part of a shared maintenance arrangement by the residents.

When higher-density dwelling configurations, such as row houses, are proposed for a cul-de-sac, the design will have to break away from the common form and introduce small road extensions from the circle. There are additional cul-de-sac forms that resemble court arrangements and usually serve a number of units. There are Private Courts, Common Courts, and Auto Courts as well (NAHB, 1986). When the density increases, more dwelling units will be accommodated and, therefore, the circulation and parking will have to increase accordingly. Having a proper setback, when such a choice is allowed, will affect the overall curb appeal of the cul-de-sac to provide appropriate human scale (Figure 6.18).

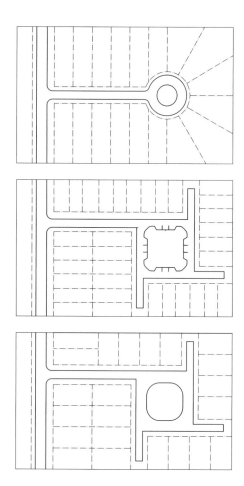

Figure 6.18 Alternative lots and road configurations on a cul-de-sac.

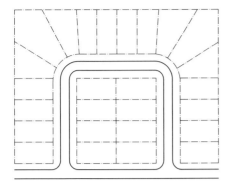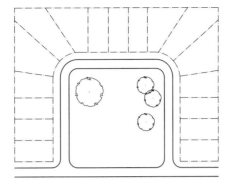

Figure 6.19
Configurations of lots
around loop roads.

Lot configurations around *loop streets* provide the privacy, safety, and economy of a dead-end street without the difficulty of turning, which results in easy circulation to and from a collector street. The loop street in various proportions and shapes provides interesting ideas for clustering homes, particularly if open space can be planned. The need to provide parking can also be accommodated with a mix of bays on the edges of the green space. It may require people to walk from their parked cars to their homes; yet, at times, it can be the only solution in a high-density situation (Figure 6.19).

BIG LOTS

When the site is divided into large plots, and several dwellings are constructed without subdividing the site, the land is owned by the occupants collectively. Design of such lots requires attention to several issues due to the close proximity between the structures. The pattern chosen for the road system within the lot will be important to consider. Cars may reach each building or may be parked in common at the periphery of the lot. It is typical to see shared parking lots in multifamily dwellings projects. Rear parking settings away from front view will, of course, be desired.

Relation to open spaces is also a critical issue in the design of high-density buildings on large lots. Allowing occupants who reside on ground to have access to private yards will be a preference. Alternatively, each structure can have its own green area, and the community as a whole will also have a space to congregate. The common space will likely be cared for by a hired contractor. The layout of the roads and the placement of the dwellings will have to consider natural features, such as trees. The placement of the homes on the lot will also depend upon the site's orientation. The buildings can be placed to ensure maximum exposure to the sun for passive solar gain.

Maintaining residents' privacy is an important concern in the design of a large lot. The structures will have to be placed on the site to prevent direct and close view between dwelling units. Preferably they will each have a view to the common area. The homes can be concentrated in one area or spread around the site. When the buildings are concentrated, the complexity and expenses associated with connecting them to the infrastructure declines.

KEY CONSIDERATIONS

- A project designed with freehold homes will limit implementing strategies for affordability. Because occupants will own the land and the home, there will be fewer sharing opportunities of utilities and open spaces.
- Subdivision to narrow lots will yield a significant economic benefit, as more units share the same infrastructure.
- A wider corner lot will permit the placement of a multifamily unit—a duplex, for example—with entrances at the front and the side.
- Angled lots create shallow formations and as a result consume less land. Homes placed on them can be closer to the street, which can save on connections to infrastructure.
- Wide-shallow, zipper, Du-Z, and pinwheel lots will contribute to greater land efficiency and cost savings.
- The placement of the home on the lot line, either on the side or the front, will foster smaller lots and reduction of infrastructure costs.
- Parking at the lot's rear, with access from a lane, will help avoid the building of a front or side garage, thereby reducing the width of the property.
- In higher-density planning, orienting the units toward common amenity spaces like parks or play areas will foster a greater sense of distance and will elevate the residents' feeling of privacy.
- In higher-density design, common amenities such as parks need to be integrated into the design, and the parking arrangements need not stigmatize the appearance of the neighborhood.
- Building on both sides of a street will be preferable, because the cost of building roads and placing the infrastructure will be shared between two rows of homes.
- Planning that integrates a variety of streets and lot patterns that correspond with the different unit types will avoid monotony.
- Narrower streets with slightly taller structures will not only save costs but foster a human scale in the community.
- Lot configurations around loop streets provide the privacy, safety, and economy of a dead-end street without the difficulty of turning, which results in easy circulation to and from a collector street.
- Maintaining residents' privacy will be an important concern in a condominium project made of large lots. The units have to be placed to prevent direct views between buildings.

7

Circulation and Infrastructure

A pproximately 30 percent of a residential development site's area is
commonly allocated to roads and parking. In a high-density, affordable housing project, careful attention should be given to these
design components—roads and parking—because they affect the overall
cost and contribute to the curb appeal of the community. Some critics and
designers argue that high-density planning needs to begin with a consideration of parking alternatives. This chapter outlines issues related to a development's traffic systems design and construction, parking arrangements,
pedestrian and cyclist paths, and the project's infrastructure.

STREETS HIERARCHY

The road network of a residential development forms part of a comprehensive movement system of a district and a region. Prior to deciding on street design pattern, issues related to fitting a local network into the outlying systems must be considered. The design of community circulation in any development, but more so in an affordable housing project, will focus on reducing reliance on cars. The network needs to give priority to pedestrian and cyclists in all decisions. The design ought to begin by identifying the built areas and the amenities that surround the site and how the community will connect with them.

Residents of existing communities are often reluctant to allow streets of a new project to link with theirs. Their main concern is that a heavier traffic load will increase noise and jeopardize safety. Linking communities, however, will not only foster social integration but make the flow of traffic efficient and cost effective. It will provide residents with easy access to existing amenities and save on building new ones. The road network of a development should, therefore, not create an isolated entity but an integrated one. The main arteries, whether pedestrian or vehicular, ought to link parks and provide access to shopping and other community facilities (Figure 7.1). The process of regional road network design also needs to bring together representatives of disciplines such as education and health when locating schools and medical clinics is considered in the master planning process.

Movement systems are designed and function hierarchically. They are distinguished from each other according to the volume of traffic they carry and their function. Links with predominantly access functions, such as getting home, are called *streets*. Those with predominantly movement functions are called *roads*. The design of the road system in an affordable housing community needs, primarily, to be safe and cost effective. The lengths, widths, and construction specifications of streets and roads are designed to respond efficiently to residents' needs. It is common to see streets in North America's low-density subdivisions with proportions that far exceed the requirements of the community. In the name of safety and access for emergency vehicles, the street width has expanded, and, as a result, street costs have grown as well (Figure 7.2). Streets should

Figure 7.1 The movement system of a new community needs to be linked to an existing one to foster social integration, increase traffic efficiency, and lower cost.

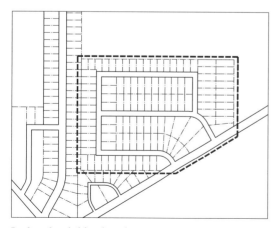

Isolated neighborhood

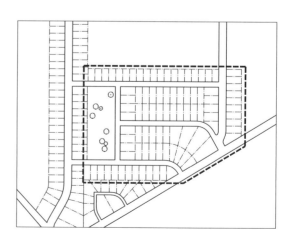

Integrated neighborhood

Figure 7.2 Street widths have expanded over the years, far beyond the daily traffic load needs of local residents.

also be designed for energy conservation, sparing motorists from driving long distances unnecessarily. They need to be designed to accommodate public transit and to control noise.

An additional feature in the design of movement systems is consideration of the site's topography and its natural features. Construction of roads should not clear natural features but incorporate them. Viewing interesting landscape vistas makes walking and driving in a community an enjoyable experience year-round. Streets also need to be designed to drain water after major storms. The site's slopes have to be well studied prior to laying down the movement network (Canada Mortgage and Housing Corporation, 1981).

One of the most important considerations in designing circulation is having a logical and simple hierarchical system. At the bottom of the hierarchy of residential streets is a *place* or a *lane*. A place is a short street, usually a cul-de-sac. It is the link between the homes and other streets. Lanes, which are also referred to as *alleys*, are built behind homes. Their origin is rooted in older cities where they provided rear service access. In recent decades, they have regained the interest of planners who see them as a way to provide homes with rear parking, thereby reducing the lot's width.

Next in the hierarchy are *subcollectors,* which are also referred to as *local streets.* They provide access to homes on smaller streets. They are designed to deter high-speed, through traffic. The daily volume of cars driving through subcollectors ranges from 2,000 to 3,000. There are rarely parking restrictions on subcollectors, except for upkeep purposes. *Collector streets* connect local and arterial streets. They are the main conduits of a residential area and carry a higher volume of traffic. It is common to see minor commercial activities like grocery or drug stores along collector roads. The traffic volume on collector streets ranges from 1,000 to 12,000 vehicles daily. Traffic signals are not usually installed, and vehicle speed is limited to 30 miles per hour (50 kilometers per hour). Top in the hierarchy is the *arterial road.* It has a high average of daily traffic, moving at

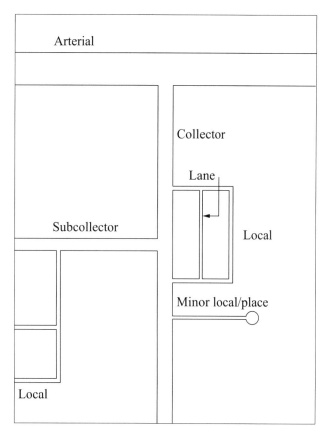

Figure 7.3 Key components of a road network in and around a residential development.

medium and high speeds. It is designed to accommodate from 5,000 to 30,000 vehicles daily (The Model Code, 1990). Arterial roads provide connections for major national and local traffic generators (Figure 7.3).

The efficiency of a road network contributes significantly to the affordability of a community's homes; therefore, several principles need to be considered. First, the proposed street type needs to reflect its use. There is no need to build more than what is needed to serve the community. Second, the driving time from a collector street to any home in the development should not exceed one minute. In addition, no more than three turns should be required between any address and the nearest collector street or arterial road (The Model Code, 1990).

With regard to public transit, at least 90 percent of all dwellings should be within 1,300 feet (400 meters) in a straight line from an existing or future bus route and not more than 1,600 feet (500 meters) from a present or future bus stop. Buses must be able to access safely the development and cross arterial roads when commuting between neighborhoods without complicated turning maneuvers (CMHC, 1981).

STREET TYPOLOGY AND INTERSECTIONS

Contemporary street configurations draw their origins from ancient towns. Modeled after the street pattern of pedestrian Roman cities, the *gridiron,* a network covering an area, lasted for centuries and suited the first suburban communities with public transit. Having straight and sometimes diagonal lines or streets, with intermediate stops at street corners was convenient for streetcars. Commercial and service functions developed around major stops. The fundamental principle behind this street configuration was the importance of public transit, which was fed by a pedestrian network (Tasker-Brown and Pogharian, 2000). This model was abandoned when reliance on public transit began to decline. Private cars enabled people to commute at their own convenience. The gridiron was no longer in need, as the invention of the cul-de-sac altered the way streets in suburban communities were designed (Figure 7.4). Over the years, this latest configuration—the cul-de-sac—further evolved to include loop streets. In addition, in the name of development efficiency, green areas and footpaths were also gradually eliminated from development designs.

	Gridiron (c. 1900)	Fragmented parallel (c. 1950)	Warped parallel (c. 1960)	Loops and lollipops (c. 1970)	Lollipops on a stick (c. 1980)
Street Patterns	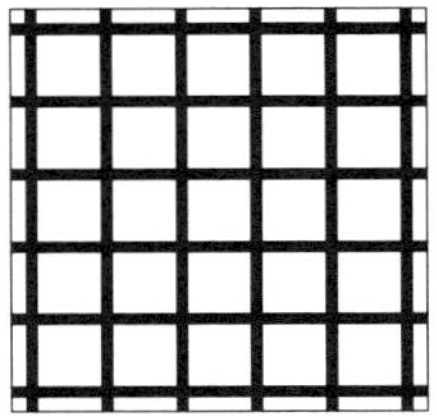	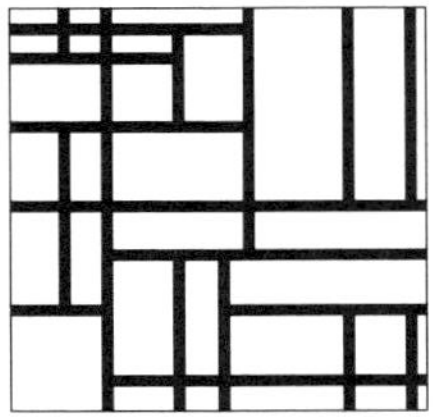		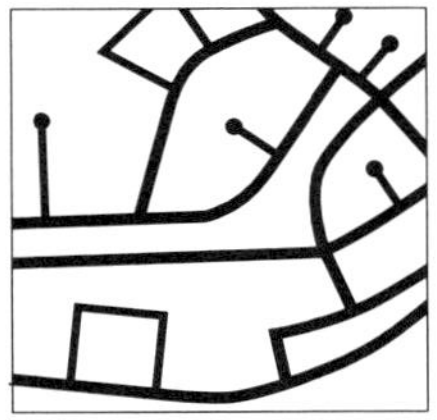	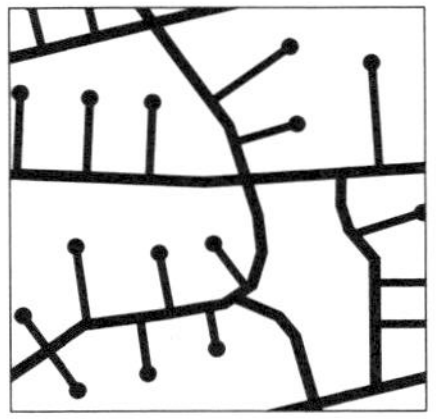
Intersections	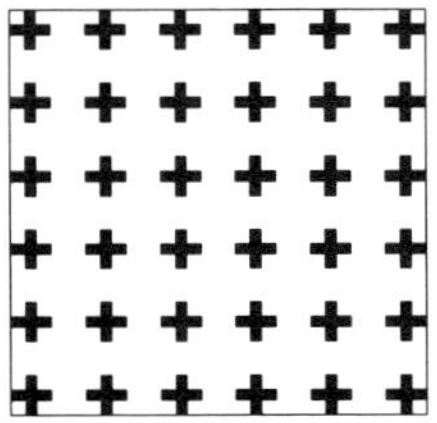	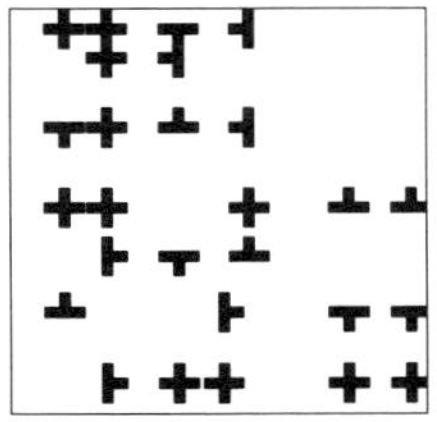	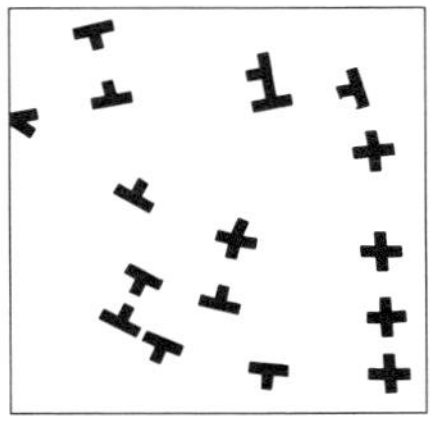	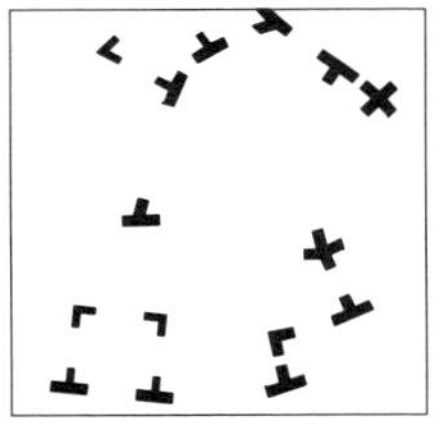	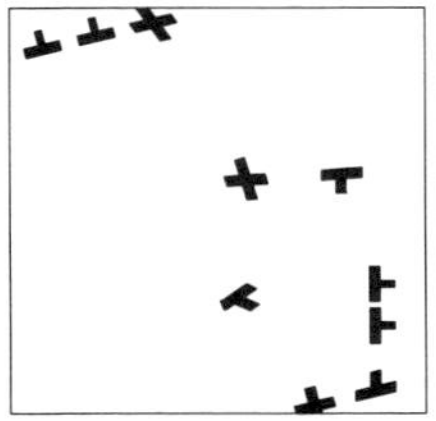
Linear Feet of Streets	20,800	19,000	16,500	15,300	15,600
# of Blocks	28	19	14	12	8
# of Intersections	26	22	14	12	8
# of Access Points	19	10	7	6	4
# of Loops & Cul-de-Sacs	0	1	2	6	24

Note: This table refers to the 100-acre unit of analysis illustrated in the diagrams. Intersections were defined as junctions of two or more through routes. Junctions with cul-de-sacs were not treated as intersections because cul-de-sacs do not lead anywhere outside the immediate area.

Figure 7.4 The evolution of street patterns since 1900 gradually accommodated cars.

Regardless of the street pattern, there are efficiency and quality principles that must be maintained in every system. A key decision that influences street design and its cost is the required "right of way." The term refers to the publicly owned land on which both motorists and pedestrians move. Thus, a cost-saving design will be a result of correlation between street function, hierarchy, and width. The functional elements commonly added to the road system's "movement" are utilities, drainage, landscaping, and street furniture; these areas should be reduced to a minimum. The street's width also needs to reflect its use. In streets with light traffic, slow speed should also be encouraged. Narrow width will not only slow motorists but save valuable land and construction costs. On such streets, pedestrian and cyclist paths can be closer to the roads; whereas, for safety reasons, a distance must be maintained between pedestrians, bikes, and cars on collector roads. With regard to land consumption, studies demonstrate that loop and cul-de-sac roads consume smaller amounts of land than the gridiron pattern (Tasker-Brown and Pogharian, 2000) (Figure 7.5).

Safety is another essential part of street design as well as a source of indirect cost reduction. The design of intersections is the most important element of street safety. Several issues need to be kept in mind during the design phase. The first is that motorists need to have a clear view of all streets. Once in the intersection, they should have an unobstructed front view of 82 feet (25 meters). The preferred angle for streets at an intersection is 70 to 110 degrees. In principle, intersections of more than two streets should be avoided, as they constitute a traffic hazard. Another important aspect of street design is the distance between intersections. According to traffic studies, this distance should not be smaller than 200 feet (60 meters). But perhaps the principal issue has to do with the number of streets that meet at an intersection. In the gridiron design, the place where two streets crossed could be considered to present the greatest safety risk. At each corner, there are 16 possible points of collision. In T-intersections, in

	Square grid (Miletus, Houston, Portland, etc.)	Oblong grid (most cities with a grid)	Oblong grid 2 (some cities or in certain areas)	Loops (subdivisions - 1950 to now)	Cul-de-sacs (Radburn - 1932 to now)
Percentage of area for streets	36.0%	35.0%	31.4%	27.4%	23.7%
Percentage of buildable area	64.0%	65.0%	68.6%	72.6%	76.3%

Note: The comparison is based on a district area of 40 acres (16 ha) that lies within a square of which the sides are 1320' (402 meters). This is the average distance for a 5-minute walk. This boundary square includes half of the perimeter road. The street ROW is assumed 65' (20 meters) for all cases. All blocks (except the first) have a depth (or width) of 200' (61 meters).

Figure 7.5 Comparison of area used for streets and buildable uses among five typical configurations.

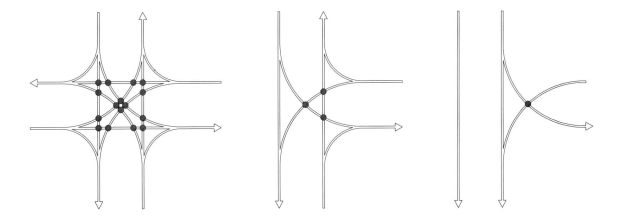

which one road meets another at a 90-degree angle, common in cul-de-sac or loop road systems, there are only three intersecting paths; they are, therefore, considered safer (Figure 7.6) (Schoenauer, 1963).

Figure 7.6 The preferred intersection design will be one that minimizes possible crossing points of vehicles and, as a result, reduces potential for accidents.

ALTERNATIVE STREET DESIGN

The steady rise in the cost of land for residential developments paralleled a similar increase in the cost of road building. In addition to a one-time construction cost, residents need to pay maintenance and upkeep fees through municipal taxes. Amelioration of standards is a prime cause of street construction and maintenance cost increases. Road width and the size of the strip of land in which utilities are buried have all expanded.

Streets in rural communities were traditionally wide, as land was inexpensive. In post–World War II suburban subdivisions, streets have gradually expanded from 24 feet (7.3 meters) to 44 feet (13 meters). Two motives drove this expansion. The first is a common notion that residents appreciate a wider street. The second has to do with concerns about access of service and emergency vehicles. Fear that, in a case of need, road entry will be limited by parked vehicles led to overdesign of roadways. The requirement for space enough for a fire truck to make a U-turn on a cul-de-sac is an example of such a concern. Wide-road standards were kept even when a loop road was designed. Cost saving in road design, therefore, requires rethinking conventional standards while not compromising safety and quality. The main issues that need to be considered are the width of right of ways and parking allocations.

Streets

The dimensions of local streets are based on the width of a motor vehicle. When large-sized cars, such as trucks or vans, are expected to pass, the road will be wider. Many municipalities, unfortunately, applied highway standards to local roads. It is not unusual to see streets with a minimum pavement width of 30 to 36 feet (9 to 11 meters). If cost-effective local streets are to be planned, traffic speed and parking allocations ought to be the factor of most influence. With low volume and low speed, it is not necessary to provide two moving lanes. If two

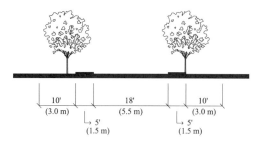

Local street without parking

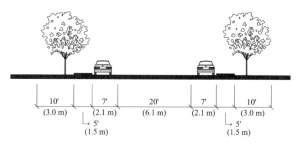

Collector or commercial road with
parking on both sides

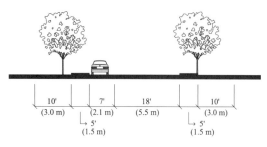

Local street with parking on one side

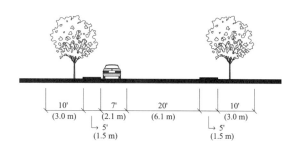

Collector or commercial road with
parking on one side

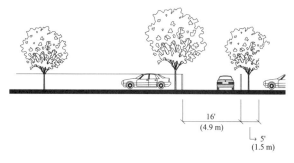

Lane

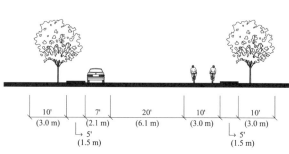

Collector or commercial road with parking on
one side and bicycle path

Figure 7.7 Alternative narrow street standards with and without on-street parking.

cars are parked across from each other, there will still be room for one moving vehicle to pull over and let another pass. Therefore, an 18- to 22-foot (5.5 to 6.7 meter) street with an 8- to 10-foot (2.4 to 3 meter) moving lane, plus two 7-foot (2 meter) parking lanes, is feasible for most residential streets (National Association of Home Builders, 1987) (Figure 7.7).

Traffic planners concerned with cost-effective design can also examine the possibility of having a single moving lane, which would be a minor inconvenience in many towns and lead to substantial cost savings. The cost of a 24-foot (7.3 meter) pavement, for example, is 15 percent less than the cost of a 28-foot (8.5 meter) pavement. The elimination of both parking lanes can contribute to further savings. Therefore, in developments where each dwelling unit has on-lot parking or a parking garage, streets can be as narrow as 18 to 20 feet (5.5 to 6 meters).

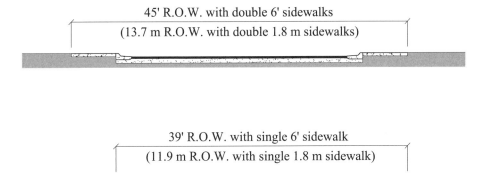

45' R.O.W. with double 6' sidewalks
(13.7 m R.O.W. with double 1.8 m sidewalks)

39' R.O.W. with single 6' sidewalk
(11.9 m R.O.W. with single 1.8 m sidewalk)

Figure 7.8 Streets can be planned with single or double sidewalks.

Narrower Sidewalks

In many instances, sidewalks can be designed below local standards, built on one side, or eliminated altogether. Decisions about whether to have one or two sidewalks, or none at all, will depend on the expected volume of the pedestrian traffic in the community. When amenities such as shops, playgrounds, or bus stops are planned for an area, sidewalks linking them with homes should be designed (Figure 7.8). In small towns with low vehicular traffic, it is common to drop requirements for sidewalks altogether. For the same reason, sidewalks have been eliminated from cul-de-sacs.

The width of the sidewalk can also vary according to the expected pedestrian traffic. Some designers tend to specify 5- to 7-foot wide (1.5 to 2 meter) sidewalks. A 3-foot wide (1 meter) sidewalk can be sufficient in most instances. In a rural setting, the width of a sidewalk can be as narrow as 24 inches (61 centimeters). In addition, driveways often interrupt sidewalks and create an effect of continuous curb cuts. Standards should, therefore, be put in place to require shared driveways and a maximum width for driveways along sidewalks (Hinshaw et al., 1998). Also, sidewalks are usually given a location within the road right-of-way. This is an unnecessary practice, and sidewalks can be located on top of the utilities that are also placed in the right-of-way.

Cul-de-Sac Street

Since the unveiling of the Radburn, New Jersey, neighborhood plan by Stein and Wright in 1929, the cul-de-sac became favored by homebuilders and residents. Safety, reduced noise, and improved curb appeal contributed to its proliferation. Yet, this popular planning configuration consumes excessive amounts of land. Many communities commonly require a cul-de-sac to have a radius of between 50 to 60 feet (15 to 18 meters). A 1994 study by the department of Housing and Urban Development (HUD) shows that 35 to 40 feet (11 to 12 meters) can be sufficient. The reduced size can adequately accommodate the turning requirement for an emergency vehicle like an ambulance or fire truck. In recent years, planners have elaborated on the traditional cul-de-sac design by adding a Y-shape, T-shape, and as well a square or circle that in some cases includes interior parking. These designs adequately consider needs for entry and turning by emergency and service vehicles (Figures 7.9 and 7.10).

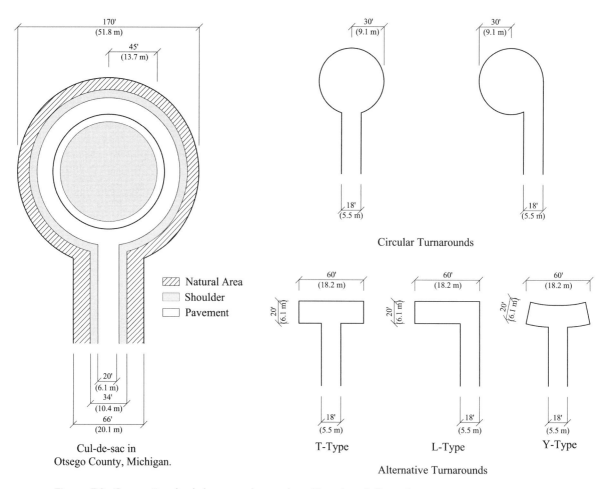

Figure 7.9 Conventional cul-de-sac and examples with reduced dimensions.

Circular Turnarounds

Alternative Turnarounds

T-Type   L-Type   Y-Type

Cul-de-sac in
Otsego County, Michigan.

Natural Area
Shoulder
Pavement

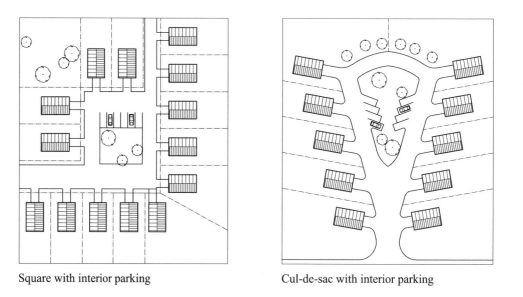

Square with interior parking   Cul-de-sac with interior parking

Figure 7.10 High-density clusters of homes arranged in alternative drive-through and cul-de-sac configurations to increase number of parking stalls and to reduce land consumption.

Avoiding Noise

Affordable housing developments are often constructed on leftover plots of land in proximity to noisy major arterial roads. In these locations, measures should be taken to ensure that barriers will be constructed to reduce noise levels. According to a number of residential design standards, the acceptable level of outdoor noise is 55 decibels. Pope (1982) explains that "This level permits conversation at close range or in a slightly raised voice most of the time. It corresponds typically to an indoor noise level of 40 dBA." Several strategies applicable to the design of affordable communities can be considered. The simplest one is to recess the dwelling from the road. This approach consumes, however, more land and, therefore, should be pursued only in high-density settings. Another approach would be to plan for a service road, with access to common parking, for example, that will separate the dwellings from the noise source. In fact, the common parking area itself can serve as a noise barrier (Figure 7.11).

Figure 7.11 Most of the common parking areas in this development were placed to act as a barrier between a busy highway and affordable dwelling units.

Another common, and in some places required, approach to noise reduction is the use of a sound wall. Noise measurements carried out indicate that a sound wall reduces noise by 6 to 7 decibels or 10 percent in the walkway between the housing and the wall (Pope, 1982). A change in topography can also contribute significantly to traffic noise reduction. When a major arterial is planned, locating it at a lower elevation from residences will be a way of reducing noise. The wall facing a freeway should be designed, if possible, with a minimum of openings or none at all. Rooms in homes in a high-noise area preferably should be located at the opposite elevation, away from the source. An earth berm can also be a noise-reduction measure. The berm can be landscaped to provide an additional measure of noise reduction (CMHC, 1981).

Streetscape

Streetscape is an all-encompassing term that refers to the street's appearance and its physical features. According to some definitions, the streetscape includes the parking, the sense the place conveys, the private and public landscaping, the pavement material, and the street furniture, such as light poles, signs, and public benches (The Model Code, 1990). In an affordable housing project, the streetscape is important to the residents' and the visitors' perception of the community. The streetscape can also lend a place its unique identity. A common notion by builders, and the public alike, is that an appealing streetscape is costly. This need not be the case. Attention to detail in the planning stage can contribute to proper curb appeal. Wider streets with large easements and setbacks not only cost more but look barren and sterile. Trees and shrubs planted at proper intervals, near narrow streets, will grow to form a canopy over the road years later. A minimum of one tree in front of each home can be mandated. Shrubs can also be placed at street corners and public areas. In some instances, a street segment can be left barren to permit vistas of unique natural views when they exist.

The street's paving material can also be designed to improve curb appeal and to serve a function at the same time. In an intersection, the pavement can be changed to include strips of interlocking pavers or bricks. Such a pavement will slow down motorists on local streets, which will provide safer passage for pedestrians or cyclists, and break the continuity of a black asphalt road (Figure 7.12).

The sidewalk design may also be reexamined for its contribution to the streetscape. It can include paving materials other than concrete and its materials integrated with the public and private landscape features. Street furniture such as lightning poles, plant-guard barrier, bus shelters, and signs should be well-designed and placed to complement each other. When fences are allowed, guidelines as to height, material, form, and colors should be put in place. Tall fences in front of each home, however, can give a neighborhood a poor image.

The façades of homes also form an important part of the streetscape. The common tendency in suburban communities is to allow some choice of styles and materials. Unlimited freedom does not work in favor of the streetscape, as it creates an uncoordinated, chaotic appearance. Guidelines can be introduced to

suggest, among others, what should be the main design features, materials, and projections. Streets should also have certain characteristics that distinguish them from other streets to avoid monotony.

Residential streets can serve purposes other than carrying vehicular or pedestrian traffic. When possible, local streets should be used for communal social activities and leisure. They can become play areas, running tracks for joggers, bicycle paths, and gathering places. To achieve multiple uses, streets need to be designed to maximize safety by creating a narrower entrance to a local road and by minimizing the pavement area. The street can be curvilinear and avoid direct links to arterial or collector streets to prevent through traffic.

Modeled after old city streets, the Woonerf Street, in the Netherlands, is a road serving motorists, a pedestrian mall, a playground, and even a public square. Planting, traffic speed regulators, and different pavement types distinguish the street from other local roads. Parking spaces for small cars are grouped and well-marked. There are no curbs in a Woonerf Street, and the entire surface is at the same level. The Woonerf Street supports commonly held beliefs that there can be more opportunities for social interaction among neighbors when there is a lower volume of traffic on a street. Turning regular streets into a meeting place can be achieved by including streetscaping features such as tree planters as part of the design. Motorists, then, will have to slow down as they proceed carefully between those elements (Figure 7.13).

Figure 7.12 Streets' intersections can be raised and paved with interlocking blocks or bricks to slow motorists and to provide safe passage for pedestrians and cyclists.

Figure 7.13 The Woonerf Street was designed to accommodate pedestrians and slow motorists down by including plantings, bumps, and different pavement types.

ROAD AND CURB CONSTRUCTION

Road design and construction specifications are largely dependent on expected use. When a heavy volume of traffic is anticipated, including large vehicles, streets must be built to sustain more wear and tear. Location is another influencing factor in road and curb design. In a place subject to varying weather conditions that include snow removal, roads are likely to deteriorate faster than roads in differing climatic conditions. Salt, which is commonly used in areas with heavy snowfall to melt ice, does not work in favor of a road's life span. Each region, therefore, has its own road construction and maintenance standards. Over the years, local governments have applied the construction standards established for roads with heavy traffic to local streets. Substantial cost savings can, therefore, be obtained by making sure that construction norms are appropriate for the anticipated use. Building heavy-duty roads for hardly-used local streets is simply unnecessary.

Road construction commonly encompasses three components: the road pavement, the road edge (known as the curb), and the sidewalk. The makeup of the road construction specification can be changed to lower cost. A 1987 HUD study suggests that consideration can be given to reducing the thickness of the base material from the traditional 8 to 12 inches (20 to 30 centimeters) as was done in Lacey, Washington (Figure 7.14). Long-distance transportation of aggregate used in construction is another item that inflates road costs. Effort should be made to use local material, when possible, to save on transport.

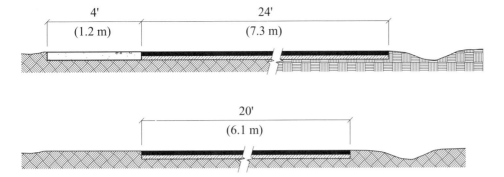

Figure 7.14
Reduced road construction standards in Lacey, Washington, contributed to substantial cost savings.

Demonstration streets

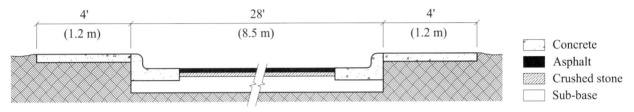

	Concrete
■	Asphalt
▨	Crushed stone
	Sub-base

Typical street

Another costly item in street construction is the road edge. Innovative approaches to curb design and construction have been introduced in recent years. They are all based on reducing the amount of concrete, a costly substance, and the amount of labor involved in constructing a curb. One approach is to simplify the curb shape. The other approach is to eliminate it altogether. It will allow runoff water to percolate through the grass, thereby reducing the amount of storm water runoff and contamination of effluent. Curbs often get damaged during house construction and utility servicing. It is essential, therefore, to select a construction method that will minimize or reduce the possibility of curb damage and thus additional cost. Delaying curb construction until the house building is complete is one such method. Also, constructing curbs with reinforcement will greatly reduce curb breakage. This has a higher initial cost, but it is worth spending more at the outset since in the long run it will result in a lower percentage of curb replacement.

Low initial costs will make housing more affordable, but the frequent maintenance and replacement costs will have to be paid by the owner in the form of municipal taxes. It is up to the municipality to decide which strategy to choose. The cost of replacing reinforced concrete curbs, for example, is usually less than half that of plain concrete curbs. Another approach will be to construct a two-stage curb, where the base is installed to the level of base course asphalt and the top poured after house construction and prior to placing the final surface layer of the asphalt. Although this method has a higher initial cost, the cost of replacement of damaged sections of the base makes this method as economical as any other method and results in a superior end product.

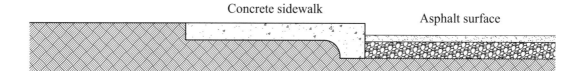

Concrete sidewalk   Asphalt surface

Figure 7.15 A cost reduction measure in road construction is integration of curb and sidewalk.

Some engineers find it more feasible to spend a little bit more at the outset and much less later on. But, since most municipalities make their decisions based on short-term rather than long-term effects, they are more likely to opt for lower initial costs. Therefore, if the municipality prefers lower initial costs and not lower future costs, then the first option to build curbs after the house construction is completed should be its first choice. A typical current standard is the construction of curbs and gutters on all new urban roads. The gutters next to the curbs ensure that runoff is directed to street catch basins where road grades are almost flat. The proposed alternative standards are curb and gutter where road grades are less than 2 percent and barrier curbs on road grades greater than 2 percent (Marshall et al., 1992). These alternative standards are cost effective because less concrete is required to construct the curb, and the cost of completing an asphalt overlay will be decreased since there is no concern about matching the gutter elevation (Figure 7.15).

PARKING

Some planners argue that the design of medium- or high-density affordable housing developments begins with the conception of parking alternatives. This notion is not far removed from reality, because the land allocated to roads and parking can in some instances amount to 50 percent of the total area. Finding parking solutions can be an even greater challenge in an infill project that is built in a highly populated urban area. What has aggravated the need to find parking solutions in recent decades is the development of a "car culture." For those who reside in low-density areas, daily activities—such as getting to work, stores, school, and social and recreational activities—are conducted by private car. The spread of lower density population does not economically justify investment in public transit, so the phenomenon of private car usage worsened as urban sprawl took hold. Cold, northern and hot, southern weather conditions can add to the desire for a more car-based lifestyle, and thus more parking. It is often impossible to walk or ride a bike over long distances in extreme cold or heat.

Large expanses of parking areas or a succession of street-facing garage doors also has aesthetic, ecological, and health ramifications. When more outdoor area is devoted to parking—a situation common in high-density projects—less is allocated to land- and streetscape. Developments with vast parking spaces are simply not pleasant to walk through or live in. Also, when it rains, grading of the parking area directs runoff to storm drains rather than to nature. In addition, in hot summer days the temperature of the pavement is several degrees higher than the soil, which is known to affect the community's overall climatic conditions and, by some accounts, public health.

The economic implications of parking provisions on residential projects, and on the cost of each home, is staggering. Litman (1999) notes that "based on typical affordable housing development costs, one parking space per unit increases costs by about 12.5 percent and two parking spaces increases costs by more than 25 percent compared with no off-street parking." The cost of parking, according to Litman (1999), consists of several components. Land for off-street parking requires about 300 square feet (28 square meters) of surface area, including access roads. One acre of land holds about 125 cars, roughly equivalent to the amount of land devoted to buildings. Since parking spots are assigned per unit, smaller units, in fact, bear the same cost as large ones. Construction and maintenance constitutes another significant expense. Underground parking can be as much as ten times more expensive than surface parking, and the annual maintenance cost of both are not negligible.

Parking design also must consider reduced potential for increased density. The higher the parking requirement ratio per unit, the lower the number of units constructed. According to Litman (1999), "increasing parking requirements from one to two spaces per unit reduces the maximum potential density for two story 500 square foot (46 square meter) bachelor apartment from 88 to 64 units per acre (220 to 160 units per hectare) representing a 37 percent decline, but only causes a 13 percent reduction in maximum density for 2000 square foot (190 square meter) townhouse" (Figure 7.16). Other expenses largely associated with parking are higher cost of dwellings, as well as elevated financing costs incurred by land developers and homebuyers. Off-street parking increases the length of the curb cut and thus reduces the amount of on-street parking (Figure 7.17).

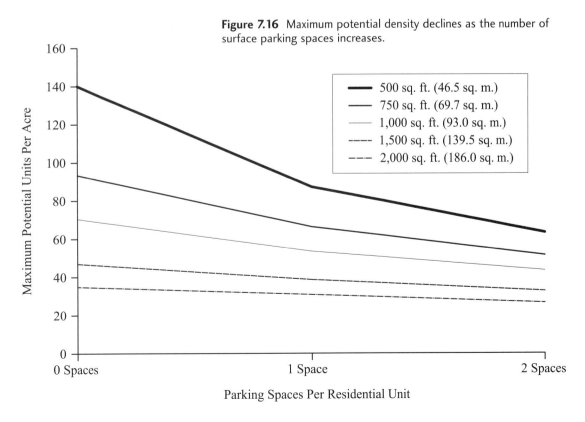

Figure 7.16 Maximum potential density declines as the number of surface parking spaces increases.

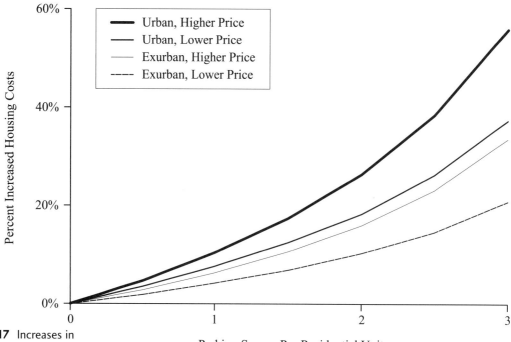

Figure 7.17 Increases in per-unit housing price are due to parking costs.

Parking requirements and their mounting costs affect affordability. A household that relies on private cars as a main mode of transit is likely to incur higher monthly expenses. It may jeopardize this household's ability to afford a home altogether. Groups likely to be affected are singles, single-parent families, and the disabled, all with modest incomes. Parking arrangement is, therefore, recognized as an essential component of the economics of housing affordability and requires a great degree of innovation in dwelling and community design.

Parking Typology

When planning parking in affordable dwellings and communities, one needs to recognize that criteria used in conventional developments need to be challenged and addressed early on. Familiarity with occupant types is important and can help determine the quantity of required parking spots. It is known, for example, that more parking space is needed by mature families with children at driving age than senior citizens or singles. The size of the dwelling is also an indication of the number of required parking spots. Larger dwellings used by more household members will entail more parking spots. Homeowners will commonly require more parking places than renters. In addition, people who reside in rural locations will rely heavily on private cars in the absence of public transit. When the site has a larger number of support facilities and amenities to which people can walk, the need for cars and parking may be lower (CMHC, 1980).

Parking solutions can be divided into two broad categories: on street and off street. In on-street situations, cars are parked on the road, whether public or private. In an off-street parking arrangement, cars are parked primarily on

Figure 7.18 Amount of resident parking needed as percentage of the type of built dwellings.

	Studio (%)	1 Bedroom (%)	2 Bedroom (%)	3+ Bedroom (%)	Assisted Senior Citizens[a] (1) (%)
Central area with good transit	25–50[b]	25–30	50–100	50–100	10
Urban area with fair transit	50–75	50–75	50–100	75–100	10–25
Suburban area with good transit	50–100	50–100	75–100	100–125[c]	10–25
Rural or suburban area with fair or poor transit	100	100–150	100–150[c]	100-200[c]	25–50

[a]Applicable to nonmarket housing, particularly where greater age and reduced income will result in reduced car ownership. Includes both studio, one- and two-bedroom apartments, and an allowance for visitor parking.

[b]The number of spaces for "mini" apartments in the core of large urban areas can be reduced to approximately 10 percent.

[c]Tandem parking arrangements are considered adequate in meeting needs greater than 100 percent. (Tandem parking provides parking stalls of sufficient length to allow cars to park one behind the other.)

private property, away from roads. Other distinguishing categories are indoor and outdoor parking arrangements. Indoor parking can be inside a dwelling—a parking garage, for example—or in an independent, enclosed structure where the car is protected from the elements. In an outdoor parking situation, the car is not sheltered. Cars can also be parked in common, in a shared arrangement. Alternatively, they can be parked individually on privately owned lots. Parking types can also be distinguished by their relationship to ground level. Cars can be parked on the ground or under it, either inside a dwelling or in common under an apartment building. Parking areas can also be distinguished according to their users. Residents' parking is different from visitors' parking. Residents will prefer to have their cars parked close to their homes, whereas visitors will likely be parking a distance from the homes of those they will be visiting.

Planners who design affordable communities will have to consider the site's parking requirements. A ratio between dwelling units and parking places is commonly used. Some of the recommended amounts of resident parking are listed in Figure 7.18. The chief criterion in the design of parking in affordable communities is the need to lower dwellings' cost through an increase in density. Some criteria related to indoor and outdoor arrangements will, therefore, be analyzed accordingly.

Indoor Parking

Avoiding long walks, guarding against theft, and keeping their vehicles warm on cold wintry days will be the prime reasons given by residents for wanting to park next to their home. The options open to designers are indoor or outdoor parking. Indoor parking is known to cost significantly more than an outdoor spot, because, in addition to allocating valuable space inside the building, driveways have to be prepared. An additional challenge faced by designers is how to place the car inside a small structure. The visual effect that parking will have on a street

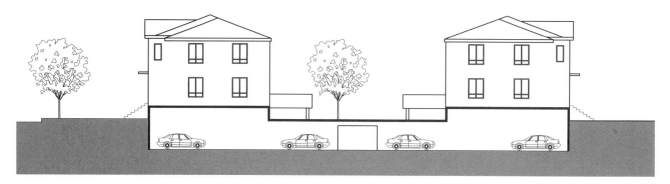

a. Common parking

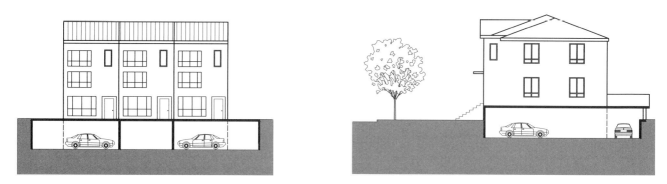

b. Parking under end units

c. Private parking with rear entrance

Figures 7.19a, b, and c Alternative underground, indoor parking solutions for higherdensity, affordable housing projects.

is also a valuable consideration. Garage doors lining the lower level of row housing, for example, will harm the street's curb appeal.

There are several effective ways, however, to park cars indoors while keeping the cost down, not jeopardizing the streetscape, and not building a separate parking structure: shared indoor parking. A concrete slab is built on top of a basement level, under a row of detached or attached homes. There will be a limited number of access points to the parking floor from which homeowners will enter their unit. The space can be subdivided into separate garages or remain undivided and open (Figure 7.19a). Joint parking solutions can also happen under the end units of a row, on-surface or underground. The end unit may not have a basement or a lower floor, but the street's curb appeal will benefit by not having a row of imposing garages (Figure 7.19b). A design can also be introduced whereby the cars will access an individual basement garage from the rear. The back balconies in these homes will be suspended over an entryway to the parking. An occupant will not have a traditional backyard in exchange for indoor parking (Figure 7.19c). The access roads to these parking arrangements can all be shared with neighboring units, leading to further cost savings. Sharing access roads can bring down the costs of parking in small-lot housing. The parking structures of detached homes can be grouped and accessed through a single road. It will not only save on land cost but on the need for curb cuts (Childs, 1999) (Figure 7.20).

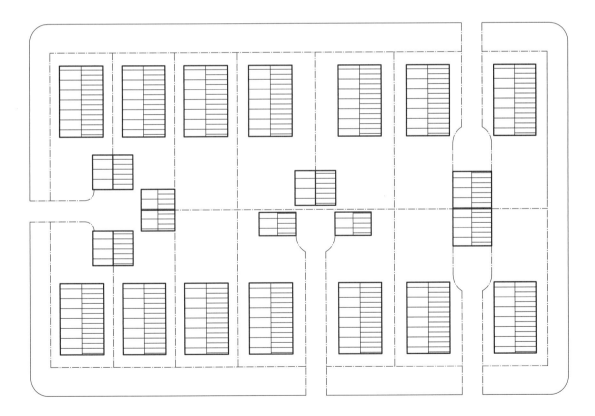

Figure 7.20 Shared access roads to grouped, individual indoor parking.

Outdoor Parking

Outdoor parking, common in affordable housing projects, requires attention to cost and the visual effect on a development. In a freehold tenure situation, cars will most probably be parked on private lots. As densities increase, group parking will be required. Careful use of land allocated to parking will therefore have to take place. The design of outdoor parking areas will depend on the size of cars. The compact economy car is likely to be more popular in urban settings and requires less parking space. In addition, cars should not be parked too close to each other, to allow all doors to open. Standards do exist for the size of stalls in a lot. Depending on the project's location, 10 percent of all stalls in a development's shared parking should be, however, allocated for large cars (CMHC, 1980) (Figure 7.21).

Wider stalls, in such a project, should be provided to residents using wheelchairs. The spots should be well-marked and close to a ramp that permits easy access to a curb. Cars can be parked perpendicular to the curb or in an angled-parking stall. Angled arrangements require narrower yet longer strips of land. The designer, therefore, needs to find a balance between width and length. Angled parking, however, is more efficient when the number of parked cars increases (CMHC, 1980).

The location of the parking area in the development is also of great importance. Residents commonly rely on their cars for daily activities. A parking stall located a long distance away from homes will not be appreciated by people carrying heavy loads. Long-walk paths must be sheltered as much as possible. Providing drop-off places in front of a dwelling, after which the car can be driven to a parking area, can be an acceptable compromise in an affordable housing project. A maximum recommended distance between the home and a parking area is 150 feet (45 meters). The distance should be reduced for senior citizens and can be increased when the path is covered (CMHC, 1980). Common parking

Figure 7.21 Sizes of parking stalls should consider the type of parked cars anticipated.

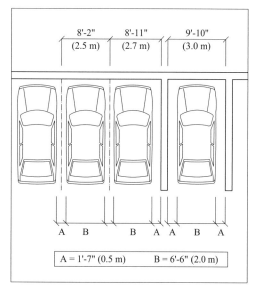

Stall sizes for standard size cars

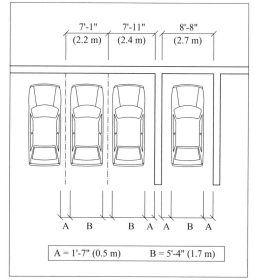

Stall sizes for small cars

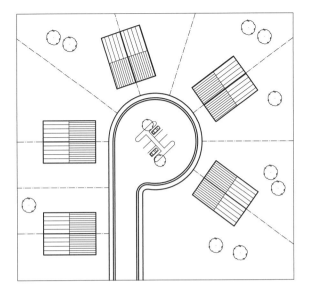 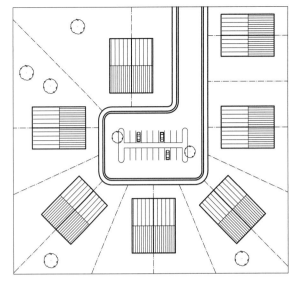

areas should not be placed, however, in close proximity to the building, as cars can generate fumes and noise as well as intrude on privacy. Shrubs, trees, or fences can help create an appropriate noise barrier between homes and parking areas. Another solution is to create a difference in elevation between the parking and the residential area.

Parking areas can be designed to serve as play areas as well. The designer will need to focus on slowing traffic by introducing speed bumps or changing the road-paving material. Visitors' parking is another key concern in high-density, affordable housing. Bylaws require allocation of parking places for visitors in addition to residents. It is common to see visitor parking placed away from the dwelling as priority is given to occupants. In such a case, a drop-off should be planned to provide easy access for a visiting elderly or disabled person. In cul-de-sac planning configurations, visitors' parking can be part of the road (Figure 7.22).

In a high-density community, parking areas can be located at the rear and integrated with public, open spaces (Figure 7.23). The challenge in such designs is to accommodate pedestrian and vehicular traffic. Pedestrian pathways, therefore, should be well-marked, well-lit, and preferably elevated from the parking level. Because they are generally open spaces, parking areas are often windswept zones. Proper planning can help create a better microclimate. A large parking area can be broken into small segments and separated by buildings that can act as windbreaks. The areas can be landscaped to shade cars and to further stop prevailing winds. The lots may contain planting strips for trees and shrubs.

When common, outdoor parking below grade is designed, the access slope should not exceed 10 percent. In cold climates, electrical plug-ins need to be provided for easy ignition on very cold days. Also, a strip of land near a parking area should be allocated for snow accumulation, and proper drainage should also be provided to prevent iced surfaces.

Figure 7.22 In cul-de-sac configurations, visitor parking can be part of the road.

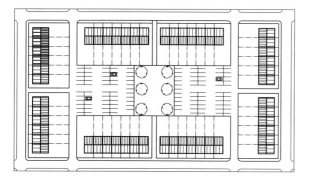
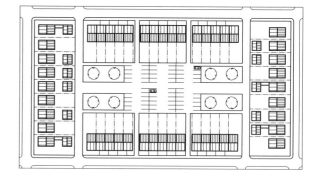
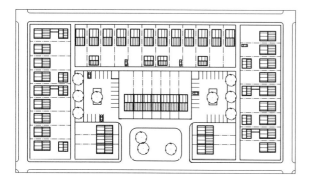
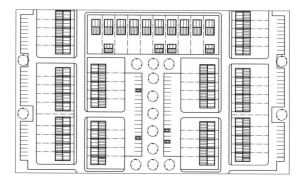

Figure 7.23 Common outdoor parking in high-density affordable communities.

Lane Parking

With the demise of the gridiron street network and the rise of the cul-de-sac in suburban communities, the alley or laneway fell out of favor. The alley is a passageway in the middle of an urban block behind homes, and it forms part of the evolution of eastern and western cities' urban history. This was the place through which coal was delivered to homes for heating purposes and where garbage was left for collection. When modern utilities—drains and electricity—were first introduced in cities, the laneway or alley was the main access. Measuring 16 to 18 feet (4.9 to 5.5 meters), alleys were also where residents housed their horse-and-carriages and, later, their cars. The popularity of suburban subdivisions saw a dramatic decline in the use of lanes. Services were introduced from the front, and cities were eager to avoid the costly responsibility of clearing both streets and rear lanes.

Alleys have gained popularity in recent years due to their potential contribution to lowering the cost of housing and are used in neotraditional developments. Lanes can contribute to reduction of the lot's width by permitting the move of the garage to the rear of the house. The costs for providing second-street access to houses are offset by the savings derived from the resulting narrower lots. Narrow lots served by rear lanes result in significant land savings of up to 50 percent compared to developments with 50-foot (15 meter) lots. As all infrastructure expanses are based on linear measurements, narrow lots mean a reduced infrastructure cost per dwelling. Therefore, there are considerable savings in reducing right-of-way width and introduction of narrower lots. In other words, in a compact development, the added cost of providing rear lanes is offset by the savings in land and infrastructure. Having lanes also contributes to nicer-looking streets, as imposing parking garages are moved from the fronts and sides of large homes to the rear.

Lanes can provide several parking alternatives depending on the type of housing. Cars can be parked outdoors on individual lots or in a group arrangement. Parking can also take place in a garage built off the laneway. Alternatively, residents can park in the dwelling itself, with rear or side entry (Figure 7.24).

Significant savings in land, roads, and infrastructure can be achieved when an alley is used innovatively in high-density housing. Whether a single-family detached home or row housing, lanes permit the parking of large numbers of vehicles in a compact form. In "planned unit development," the alleys will be maintained privately (Figure 7.25).

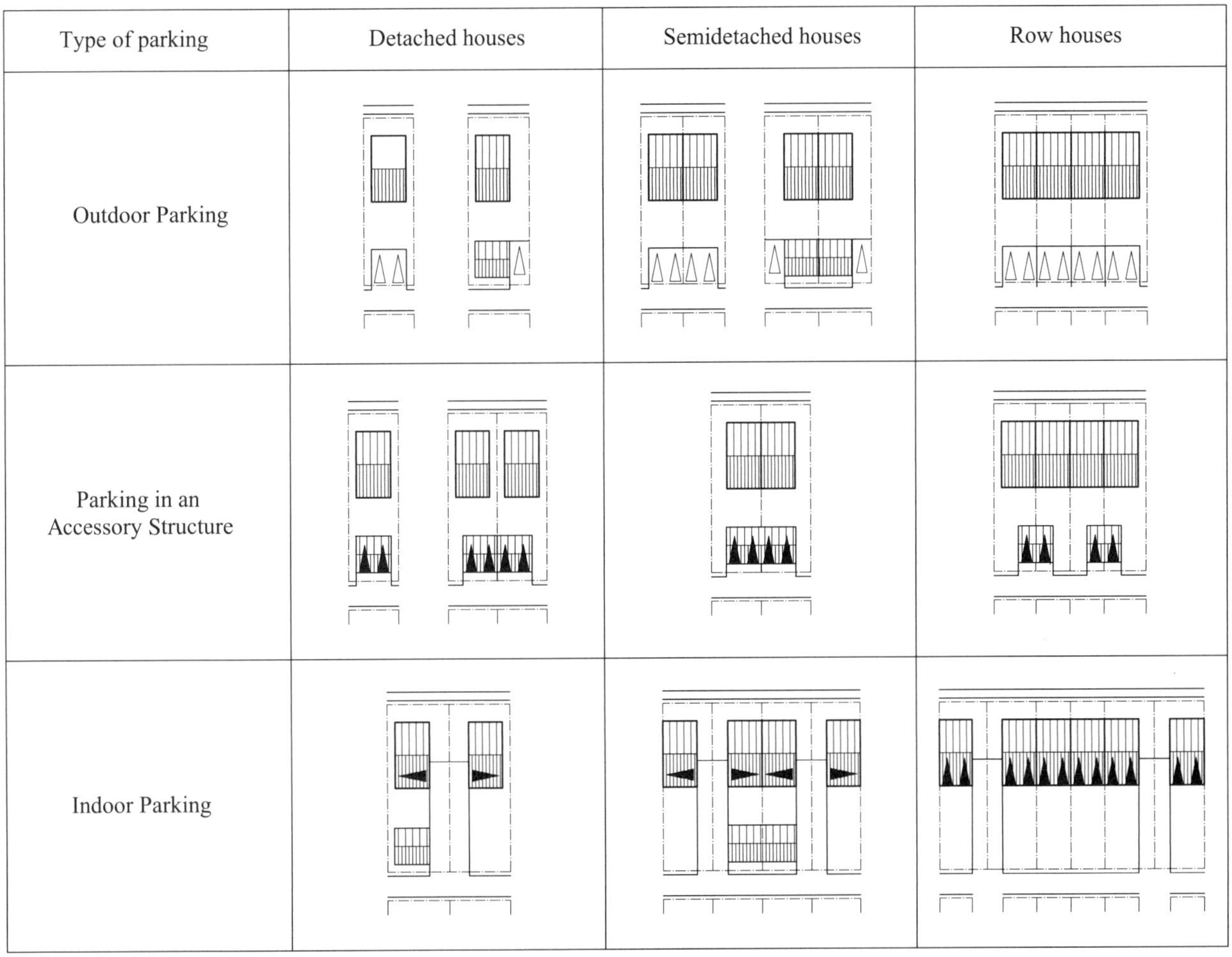

Type of parking	Detached houses	Semidetached houses	Row houses
Outdoor Parking			
Parking in an Accessory Structure			
Indoor Parking			

Figure 7.24 Parking alternatives with access to several housing types from a lane.

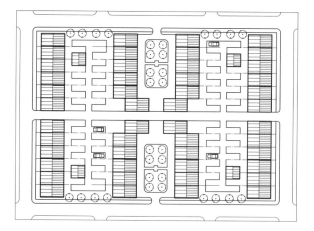

Private

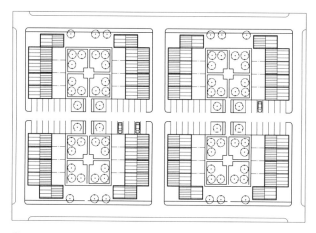

Common

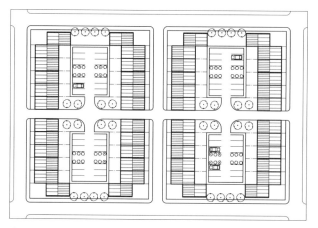

Common

Figure 7.25 Lanes provide opportunities for convenient parking in a high-density housing pattern.

FOOTPATHS, BICYCLE PATHS, AND PUBLIC TRANSIT

Reduced reliance on cars not only saves on building and maintenance of roads but creates healthy communities and fosters stronger bonds between neighbors who stand a greater chance of meeting each other. While traditional towns accommodated pedestrians, present-day subdivisions are designed with drivers in mind. The reintroduction of foot and bicycle paths, along with amenities integrated as part of the community, can help reduce the number of cars and the area allocated to parking. Providing easily accessible and reliable public transit will also help link neighborhoods with regional services.

Footpaths

Footpaths can be divided into three categories. The first includes walkways that link homes to daily utilitarian functions such as parking and refuse disposals. The second category consists of paths between dwellings. The final category is a network that connects homes to commercial and community amenities, such as parks and schools. These pedestrian systems are designed and constructed as are sidewalks (NAHB, 1986). The width of pathways depends on their expected use. It is, therefore, important that they are strategically positioned in the project and link important urban features. They also need to be well designed. Locating a path in an isolated, wooded area, away from viewers, may raise safety issues. Similarly, a path in an unsheltered area that is exposed to harsh sun and wind will be rarely used. Footpaths need to be designed for use by people of all ages, as well as be proposed as a recreational feature that includes benches for rest. In winter, footpaths should be kept snow-free to allow year-round use. They also need to accommodate parents pushing strollers and people using wheelchairs; consequently, curb cuts need to be part of the design. They also need to be well-marked, indicating the type of users and uses allowed. Footpaths are most effective when they are designed for use day and night. Safe routes and light pools along the path are, therefore, mandatory. Preferably, they will be located in places easily viewed from buildings (CMHC, 1981).

A place worth special attention is an intersection between a path and a road. When budget permits, the path can be routed under the street. Otherwise, a clear signalling of an upcoming intersection should be provided for motorist, pedestrians, and cyclists. In advance of the intersection, bumps, or other changes of pavement material can alert drivers that a crossing place is ahead, and they should slow down. When a street with heavy traffic crosses a path, traffic lights should be part of the design. In new suburban subdivisions, a path is rarely designed between homes to permit passage from one cul-de-sac to another. Pedestrians need to walk long distances to reach neighboring homes on streets that often are constructed without sidewalks. Combining cross paths through a project and linking clusters of homes will reduce reliance on cars, increase safety, and encourage activities that contribute to a healthy community.

Bicycle Paths

Bicycle paths can be used for leisure or have a utilitarian purpose. They enable residents to cross longer distances while transporting small objects. They can also be used by people of almost all ages. The path can be part of a special network distinguished from a road or be made part of it. When it is part of the street it ought to be separated by special markings and allow cyclists to ride in both directions. Unlike pedestrian paths, bicycle paths can span longer distances. They may link homes with regional amenities such as libraries, sports centers, and schools. Bike racks for safekeeping can be put near such amenities.

Public Transit

The proliferation of private cars contributed to the decline of use and the availability of public transit. Most municipalities argue that the system needs to be economically self-sustaining, something that is hard to achieve. Public transit is arguably a tool that helps achieve housing affordability, as it prevents the need to own and maintain a car. Buses, therefore, need to be an integral part of the region and the neighborhood planning process. When designing a public transit network, it should be done in conjunction with a street and paths' circulation system designed for maximum use. The transit system needs to be hierarchical-

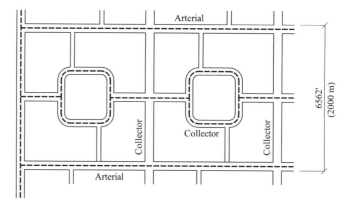

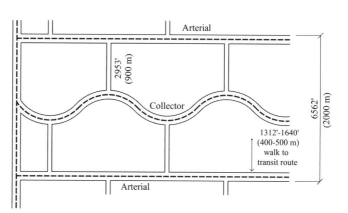

Figure 7.26 Preferred walking distances and street configurations that integrate public transit in residential communities.

ly organized, allowing residents to reach other bus or train lines connecting neighborhoods with major urban centers. Public transit networks should be designed for easy and convenient access by everyone in the development. It would preferably serve both sides of the street, avoiding risky left-hand turns and connecting with pedestrian paths.

In older, denser communities, bus stops should be located approximately every 3,300 feet (1,000 meters) fostering an average walk of half that distance to a stop. In new low-density subdivisions, the distance may be twice as long. The common approach to public transit planning in such communities is to have "local bus routes that connect with downtown truck routes at main activity points such as shopping centers" (CMHC, 1981) (Figure 7.26).

Sheltering those waiting for a bus is necessary in a barren new subdivision. It protects people from the elements as well as acts as a meeting point. Land for a shelter can be acquired early on, and its construction and maintenance can be, when possible, financed through advertisements. The shelter needs to have a bench, bus schedule, and a map showing neighborhood streets and a regional bus transit system. In areas with harshly cold climates, the shelter may be heated. It can also be located near a convenience store, when there is one.

INFRASTRUCTURE

In the built environment, the term *infrastructure* commonly refers to the visible and hidden networks, systems, and structures that permit convenience and comfort at home. They include roads, bridges, train and subway lines, and the water and waste treatment plants. In residential communities, these very same systems are reduced in scale to connect each dwelling unit to the main networks. Infrastructure, in this section, will refer to several elements that affect the cost of a community plan and each home within it.

Along with a rise in the quality of home building, in recent decades, infrastructure has improved as well. Homes are now connected to more services and utilities than in the past. In addition to a fresh water supply, water and sewer drainage, and electricity, homes are provided with cable TV, Internet, and telephones. Roads are equipped with storm sewers, to keep them dry, as well as fire hydrants. The cost of building these systems has risen in recent years. Once built, they have to be maintained by funds collected through taxes. Building neighborhoods away from the city center, in sparsely populated settings, implied extending these networks, which increased their costs per dwelling. To construct affordable infrastructure, some of the conventions and traditions involved in their planning need to be reconsidered. Designing while watching cost implications in the short- and long-run is the key to their successful conception.

Storm Drainage System

The *storm drainage system* collects and directs rainfall away from homes and streets. Each home, primarily in urban settings, transfers water collected around its perimeter to the system. When proper grading of soil is done, rainwater from

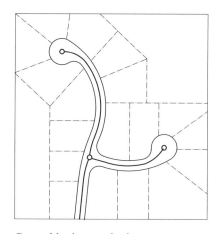

Figure 7.27 By employing a curved storm-sewer pipe laying method, the number of manholes can be reduced.

Conventional   Curved laying method

each lot will be directed into the street and to *catch basins,* which will further move the rainfall through pipes into a large body of water, such as a river. The catch basins are spaced apart on the street close to the curb.

When cost reduction of storm drainage systems is explored, an underlying principle of all strategies needs to be reduction or even elimination of costly pipe networks. Once built, they have to be equipped with manholes and constantly maintained. Their elimination can be achieved by proper grading of soil to natural features such as landscaped areas.

In addition, two-tier systems can be conceived: a system that can handle rain from a minor storm that happens every year or two and serves a residential area, and another sytem that can handle major storms that occur every five to ten years, which will be constructed around major traffic arteries and commercial areas (CMHC, 1981). Another economic approach to handling storm water is the creation of retaining ponds, which are far less expensive than a drain system. Having ponds or lakes at the center or the periphery of a development can provide a recreation facility for a community. Another economic strategy is the building of a continuous retention ditch at the side of the road. With proper grading, the ditch—which may also have a landscaped berm—will absorb the water or, in the case of an overflow, lead it to a retaining pond.

When conventional storm drain systems with pipes and manholes are planned, less-costly materials and construction techniques can be used. With the invention and proliferation of plastics, the traditional metal and reinforced concrete are being phased out. Polyvinyl chloride (PVC) also has corrosion-resistant qualities and can be installed in most "minor" storm systems (HUD, 1987). The spacing and construction techniques of manholes can also be questioned. Some municipalities still require use of the old standard of spacing manholes 200 feet (60 meters) apart. Improved construction methods permit extending them to between 600 to 800 feet (180 to 240 meters). Some manholes can be eliminated altogether by constructing curved sections of pipes (Figure 7.27). The use of a single-unit, precast concrete manhole can also yield savings.

Sanitary Sewers

Sanitary sewer systems drain the home's waste water into treatment plants. Many of the components of such a system are similar to those of the storm sewer system, and, therefore, cost-saving methods in both are quite similar. In storm sewers, the water can be retained in open ponds; however, the contents of sanitary sewers must be contained and treated to prevent public health risks. The system will, therefore, be made cost-effective by reducing outdated, oversized standards and taking advantage of new building techniques and materials. Here, too, encouraging curvilinear sewer design will save money by reducing the number of necessary manholes. The spacing of manholes can also be challenged. They can be spaced every 600 feet (180 meters) rather than every 200 to 400 feet (60 to 120 meters), as is the standard in some communities. A 1987 HUD report notes that "special flush trucks capable of cleaning sewer lines 600 to 800 feet (180 to 240 meters) in length are now standard equipment for many public works departments." Manholes may, however, be required at a slope change or at a meeting place of several pipes. The pipe material can be plastic, which is corrosion resistant and less costly than reinforced concrete or cast-iron pipes. At times, the standards themselves are overdesigned. When a line serves only a few homes, the diameter of the pipe can be smaller than the customary 8 inches (20 centimeters).

Most communities will charge fees for connecting the home's sanitary system to the main network. Savings can be achieved by joining the connections of two homes (Figure 7.28). HUD explains that "when a standard Y fitting is installed at the junction of the individual building drains, the pipe length is decreased by almost 50 percent since every other lateral is eliminated." In rural areas, methods other than pipes can be explored. Recent evolution in septic-tank technology makes it a viable and highly cost effective alternative to the conventional approach. Septic tanks can be used in areas where the soil is suitable for such an installation.

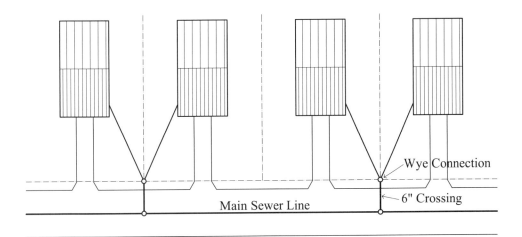

Figure 7.28 Two homes are connected to a common sewer lateral.

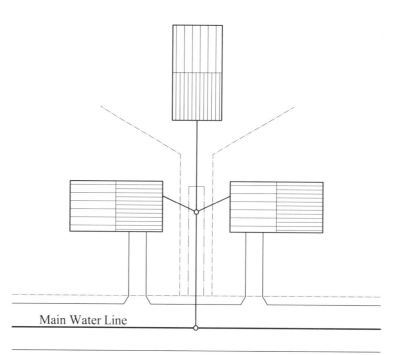

Figure 7.29 A multiple connection to a single waterline can lead to cost savings.

Main Water Line

Water Supply

Unlike the previous systems discussed in this section, *water supply* brings water into the dwelling. Here, as well, new techniques and materials can be taken advantage of for cost-reduction purposes. The use of PVC can replace cast-iron or asbestos-cement pipes. The mostly dry connection of these pipes reduces costly labor and maintenance. Multiple connections should also be questioned. A single water connection can be installed along the common property line and a standard Y or T used to branch off to each home (HUD, 1987), as shown in Figure 7.29. The arrangement can be metered by a single box containing several meters.

Grouping Utilities

For underground services, utility companies are major users of the allocated space within the right-of-way. This in turn increases the road's width, making it difficult to design a high-density development. A compact development is desired when the cost of infrastructure is to be distributed among a larger number of residents, thus improving housing affordability. Due to the nature of their installation, utilities are typically located on both sides of the right-of-way. Separate spaces are allocated for telephone, hydroelectric power, gas, Internet, and cable TV, although it is a general practice to install utilities in a common trench, leaving four space allocations—two on each side of the road—unused. These spaces are reserved for future uses, and their necessity should be questioned. To accommodate a reduced right-of-way width, utilities should be installed in common trenches, and space for future installations should only be reserved if there is a future, realistic need.

In most municipalities, sidewalks occupy an exclusive position in the road right-of-way width. Constructing services under the sidewalks should be done in concrete-encased duct banks with manholes. These utilities should be installed before the construction of sidewalks, which is easily achievable since sidewalks are usually constructed after the development's buildings are complete. This would avoid the cost of removing and then rebuilding the sidewalks after the utilities have been installed, which sometimes happens.

Transformers are used to reduce the voltage in the electrical system from the primary distribution voltage to the secondary voltage required for houses and street lighting. They present a significant constraint in the design of high-density residential neighborhoods, because they are large and must be accessible for inspection and maintenance. There is also a maximum practical distance that separates houses from transformers, and, due to safety reasons, electrical authorities prefer not to have transformers too close to the roadway, sidewalk, or other utilities. Several options can be considered to prevent transformers from increasing the road right-of-way width and to improve the distribution of infrastructure costs among an increased number of residents. A choice of transformer location that fits into the plan of the subdivision without affecting lots, such as in front of schools, parks, open spaces, or other nonresidential land uses, can be made. Also, the transformer can be located adjacent to the right-of-way on the front or on either an easement or a local widening of the right-of-way. If there are rear lanes, then the hydroelectric services can be located in the lane and the transformers in adjacent widenings or easements. If there are no lanes, the transformers can be located in rear-yard easements (Marshall et al., 1994).

KEY CONSIDERATIONS

- The principle in the design of circulation in an affordable housing project should be of reduced reliance on private cars. The network needs to give priority to pedestrians and cyclists in all decisions.
- Linking the roads of existing and new communities not only will foster social integration but make the flow of traffic efficient and cost-effective.
- Streets should be designed for energy conservation, sparing motorists from driving long distances unnecessarily.
- Construction of roads should not clear natural features but incorporate them for cost savings and viewing enjoyment.
- Designing circulation to be a logical and simple hierarchical system is a crucial part of designing an affordable community.
- At least 90 percent of all dwellings should be within 1,300 feet (400 meters), straight-line distance, from an existing or future bus route (CMHC, 1981).
- Cost-effective design of streets will be the result of correlation between the street function, hierarchy, and width. Narrow width not only will slow motorists down but save valuable land and construction costs.
- In principle, intersections of more than two streets should be avoided, as they constitute a traffic hazard.
- In areas with low-traffic volume and low speed, it is not necessary to design streets with two moving lanes. If two cars are parked across from each other, there will still be room for one moving vehicle to move over and let the other pass.

- In many instances, sidewalks can be designed below local standards, built on one side, or eliminated altogether.

- To increase their effectiveness, local streets with low-volume traffic can become play areas, running tracks, bicycle paths, and, on special occasions, gathering places.

- Substantial cost savings can be obtained by making sure that construction norms are appropriate for the anticipated use. Building heavy-duty roads for hardly used local streets is simply unnecessary.

- Delaying curb construction until buildings are complete will minimize the possibility of damage and unnecessary expenditure.

- The economic implications of parking provisions is staggering. For example, Litman (1999) notes that "one parking space per unit increases cost by about 12.5 percent…compared to on-street parking." The need to select an appropriate parking solution in affordable housing is, therefore, of utmost importance.

- Underground parking can be as much as ten times more expensive than surface parking. In most affordable housing projects, the common solution is outdoors parking.

- Familiarity with the type of occupants is important in determining the quantity of parking spots needed. More parking will be needed, for example, by mature families with children at driving age than by senior citizens and singles.

- Money can be saved by sharing access roads to parking spots in small-lot housing and by grouping parking structures.

- The compact economy car is likely to be more popular in urban settings and requires less parking space. Depending on the project's location, 10 percent of all the stalls in shared parking should be allocated to large cars (CMHC, 1980).

- For visual and climatic purposes, a large parking area should be broken into small segments separated by buildings. The area can be landscaped to shade cars and to stop prevailing winds.

- Narrow lots served by rear lanes result in significant land savings of up to 50 percent compared to developments with 50-foot (15 meter) lots.

- Footpaths need to be located to connect key points in the community. They should be designed to be used by people of all ages and accommodate disabled users, and they should be well marked and maintained.

- Building a continuous retention ditch at the side of the road to absorb rainfall is a simple yet effective cost-reduction alternative for storm drainage systems.

- Improved construction methods permit placing manholes at wider distances. Some manholes can be eliminated altogether by constructing curved sections of pipes.

- When a standard Y fitting is used to connect two dwellings to a single city drainpipe, the pipe length can be decreased by as much as 50 percent (HUD, 1987).

- To accommodate a reduced street right-of-way width, utilities can be installed in common trenches and space for future installation should only be reserved if there is a future, realistic need.

Open Spaces

O pen spaces are the communal or private areas used for outdoor and leisure activities in a housing development; they are also known as green spaces. As housing density increases, so does the functional and psychological importance of open space between dwelling units. It is, therefore, crucial that they not be treated as leftover areas but designed to foster a sense of identity and unity while providing privacy for individuals and families. This chapter recalls the roots and evolution of open-space use and describes some types. Design strategies for energy conservation are outlined. Finally site landscaping and grading are discussed.

ROOTS AND EVOLUTION

The inclusion of public open spaces as an integral part of the design of housing developments accessible to all is a relatively recent practice. At the dawn of the nineteenth century, private recreational gardens were not common; where they existed, they were used by their owners and guests. Public green spaces formed parts of large estates; they welcomed only middle- and upper-class residents and played an important social role. With modern medicine at its infancy, fresh air and natural light were regarded as the prime cures for diseases brought about by the poor hygiene of the city. Therefore, being away from the city, in proximity to nature, was seen as a remedy. The seed of suburban communities—places where residences are surrounded by green, open spaces—was planted.

With the proliferation of trains and railway lines, the exodus of the wealthy was followed by the middle class, and communities eventually began to develop a distance away from congested cities. Ebenezer Howard's *Garden City*–planning concept, which was published in 1898, placed green space in the center of a planned community. Commerce, followed by residences, radiated from a central park, all surrounded by a belt of farmland. Allocation of land to common green space was put into practice by Raymond Unwin and Barry Parker's design of the town of Letchworth, England, several years later.

In North America, the organic plan proposed by Frederick Law Olmsted and Calvert Vaux in 1869 for the community of Riverside, Illinois, included a number of green-space principles (Olmsted, 1992). Public spaces separated clusters of residential lots, permitting leisure walks in between. The curvilinear streets were full of trees and contributed to the green image of the community (Figure 8.1). The need to locate suburban communities in proximity to rail lines was changed with the proliferation of private cars. Common green space remained, however, part of the design. It was best manifested in the design of Radburn, New Jersey, the archetype of today's suburban neighborhoods. Homes faced a paved cul-de-sac, which acted as open space, yet the common civic space was gone. These principles evolved over the years, yet they remained central to the conception of public open spaces in residential communities.

The post–World War II quest for planning and building efficiency saw the disappearance of Radburn's common, open spaces that surrounded homes. Residences have now been confined to private lots containing both the habitable and green areas. As planning acts became laws, land developers were mandated to allocate between 5 and 10 percent of the project area to common green space with hierarchical ordering of open spaces. In recent decades there have been attempts to reintroduce the park as a central civic feature in town planning. From the early 1980s, the movement for New Urbanism regarded traditional towns as models of contemporary residential development. Lining streets with trees, providing easy access to common green spaces, and creating a civic square are some of the elements of the movement's design principles.

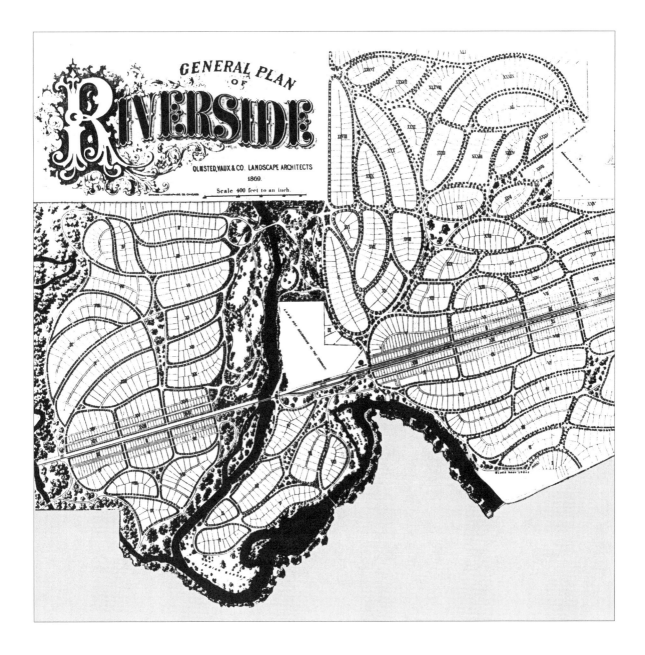

OPEN-SPACE SYSTEMS

Open spaces in communities can be regarded as a system where an easily accessible network of green areas that range from the regional to individual unit levels is created. Large scale parks, located outside the development, form the most public of these spaces. Enclosed outdoor areas, on the other end, are the most private. Within these two extremes are neighborhood parks and communal areas for clusters of homes. Despite planning for high density, affordable housing communities need to provide a variety of outdoor spaces for both active and passive recreation.

Figure 8.1 Green open spaces were included in the design of Riverside, Illinois, by Frederick Law Olmsted and Calvert Vaux in 1869.

The spaces themselves, regardless of their place in the hierarchy, can be designed along several key, guiding principles:

- Incorporate natural features.
- Design for accessibility from all homes.
- Make the spaces the green lungs of the neighborhood.
- Let sunlight into the heart of the neighborhood.
- Integrate storm-water management systems when feasible.
- Ensure that large regional play areas are well served by public transit.
- Incorporate noise and privacy protection for homes built near common, open spaces.
- Ensure that each open space contributes to the well-being and health of the community it serves.
- Make all play areas for children, fields and courts, paths for jogging and bicycling available for active recreation.
- Provide spaces for passive activities such as sunbathing, reading, and simple get-togethers.
- Accommodate the needs of people of all ages and mobilities.

Linking the various spaces to form a system while providing varying degrees of privacy in each is a fundamental principle of planning open spaces in affordable communities. Several patterns for the design of open-space systems have evolved and proven successful as guidelines for the organization of these places. They include separate patch, composite urban, hierarchical, and green belt (Wei, 2003). Their principles will be outlined below (Figure 8.2).

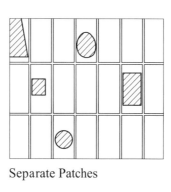

Separate Patches   Composite Urban

Figure 8.2 Several design patterns for organization of open-space systems are commonly used by planners.

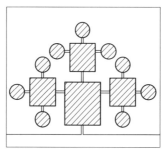

Hierarchy

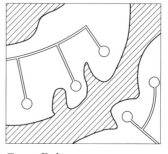

Green Belt

The *separate patch* system is often used in gridiron street patterns, and in recent times was applied in the rehabilitation of older neighborhoods. Its key attribute is the creation of a street-oriented community life. There is, however, a lack of continuity between the patches, which can be accessed from streets or alleys only. Patches form well-defined gathering places in neighborhoods. They may include a prominent feature, such as a bandstand or water fountain, and can be landscaped in a variety of ways. The separate patch system constitutes the traditional town square.

The *composite urban* pattern has a more structured design. It is recognized by its geometric forms and is often associated with New Urbanists' residential schemes. The main arteries connect housing clusters to communal facilities and public plazas, and the dwellings are oriented according to the geometry of the overall plan. It is a more rigid design pattern and best suited for large, new housing developments rather than the rehabilitation of old districts. The strong, formal geometry dictates the organization and the orientation of the dwellings, which may not correspond with sitings that take advantage of passive solar gain, topography, or ecological preservation. This pattern is nonetheless beneficial when it comes to high-density design with potential to contribute to lower cost housing. Another notable advantage rests with accessibility to and from the open spaces. Networks of roads and boulevards form vital parts of these schemes.

Formal in nature, the *hierarchical system* organizes open spaces based on their order of public, semipublic, and private areas. With its roots in ancient settlements, the system combines public plazas with courts and yards. Its design is visibly more flexible than the systems outlined above. The hierarchy system allows for a variety of different open spaces within a relatively short distance from each other by accommodating diverse needs of community members. Spaces are provided for large gatherings and intimate private encounters. Despite the notion that hierarchies lead to formality, the pattern can also take on a more free-form design in higher-density residential configurations with affordable housing.

The *green belt* pattern design regards the natural characteristics of the site in planning the open-systems area. The approach resembles the one used by Howard in the Garden City design and later by Henry Wright and Clarence Staine in Radburn, New Jersey. The residential areas are often bordered by amorphic, green spaces. The areas may be never-planted green patches or newly planted. The scheme is highly suitable to developments based on ideas that privilege natural drainage and ecological corridors and living in organic settings. The pattern is not suitable, however, for high-density residential configurations unless multifamily, rather than single-family, dwellings are designed.

Some of the systems that were described above are more suitable than others for high-density affordable housing. All of them, however, can be reconfigured for such designs by proper planning of their lesser elements, which are described and analyzed below.

Regional Parks

Regional parks are located and designed to serve a wider area and are shared by several neighborhoods. They form an important part of an affordable housing project's planning strategy by providing amenities that are not available in each neighborhood. They are built and maintained by a municipal government, and they are accessible to all. Regional parks can be built on existing natural areas such as forests or riverbanks. They may include scenic or ecological features not available in the communities themselves. The park must be part of the district's movement system and accessible by pedestrian and bicycling paths, or by public transit, at the very least. Regional parks can also form part of a green belt that binds several neighborhoods. When properly planned, they can contain amenities such as school, nature conservatories, and sports centers. By siting an affordable-housing project near an already existing regional park and providing easy access for residents, the demand for large, communal spaces within the neighborhood itself will be lessened, and the land allocated to open space can be reduced. Another objective of such spaces is to provide a place for residents of several communities to meet for sporting activities and on holidays.

Neighborhood Parks

Whereas a regional park serves a large area and is accessible to residents of several communities, a neighborhood park serves one neighborhood only. It provides space for various types of organized and unorganized sports, play, and relaxation activities. There are various standards dictating what should be the size of such a space. A common requirement is that 5 to 10 percent of the development's gross area be allocated to open space. This standard may apply to low-density developments, and its relevancy may be questioned in medium- to high-density housing projects. In such projects, one acre (0.4 hectares) for every 120 homes might be more suitable. The area allocated to open space may, therefore, be smaller in size, yet innovatively designed when it is made part of an affordable housing community (CMHC, 1981).

The location of a park in the neighborhood needs to take into consideration the needs of all residents. Ideally, it will be centrally located within walking distance from every dwelling. Alternatively, the area allocated to a neighborhood park can be divided into several segments around which homes will be constructed. The latter is at times a better option since it offers views into a green space to a larger number of dwellings. It also provides parents the opportunity to watch their children play (Figure 8.3).

The design of neighborhood parks in medium- or high-density communities offers several design challenges and opportunities that must be addressed in the master planning stage. The park can become an extended backyard to some of the homes and provide an addition to the dwellings' own outdoor, private spaces. The homes then need to be constructed to enclose the park. The density of these dwellings can be increased and they can be multifamily, multistory buildings and offer a view to occupants of upper floors who may not have access to a yard. On the other hand, consideration should be taken so that the privacy of ground-floor residents will not be compromised. Those using the outdoor space should not have a direct view into lower floor dwellings. This privacy and accessibility ideal can be achieved through changing elevations and proper landscaping. Another concern has to do with noise caused by users of the play area. Here, too, similar strategies may be used to prevent high-noise levels.

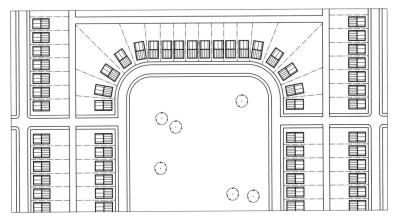

Central neighborhood park

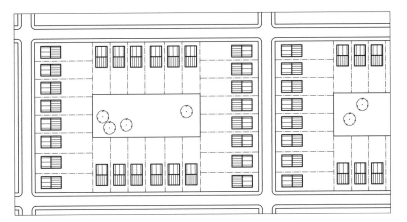

Open space on each block

Figure 8.3
Neighborhood parks can be centralized or fragmented throughout the community.

At times, as a result of the high cost of land for an affordable housing project, no large area will be allocated for a neighborhood park. Planners will then consider having smaller-size open spaces known as *parkettes*. The spaces are commonly designed as play areas for children of different ages and landscaped and furnished accordingly. Fliess (1980) recommends that for a freehold housing development of 300 units or more at medium density, a parkette of 1½ to 2 acres (0.6 to 0.8 hectares) should be provided within 820 feet (250 meters) of the homes.

Communal Areas for Clusters of Homes

While neighborhood parks are to be shared and enjoyed by all members of a housing development, smaller communal areas can form a more private setting for small clusters of dwellings. One of the best contributing aspects for the design of such spaces is the height-to-width ratio. It will define the space and affect its level of privacy and intimacy. In medium- to high-density affordable housing units, this common space typically has a height-to-width ratio between 1:5 and 1:3 (Figure 8.4). For example, in a project with housing clusters that are

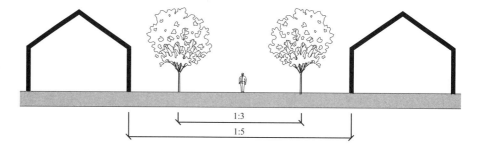

Figure 8.4 To foster privacy and a human scale, the desired height to width ratio of open spaces in an affordable-housing development ranges between 1:5 and 1:3.

30 feet (9 meters) high, the common space in between clusters should be about 90–180 feet (27–54 meters) across. These communal areas for clusters of homes help to increase the affordability of housing projects by creating semiprivate areas for residents and reducing the need for large, private yards for individual units. Generally, the smaller the private area for individual dwellings, the larger the communal areas should be (Svensson, 1998).

Several models for the design of open spaces have been proposed in an Ontario Ministry of Housing study. The models provide a variety of options for a range of privacy levels and interaction between residents (Figure 8.5).

While communal areas provide both functional and cost benefits, a completely screened private, outdoor living space is preferred by most users. Accordingly, one strategy for developing the area in between clusters of housing units is to maximize enclosed private space and eliminate communal areas altogether. Such an arrangement is called the *closed model* (Figure 8.5a). The benefits of the closed model include the maximization of private, outdoor spaces and a reduction of communal maintenance charges. In such a design, incorporating landscaping elements like raised flower beds, trellises, and shrubs to form visual screens and dividers between dwellings, rather than just fences, becomes essential to preventing occupants from feeling "caged-in" (Lynch-Tresch, 1984). This model, however, can create a sense of detachment from neighbors and fails to take advantage of the opportunity to create a parklike environment that can be easily supervised from within the dwellings themselves. In terms of affordability, the closed model can provide cost-savings by eliminating common open spaces altogether and transferring the care of those areas to individual homeowners.

The *combined model* incorporates smaller enclosed outdoor spaces for individual units with a communal outdoor living area. The screened private gardens occupy only a portion of the outdoor space provided to each unit, and the remaining land becomes part of a communal system that is accessible to all the project's residents. The advantage of such a design lies in the opportunity that the hybrid situation allows, whereby privacy is given to each resident, yet communal interaction between neighbors is still possible. In addition, children can play with easy supervision from the dwellings and without danger of passing traffic. The drawbacks of the model include reduction in the size of private outdoor spaces and the need to spend more on the maintenance of the common areas (Figure 8.5b).

To increase the size of private, outdoor spaces and to bring down maintenance costs while still preserving a communal space, a *walk-through model* is

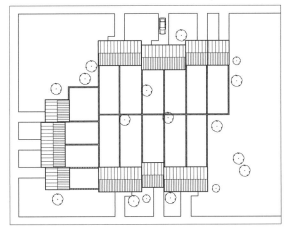

a. Closed Model

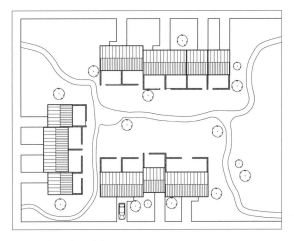

b. Combined Model

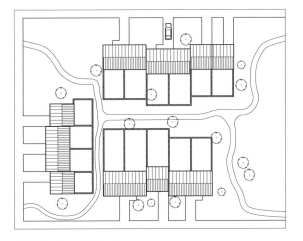

c. Walk-through Model

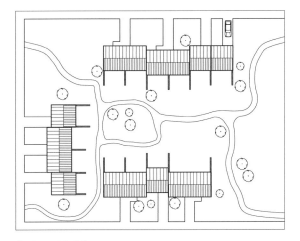

d. Open Model

proposed. The communal space can be reduced to a paved walkway system that may widen at points to small sitting and play areas. This model reduces communal maintenance costs to a minimum, optimizes private areas, and retains many of the advantages of a safe pedestrian and play area system (Figure 8.5c).

At the opposite extreme of the closed model is the *open model*. In the open model, all of the open space adjacent to the unit is communal, and screens are only provided between adjacent units. For this system to be successful, the grouping of and space between units, the land form, and the landscaping must provide privacy to units facing each other. Additionally, the landscaping must be attractive and sufficiently intensive to create a park-like setting that provides adequate compensation for the lack of enclosed private spaces (Figure 8.5d).

The open model is best suited for apartments and other forms of multi-attached housing where balconies and decks overlook a large central space. Landscaping occupies an important role in creating some degree of territorial privacy, as well as designating areas for different activities, such as playing or sit-

Figure 8.5 Design models for open-space areas for clusters of homes.

Figure 8.6 Communal planting gardens can form part of the neighborhood open spaces.

ting. Without proper treatment, large interior open spaces can become a wasteland receiving little use by residents.

Another form of shared open space can be *communal planting gardens*. An area can be sectioned near the dwelling and platted for each dwelling. Residents can grow seasonal green produce for self-use and foster better relationships among themselves. The area needs to be equipped with a tool shed and water pipe (Figure 8.6).

Selecting the model that best meets the needs of residents while maintaining affordability requires a thorough analysis of both the site and the population for whom the housing is being built. For example, a housing project for mainly elderly retirees that is located close to a regional park would probably benefit most from the closed model, as seniors tend to prefer private space and the nearby park could accommodate more social recreation. Developments for young families with small children, however, may favor the added convenience of a park right outside their dwellings. Young families may appreciate the increased opportunities for social interaction between neighbors that the combined model provides.

Private Outdoor Spaces for Individual Units

In affordable homes where interior space is often reduced to cut costs, private outdoor spaces can be regarded as outdoor rooms (Svensson, 1998). Some form of easily accessible, private outdoor space should be part of all dwelling units.

Fencing, shrubs, or other screening devices can provide both visual privacy and a clear demarcation of the edges of the private area.

When the private outdoor living space is completely enclosed, as in the closed model, outlined above, it should be large enough to provide space for different activities, such as sitting and gardening. Creating difference spaces helps create a psychologically pleasing environment, and ensuring that the area is large enough helps prevent a sense of a lack of space. Fliess (1980) recommends that a minimum of 480 square feet (45 square meters) is necessary to achieve a well-balanced design (Figure 8.7a).

Private spaces within the combined model can be smaller, from 270 to 480 square feet (25 to 45 square meters). Varying the material used for the enclosure is increasingly important. While wooden or stone walls are preferable, hedges, trellises, or raised flower beds combined with the landscaping of the communal area can provide adequate privacy while avoiding a boxed-in effect. Ground-level exterior spaces function best as extensions of indoor living spaces when attached to the living room or kitchen of the dwelling. Designing a kitchen window that looks onto the enclosed, outdoor space provides opportunity for children's play supervision (Figure 8.7b). At times, in small homes, the outdoor living space, which acts as an extension of the dwelling itself, may not be completely enclosed for privacy. The size of that space should then have a minimum area of 600 square feet (54 square meters) for privacy reasons (Fliess, 1980) (Figure 8.7c).

In dwelling units without direct access to the ground-level—such as triplexes—decks or balconies can serve as private outdoor space and connect directly to the home's living areas such as the living room and dining room. For one-bedroom apartments, balconies should be at least 6 feet (1.8 meters) deep and have

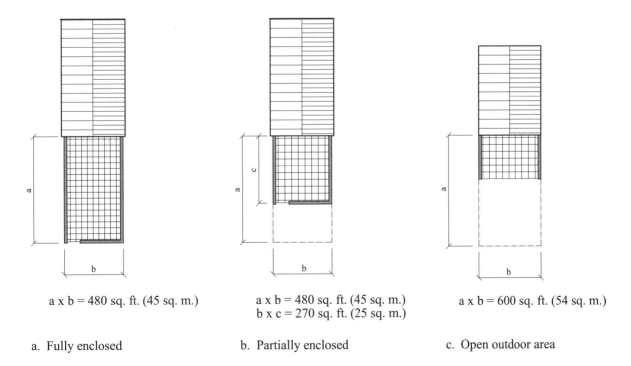

a x b = 480 sq. ft. (45 sq. m.)

a x b = 480 sq. ft. (45 sq. m.)
b x c = 270 sq. ft. (25 sq. m.)

a x b = 600 sq. ft. (54 sq. m.)

a. Fully enclosed

b. Partially enclosed

c. Open outdoor area

Figure 8.7 Suggested spatial arrangement and dimensions of private outdoor spaces for individual units.

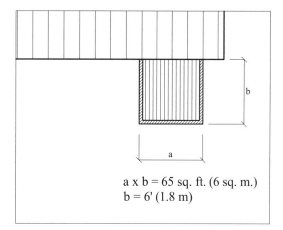
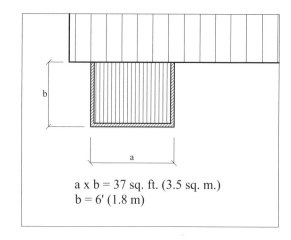

a x b = 65 sq. ft. (6 sq. m.)
b = 6' (1.8 m)

a x b = 37 sq. ft. (3.5 sq. m.)
b = 6' (1.8 m)

Figure 8.8
Balconies can provide an extension to the home's living area when properly dimensioned.

a minimum area of 65 square feet (6 square meters). Ideally, balconies should be recessed into the building to create a sense of privacy, and a minimum of 60 feet (18 meters) should separate facing balconies with no other source of visual screening (Fliess, 1980) (Figure 8.8).

While most private, outdoor spaces tend to be located at the back of the house, front yard space, however small, serves an important communal function. It acts as a transition between the public and the private realms and defines the owner's identity. In the front yard, residents can put up trees, help create a more private space, or place a flower bed. Svensson (1998) suggests that it is residents' own design of the semipublic zone that determines the degree of human contact in these surroundings.

With the limited space available for private, open space in affordable housing developments, creating well-designed dynamic spaces that can accommodate a wide variety of functional and psychological needs is essential. Communal spaces can help compensate for lack of private space; but, ultimately, both spaces are necessary to establish a sense of individual and community identity.

Open Spaces for People with Reduced Mobility

Design of open spaces in affordable housing ought to consider the needs of people with reduced mobility. All residents, whether disabled or elderly, should have easy access to comfortable, safe outdoor spaces. These spaces have particular importance in the life of the elderly, as they tend to spend more time outdoors meeting others. Carstens (1992) suggests that the spaces should reinforce both actual and perceived safety and security. It can be achieved by arranging the dwellings to create enclosures that will not be overly "boxed-in." A clear demarcation between more private areas and public neighborhood areas also helps to create a psychological sense of safety. Care should be taken to ensure that small, intimate spaces are provided for quiet retreats, but that these spaces are close to and partially visible from more crowded public spaces to ensure adequate security.

When outdoor spaces are designed with the elderly in mind, the designer should create a desirable microclimate through siting and landscaping, as the elderly are particularly susceptible to changes in temperature, excessive windiness, and glare. Areas more often used in the afternoon or evenings should maximize late-day sun exposure and provide protection from cold night winds.

When attached to the main living areas, private balconies can create a particularly desirable outdoor space for the elderly. Residents can access nature on a daily basis even with very limited mobility. Many seniors favor spending time outdoors in solitude, and private balconies are an effective and affordable means to do this. The balconies should be designed to face each other across a large landscaped area or look onto a well-used public outdoor space (Carstens, 1992). This arrangement creates a sense of participation within the larger community, even if one is not physically able to access all public areas.

The paths in between dwellings and open spaces should be well-marked and use nonslip surfaces and nonglare materials, such as stained, broom-finished concrete. Dramatic changes in grade should be avoided, as well as any irregularities in paths that could pose a safety hazard. Raised planters prevent soil from spilling onto paths and also offer an opportunity for residents in wheelchairs to participate in gardening. Handrails and benches should be located along paths at short intervals to allow for brief pauses and longer rests (Carstens, 1992).

Play Areas for Children

Since children are some of the primary users of outdoor spaces in affordable housing, much care should be taken to ensure that the play areas are conducive to healthy and engaging play. Areas for organized sports, such as a baseball diamond or soccer field, should be provided in parks, as well as informal, flat grassy areas for unstructured play. Including natural environments and sturdy trees for climbing, as well as more intimate spaces screened by low shrubs or walls, creates opportunities for quiet, creative play. Large, empty, sterile environments are seldom used or enjoyed, and they can cause passive, static, bored, or even aggressive behavior in children (Hill, 1970).

The cost of playground equipment can be greatly reduced by using recycled and naturally occurring objects such as trees. Loose materials for construction, such as boxes, old boards, and rocks encourage imaginative play, while old tires, logs, and chains can be used to create climbing structures as long as safety precautions are taken. In Denmark, "junk playgrounds," where children can build structures out of old construction materials, are extremely popular. Another money-saving option is to give control of the design and maintenance of the neighborhood parks to the residents. Parks and recreational areas supervised by the residents themselves are run in a cost-effective manner, more frequently used, and better maintained than parks cared for by an outside authority (Svensson, 1998). Furthermore, this arrangement allows outdoor spaces to become symbols of community unity and identity.

Where open green spaces are extremely limited, paved areas such as parking lots and cul-de-sacs can be treated as potential play areas for children. Because these areas are primarily used by automobiles, great care must be taken to ensure that safety is maintained for children who may use these areas. Devices such as curved roads and speed bumps can ensure that traffic stays slow around play areas. Creating areas of trees and other plantings within a paved parking area helps to claim the site as a recreational area.

DESIGNING WITH NATURE

Once created, open space can be landscaped or existing natural features can be integrated with the design. The latter can not only foster attractive environments but lead to cost reduction. The tendency to want to reshape the site's nature, therefore, needs to be rethought in the design of affordable homes. The project can be designed around nature rather than altering it where relevant. The approach is often referred to as *conservation design*.

A conservation design approach is best suited to the design of new, affordable housing communities. In a conventionally designed subdivision, all of the land is cleared, levelled, and then subdivided into lots and streets. If any land remains undeveloped, it is usually wetlands, steep slopes, floodplains, or storm-water management areas. Conservation designs, however, require that one-half or more of buildable land be designated for undivided permanent open space (Arendt, 1996). The approach often raises questions of density, which challenges the project's economic viability. A balance, therefore, needs to be found between the project's monetary goals and the existing natural conditions.

Creating a conservation development can be broken down into a comprehensive background stage and then a design stage. During the background stage, the condition of the site is carefully examined. Wetlands and floodplains are identified, preferably during spring thaw when areas are most likely to be saturated, and vegetation is documented. From these different layers of information, objectives are formed and prioritized for the design stage. During the design stage, different conservation areas are identified. Conservation areas can fall into either of two categories: primary or secondary conservation areas. *Primary conservation areas* include unbuildable wetlands, bodies of water, floodplains, and steep slopes. Once these areas are mapped on the site, *secondary conservation areas* are located, which include mature woodlands, upland buffers for wetlands and bodies of water, prime farmland, natural meadows, critical wildlife habitat, and sites of cultural, historical, or archaeological significance (Arendt, 1996). These areas should be conserved wherever possible.

Once the primary and secondary conservation areas are located, potential house sites can be laid out. In locating the individual dwellings, great care must be taken to ensure that a maximum number of homes have access to an open view and that the views do not look onto neighbors' backyards (Figure 8.9). Designing with zero-lot line can help ease this problem, by putting detached dwellings very close together along one windowless side. This side can be used for stairs and services. Unit placement should be close to roads unless mature vegetation sits near paving lines. Also, maximizing tree preservation within the housing clusters enhances the experience of living in a woodland (Figure 8.10).

Once house sites have been located, street alignments and trails can be designed. Street widths should be kept to a minimum, and curved streets are preferred to straight because they offer better views and help reduce car speeds in residential areas. In landscaped areas, road design should follow areas of younger growth, to preserve mature trees. Additionally, the edge of the vegetation along the road should be staggered and varied to create greater aesthetic appeal and prevent monotony. Sidewalks along streets should also be narrow and at the same level as the street's asphalt surface, allowing rainwater to return

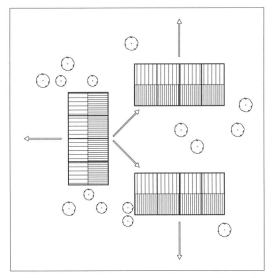
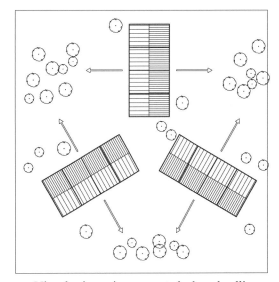

Visual privacy is reduced when dwelling units face one another.

Visual privacy is augmented when dwelling units face away from one another.

Figure 8.9 In conservation design, due to the proximity of the dwellings to each other, care must be taken to ensure that the units will have an uninterrupted view of natural features.

Figure 8.10 Maximizing tree preservation within the housing clusters will enhance the experience of living in woodlands.

to nature. Parking can be located in unpaved areas under trees. This arrangement reduces the amount of paved areas on the site, which aids in maintaining natural storm-water patterns. After the houses and streets have been located, the lot lines can be drawn in. During construction, only trees that the building footprint touches should be cut down while the rest of the trees on the lot should be protected against damage caused by heavy machinery.

Conservation design also stipulates that the land be developed in a *density-neutral* manner, meaning that the project will contain the same number of dwellings as would be in a conventional layout for the same area. It requires that lot sizes be reduced in exchange for a greater percentage of open spaces. Since the vegetation in open spaces is conserved, landscaping costs for green areas are eliminated or significantly reduced. The smaller lot sizes, when properly laid out, can greatly reduce infrastructure, engineering, and construction costs, as 50 to 75 percent of the area typically remains undeveloped (Arendt, 1996). While the decreased lot size may deter some would-be homebuyers, well laid out lots can maintain views of open spaces and alleviate lack of privacy concerns. The open spaces also provide more opportunities for informal social interaction between neighbors. In a survey of 39 qualities sought in developments, homebuyers ranked "lots of natural open space" and plenty of "walking and biking paths" as second and third most desirable qualities of a housing community (Arendt, 1996). Conservation developments seek to provide these amenities while keeping the environment intact and house prices affordable.

By choosing an environmentally oriented marketing strategy, conservation developments can attract homebuyers and gain support of local governments while maintaining affordability. To counter complaints about small lot sizes, developments can advertise that for every one-acre lot (0.4 hectares), the buyer actually gets 80 acres (32 hectares) of woodland, meadows, ponds, and trails. Creating such a large amount of undivided open space also reduces demand for new public parkland. If developments can meet their own recreational space needs, fewer demands will be made on local governments to provide and maintain larger community and regional parks. Additionally, Arendt (1996) suggests that local communities will benefit from cleaner water, greater wildlife habitat, and more attractive natural surroundings.

Conservation developments, therefore, become more attractive to local governmental bodies that could, in turn, offer bonuses for including affordable homes in the developments. These bonuses could then be used by developers to build affordable dwellings that can be more appealing during a municipal review process. The initial background stage of the project requires a rigorous examination of the land and leads to an understanding of its locational context, and an auditing of its natural, cultural, and historic features. By the time a project is ready to be reviewed by pertinent regulatory bodies, the design is already well thought out and potential design problems anticipated.

Affordable Landscapes

In individual lots and new housing developments, landscapes can be designed to reduce maintenance costs and irrigation needs. The typical North American urban or suburban neighborhood landscape consists primarily of neatly trimmed green lawns with a few scattered trees and shrubs and some decora-

tive annual flowers. Such landscapes require large doses of water, energy, synthetic fertilizer, herbicides, and pesticides to keep plants green and healthy and result in significant annual costs for the consumer. Moreover, the quality of water, soil, and air is degraded as these resources are consumed (Fisher, 1994).

Despite the North American tradition of a well-maintained lawn, homeowners and municipalities are beginning to explore more environmentally friendly landscape alternatives. *Xeriscapes,* from the Greek *xeros* for "dry," create landscapes using a variety of indigenous plant species that seek to reduce water and fertilizing needs. Central to the design of xeriscapes is limiting turf area to the amount necessary for specific social and recreational functions. This requires that lawn never be used as a purely visual ground cover. Instead, water-efficient plants suited to local site conditions should be used for ground cover (Fisher, 1994).

For affordable housing projects, regional economic incentives are necessary for the implementation of a successful xeriscape; however, the reduction in maintenance and the environmental benefits make such landscapes an important investment. Maximizing the use of a variety of hard but porous surfaces in landscaping, such as river stones or bricks, can provide an inexpensive and almost maintenance-free alternative to native trees and plants in some areas, although for aesthetic reasons, some plantings are still desirable.

To relieve water stress, resulting from insufficient rainfall, trees, shrubs, and ground cover should be grouped together in beds rather than planted alone. This arrangement reduces water loss from runoff and evaporation. Trees planted in isolation have water requirements two to three times that of trees in grouped beds (Harris, 1983). Mulching between plants also helps reduce evaporation and prevent weed growth, which reduces labor costs, and as the mulch decomposes, it becomes a natural fertilizer for the soil. To capture rainwater and to prevent excess runoff, plant beds can be built to incorporate a small depression. Improving soil conditions at the time of planting can also reduce irrigation needs by increasing the soil's water-holding capacity (Granger, 1991) (Figure 8.11).

Figure 8.11 Grouping trees and shrubs, as well as creating small landscaped depressions, will help save water and lower maintenance costs.

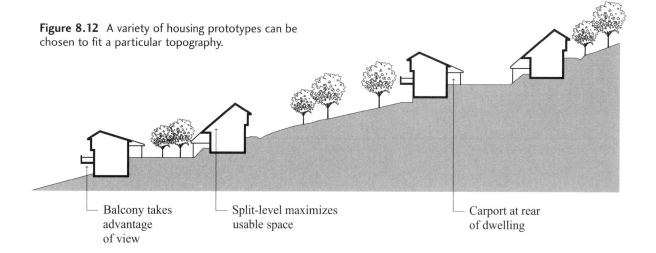

Figure 8.12 A variety of housing prototypes can be chosen to fit a particular topography.

Balcony takes advantage of view

Split-level maximizes usable space

Carport at rear of dwelling

GRADING

Site grading can have a substantial impact on the cost of a development, for both the developer and residents. Therefore, built developments need to be arranged in accordance with natural slopes. Proper site grading will help turn existing topography into a usable and easily maintainable ground surface for a housing project (Figure 8.12). Grading should start with designing roads that follow the contours of the existing topography. This approach results in roads that are significantly less steep than they would be if cut linearly through the site and less costly to build. These roads should comply with existing grades and seek to minimize the need for excessive cuts or fills, preserving natural drainage systems and creating a more aesthetically pleasing environment for residents. Split-side and detached housing can then be arranged along the south, to maximize passive solar gain.

In less than ideal circumstances, when existing roads must be preserved, four types of building sites may occur: *level sites, below-the-road sites, above-the-road sites,* and *sloping-road sites* (CMHC, 1981). Awareness of the type and specific needs of a given site's topography will allow buildings to be better designed to make the most of naturally occurring slopes. For *level sites,* grading can provide drainage to either the street or the rear of the lot. In rocky areas or areas with high-water tables, basements can be eliminated and houses can be constructed with just a crawl space or slab-on-grade, either of which greatly reduces excavation and construction costs. *Below-the-road sites* require drainage to the rear. Creating a walk-out basement or back-split house design allows a change in elevation through the building of up to 8.2 feet (2.5 meters) and increases interior living space. Providing an exterior finish on the basement that coordinates well with the rest of the exterior material helps to improve the appearance of this design (CMHC, 1981).

Contrary to the below-the-road design, *above-the-road sites* require drainage from the rear of the lot to the street. A front-split design or fully raised basement can be used for parking and permits a change in elevation of the building of up to 8.2 feet (2.5 meters). *Sloping-road sites* require a combination of grading techniques. Through a mix of side-split homes with alternating garage locations, even large street grades can be easily accommodated. Drainage can be directed either to the road or to swales in between houses or along a small slope to the rear of the lot.

For residential projects, the total drainage of the site should always be away from the dwellings, with gradients of at least 2 percent of grass-covered areas and 1 percent for hard surfaces. Driveways will have a slope not greater than 12 percent, although a smaller maximum slope should be considered in regions where winter conditions may make such slopes difficult for cars. Outdoor living areas should have gradients between 1.5 and 5 percent for effective drainage away from the building and for practical use by residents (CMHC, 1981).

To avoid incurring excavated earth transportation costs and to maintain balanced earthwork, the basement excavation should approximately equal the amount of fill required to complete the grading of each lot. When designing affordable homes, lots tend to be small; so initial rough grades should be kept low, since only a small area around the dwelling's footprint is available to contain the excavated material. In larger developments, mass grading is sometimes necessary, as it is not always possible to achieve an ideal balance between cut and fill requirements on each individual lot. To minimize costs, mass grading should be carried out before the installation of underground services and construction stats, when less-precise, cheaper equipment can be used (CMHC, 1981).

DESIGNING FOR ENERGY CONSERVATION

Well-designed open spaces can lend themselves to increasing the value of a project without dramatically increasing its cost. These spaces can also be designed to increase affordability and sustainability indirectly, through savings in infrastructure and energy costs. Open spaces and the landscaping within them have the potential to reduce maintenance costs of developments, lower the initial cost of the project's infrastructure, and reduce energy bills for residents.

Passive Solar Gain

Thoughtfully planned developments can utilize the sun, both actively and passively, to reduce lighting, heating, and cooling expenses. When properly designed, even projects in upper latitudes can see significant reductions in energy consumption. To capitalize on the sun's free energy, siting of the housing is the most important factor. Solar-siting strategies can be broken down into three categories: orientation, location, and configuration (Numbers, 1995). A home's orientation determines where it faces. Ideally, homes should be oriented with their long side facing south, or within 15 degrees of south (Figure 8.13). For this siting, it is important to make measurements based on true north rather than magnet-

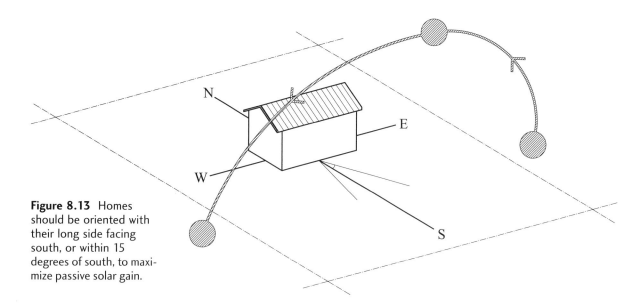

Figure 8.13 Homes should be oriented with their long side facing south, or within 15 degrees of south, to maximize passive solar gain.

ic north, as these measurements can vary by up to 20 degrees in some areas (Numbers, 1995).

Homes sited on south-facing slopes receive more of winter's low-angled sun than homes on level ground. Locating a housing community on a south-facing slope increases winter sun exposure and also reduces the space necessary to prevent shadowing between groups of homes. This effect is reversed on north-facing slopes, reducing the amount of winter sun that reaches homes and increasing the necessary distance between homes, which then reduces density. In colder climates, especially, using north-facing slopes as home sites should be avoided. Trees around the homes can also dramatically affect the solar potential of a project, especially coniferous trees, which shade houses in winter, when direct sunlight is desired. Buildings located around the site can similarly reduce the solar potential of homes.

A home's configuration determines both its outside shape and the interior arrangement of rooms. Living spaces, such as the living room and kitchen, should be located along the south-facing side of a house, while less-used, private spaces, such as the garage, bedrooms, and hallways should be along the north-facing side. This arrangement allows the less-used spaces to act as a buffer between the cold, windy north exterior and the warmer, more-used rooms along the south-facing side.

The overall shape of a dwelling also bears heavily on its energy-saving potential. Compact, simple rectangular forms minimize exterior wall exposure and, therefore, reduce heat loss and thus energy costs. The very same attributes work toward the goal of reducing the overall cost of a home. For cold climates, the long dimension of a house should be between 1.1 and 1.3 times that of the short dimension, with the long side oriented approximately along the east-west axis. For temperate climates, the ratio between long and short sides can be 1.6:1 and 2.4:1. For hot, arid climates, the ratio can be 1.3:1 to 1.6:1, and for hot, humid climates, where high air circulation is essential, between 1.7:1 and 3:1 (Numbers, 1995).

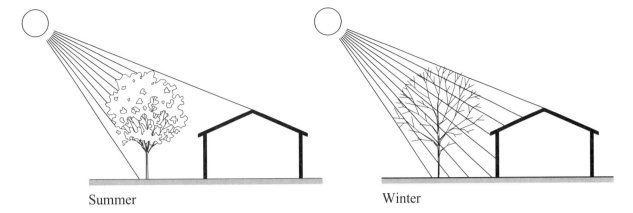

Summer   Winter

Deciduous trees on the site can also help reduce energy costs by providing shade in the summer and allowing sun to pass through in the winter (Figure 8.14). Trees should be placed close to the house to provide shade in the proper location, and care should be taken to select the proper tree for the climate and soil type, as well as the projected size and shape. Additionally, the layout of the interior as well as overhangs and other shading devices can be used to control passive solar heating and natural lighting within the house. Adjustable louvers, for example, can be used to control when and how much light is permitted to enter a space. This system allows winter light to enter and warm a dwelling, while summer light can be kept out to avoid overheating. Light-control systems, such as louvers and blinds, best shield the summer sun when located outside of the home, preventing the light from entering the home and heating the air around the window.

Figure 8.14 Deciduous trees on the site help to reduce energy costs by providing shade in the summer and allowing sun to pass through in the winter.

Considering Wind

When used in conjunction with passive solar heating, wind can produce a microclimate that creates a system of natural heating, cooling, and ventilation in all seasons. In the temperate zone, locations on slopes must take into account both summer and winter winds. Desirable slope exposure should be southeastern, and the upper portions of slopes that still provide winter wind protection are the most advantageous. Consideration must also be given to cooling summer breezes, which do not normally cross a site in the same direction as winter winds (NAHB, 1986).

Local wind patterns are determined by three main factors. First, wind velocity picks up over flat surfaces, such as fields or large bodies of water, and wind decelerates over rough terrain. Second, during the daytime, breezes flow inland from bodies of water and reverse their direction at night due to temperature and pressure changes. Lastly, wind flows uphill over mountains and ridges during the day and downhill toward valleys and lowlands at night. Public spaces in areas that can anticipate high-wind activity should provide wind barriers in the form of walls, trees, and other vegetation. A wide screen of evergreens on the northwest side of a house will block winter winds. The effects of a vegetation-shelter belt can cut wind speeds by more than a half for a distance twelve times the height of the belt (NAHB, 1986).

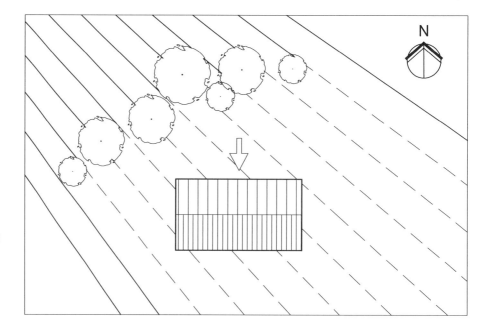

Figure 8.15 Northern entrances should be protected from cold winter winds with earth mounds or coniferous trees.

Steeply pitched roofs on the windward side of a house reduce the roof area affected by winds. North entrances should be protected from cold winter winds with earth mounds, coniferous trees, and walls or fences (Figure 8.15). In addition, homes can be built into hillsides or otherwise partially covered with earth and plantings to reduce wind exposure and to provide natural insulation.

KEY CONSIDERATIONS

- Open spaces in communities can be regarded as a system where an easily accessible network of green areas that range from the regional to individual unit levels is created.
- Green spaces need to incorporate natural features, be easily accessible from all homes, become the green lungs of the neighborhood, and let plenty of sunlight into the community's heart.
- Regional parks must be part of the district's movement system and must be accessible by pedestrian and bike paths or by public transit, at the very least.
- The neighborhood park can become an extended backyard to some of the homes and provide an addition to a home's outdoor, private space.
- For a freehold housing development of 300 units or more, at medium density, smaller-size open spaces of 1½ to 2 acres (0.6 to 0.8 hectares) should be provided within 820 feet (250 meters) of the homes.
- Communal areas for clusters of homes increase the affordability of housing projects by creating semiprivate areas for residents and reducing the need for large private yards for individual units.

- Communal planting gardens, where residents can grow seasonal green produce for self-use, can be a form of open space.

- Some form of easily accessible, private, outdoor space should be part of all dwelling units. Fencing, shrubs, or other screening devices can provide both visual privacy and a clear demarcation of the private area.

- In dwelling units without direct access to the ground level, such as triplexes, decks or balconies can serve as private, outdoor space and can connect directly to the home's living area.

- Design of open spaces in affordable housing ought to consider the needs of people with reduced mobility. All residents, whether disabled or elderly, should have easy access to comfortable, safe, outdoor spaces.

- The cost of children's playground equipment can be greatly reduced by using recycled and naturally occurring objects such as trees.

- In conservation design, lot sizes are reduced in exchange for a greater percentage of open spaces. While the decreased lot size may deter some would-be homebuyers, well laid out lots can maintain open space views and alleviate lack of privacy concerns.

- Maximizing the use of a variety of hard but porous surfaces, such as river stone or brick, in landscaping can provide an inexpensive and almost maintenance-free alternative to native trees and plants in some areas.

- For residential projects, the total drainage of the site should always be positive, away from the dwellings with gradients of at least 2 percent of grass-covered areas and 1 percent for hard surfaces (CMHC, 1981).

- To benefit from maximum passive solar gain and lower heating bills, homes should be oriented with their long side facing south or within 15 degrees of south (Numbers, 1994).

- Living spaces, such as the living room and kitchen, should be located along the south-facing side of a house while less-used private spaces such as garages, bedrooms, and hallways should be along the north-facing side.

- Deciduous trees on the site can help to reduce energy costs by providing shade in the summer and allowing the sun to pass through in the winter.

Infill Housing

A n *infill housing project* is built on vacant land within an already developed area. While such projects might commonly be found in dense urban areas, the project can nonetheless be located on vacant land in a suburban location. For a variety of reasons, a single lot or a large area is left vacant in a built community. Such lots or open areas sometimes prompt an interest in developers to fill in the gap. The resulting homes are termed *infill housing*. An infill project may also include the building of residences on previously designed industrial land, known as *brownfields*. Some brownfields may include existing industrial structures that can be converted into residences.

Vacant land within built areas offers opportunities and challenges to initiators of affordable housing projects. Ease of linkage with nearby roads and utilities and rehabilitation of a rundown neighborhood are some valuable advantages. The likelihood of encountering contaminated soil, designing for odd-sized lots, and facing NIMBY ("not in my backyard") sentiments are some of the drawbacks. The need to curb urban sprawl, to adopt smart growth strategies, and to lower dwelling costs makes infill housing worth considering. This chapter elaborates on issues related to infill housing and dwells on strategies for planning and designing a community of infill housing.

THE UNIQUENESS OF INFILL HOUSING

Infill housing developments can take any form. Dwellings in such projects might be a single detached home, a cluster of dwellings built in high-density configurations, or apartment blocks. Yet the specific characteristics of such projects, built in urban areas, make row housing one of the most common types in such projects. Essential to the expanded definition of infill housing is the notion of the new development as part of an existing fabric. This insertion can be thought of as a careful consideration of various physical and social factors to create a seamless transition between the new or converted project and the community around it. A report by the New York State Council on the Arts (1988) touches upon the human aspect of infill, defining such projects as "the integration of buildings — and their residents — into the existing social fabric, not their separation and exclusion." According to this definition, infill housing projects should respect current lifestyle patterns rather than make effect to reform them.

The availability of land for infill housing primarily in urban areas can be attributed to the increased popularity of suburbia and the demise of the city. Homeownership and privacy were two of the catalysts that made people leave cities. Escape from crowded and unhygienic conditions of the city were some of the other incentives to move. From the middle of the twentieth century, cities, primarily large city centers, fell from favor. Mobility was class associated. The well-to-do left first, followed by the middle class, leaving behind the poor. With residents moving away, cities had become primarily hubs of employment. Office towers or manufacturing plants drew people during the day and remained vacant after hours.

With the relocation of a substantial portion of the residential population to the suburbs, many North American cities have succumbed to urban depression following the exodus from the central, residential neighborhoods. With fewer people living within cities, downtown areas experienced reduced retail activity, increased crime levels, and a general diminishment of vibrancy, therby reducing the quality of city life. To support the essential services of a large city, a solid base of property tax–paying citizens is crucial. Yet, when the population dropped and the tax base followed, civic upkeep and maintenance suffered — civic quality declined, and even more people departed.

As their population declined, cities lost the electoral power that they once had. It made more political sense to invest in suburbia rather than repair deteriorating infrastructure in cities. In addition, as cities remained the place of residency for lower income, primarily renting population groups, landlords stopped spending on maintenance. Homes quickly fell into a state of disrepair, leaving many core urban neighborhoods rundown. With less money spent on welfare, some communities experienced severe social problems.

The transformation in methods of industrial production and the preference to locate plants next to busy highways rather than the city core vacated a large number of plots of land and multistory factories in cities. The departure of industry often left a noticeable scar in urban areas with empty, boarded buildings. Investments needed to bring these buildings to an acceptable environmental standard were often too high and unjustifiable.

Societal and economic changes make consideration of infill housing projects, primarily in the urban core, highly relevant. Perhaps the greatest contribution of building on vacant land to regions is the opportunity to curb rampant urban sprawl. While suburban developments may appear to offer a more attractive standard of living to residents, this standard comes at a great cost. As sprawl pushes outward onto unspoiled land, the cost of constructing each dwelling increases. Much of this cost increase can be attributed to creating or extending existing infrastructure for the new homes.

Infill housing has the potential to reduce many of these costs. Ideally, infill housing projects will connect to existing infrastructure and circulation arteries. Such projects can also capitalize on public transportation routes already in place, reducing autodependency. By building within existing communities, local commerce can provide immediate resources for residents, removing the need for development of new centers. Additionally, infill developments can take advantage of local green spaces and regional parks and reduce the need for developers to provide and landscape community parks, further reducing housing costs.

Demographic changes offer another opportunity for initiators of infill housing. Traditional nuclear families no longer constitute the majority among North American households. Singles, single-parent families, and the elderly are more inclined to look for and to afford smaller, lower-cost dwellings built in higher-density settings. Living next to existing amenities and not relying entirely on private cars might be an additional attraction.

Another potential benefit of infill housing is its effect on the surrounding area. Well-designed infill housing can help revitalize a neighborhood. By attracting more residents to the site, new developments can broaden an area's tax base and attract new business. By providing a mix of housing types, a greater variety of residents with a wider range of incomes can occupy the same neighborhood. This diversity of residents creates a vibrant street scene in successful cities. When permitted by zoning laws, infill housing also provides the opportunity for mixed-use projects that combine residential, retail, and community functions within the same development. Mixed uses further diversifies city life. By removing patches of slums from a city, infill projects can, little by little, help promote a sense of safety that creates a continuous network of pedestrian-friendly streets (Jacobs, 1961).

CHALLENGES OF INFILL HOUSING

Despite the many advantages of infill housing and its contribution to repairing social and urban fabrics, problems surrounding it make these projects difficult to build. When an entire area or a single plot of land has remained vacant, there is usually a good reason for it. Prior to acquiring such a lot and engaging in its design, the initiator needs to assess carefully these potential challenges.

Soil contamination is a challenge in infill affordable housing developments. When the site is the former location of a manufacturing plant or storage facility, poisonous materials may find their way into the ground, and these materials may pose a risk to the people who will inhabit future homes. The soil, therefore, needs to be tested and decisions made as to the method of clean-up. When an industrial building is located on the site and cannot be converted, it must be demolished and cleared. There commonly are fees associated with disposing of the building's debris. When the building is to be preserved, it also needs to be inspected for contaminants prior to beginning work. Dangerous substances could have been stored on the floors and may have been absorbed by the building's structure. At times, a seemingly clean site—on which there was no industrial activity—was a dumping ground for contaminants from other sites and will need to be cleared.

The size, shape, and location of the site may also make infill housing projects more challenging to design and costly to build. At times, such sites can be leftovers of a larger plot of land. To design these odd shapes efficiently into homes is a great challenge; lot shapes may lead to substantial waste, casting doubt on the viability of the entire project. The lot's shape may also form challenges to the logistics of home construction. When the site is too small, manipulating machinery and materials will be difficult and, therefore, costly. When construction begins, noise and pollution may disturb neighboring homes and halt work.

Local opposition to an affordable housing infill project may arise long before construction has begun. While most people fully support the idea of affordable housing, this support quickly fades at the prospect that affordable housing might be built near them. Much of the fear can be attributed to the fact that the introduction of an affordable housing project into a given neighborhood will in some way alter its character. This could be due to the introduction of higher-density housing or the fear that the new project and its inhabitants would not "fit in" with the existing community. Community involvement and education, preferably in the early stages of the design process, can help remove these fears. Innovative design can ensure that infill housing will complement the neighborhood and will not disrupt the existing quality of life.

Zoning bylaws can further jeopardize the feasibility of infill housing projects. Zoning was originally developed in Europe during the nineteenth century to separate industrial land uses from residential uses to cure severe respiratory problems. Whereas past zoning served to separate incompatible land uses, today's zoning laws are more specific. Different housing densities and types are separated from each other, residences are separated from offices, and one type of commercial activity is separated from another. This sort of zoning is especially prevalent in suburban developments; it no longer simply separates based on uses but has evolved to become a tool of economic and, at times, racial discrimination (Duany et al., 2000). Working with local governments to ease zoning laws for an infill project can create opportunities for more diverse and lively communities.

DESIGNING INFILL SITES

Selecting a Site

Since affordable infill housing can be built in a variety of configurations, the choice of unit type and site location is a highly important decision. Some site considerations have been outlined above, yet a designer needs to bear in mind that the project will be woven into both the physical and the social fabric of an existing community. Several issues, therefore, need to be considered when selecting a site.

The socioeconomic profile of the area should accommodate anticipated users. Proposing a project for low-income users in an area with costly services and amenities will be a poor decision. Preferably, the residents will live in close proximity to sources of employment. When there are few jobs in the area, a mixed-use project with integrated commerce can be proposed to employ some of the project's inhabitants. It is also likely that low-income users will have fewer cars per family or none at all. Therefore, ensuring existing public transit or extending it to the new development and installing bus shelters is a step toward integration into the existing community.

Selecting a site in which the dwellings can be oriented for passive solar gain is another necessary attribute. Every measure that will contribute to reduction in maintenance and upkeep costs of homes will make living in the development more affordable (Figure 9.1).

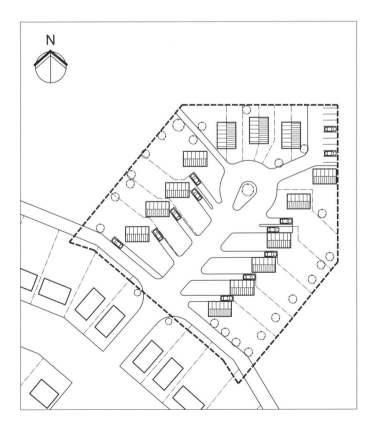

Figure 9.1 Most of the dwellings in this infill, affordable housing project were oriented toward the south to maximize passive solar gain.

Since infill projects can vary greatly in size, from a single row house to a large development with hundreds of units, an often-asked question is what the size for such a project should be. While there is no exact formula for the optimal size of affordable infill housing projects, it is clear that projects that consolidate an area's poor into one development tend to create impoverished ghettos that perpetuate rather than solve a city's housing problem. Infill housing can avoid this predicament by introducing affordable housing into existing communities in a more incremental and dispersed manner. In *A Pattern Language,* Alexander (1977) notes that attractive cities and towns have organic internal structures that have grown gradually through a process based on a sequence of patterns and spatial relationships and that this pattern is piecemeal and coherent. By concerning itself with the existing structural context of an area in terms of spatial configuration and architectural vocabulary, infill housing can succeed in continuing an area's organic growth.

Duany et al. suggest introducing affordable housing into a community with a 1-in-10 ratio, providing one unit of affordable housing for every ten units of regular market housing. This distribution can "provide models for the poor while mitigating against the close-mindedness of the wealthy" (Duany et al., 2000). Such a strategy for the implementation of low-cost housing requires greater investment, as each unit must be designed to fit into its particular site and the small scale of the project offers fewer opportunities for mass-production savings. This investment, however, is essential in creating housing that is socially sustainable and well integrated.

For sites with a larger amount of housing, efforts should be made to vary the types and costs of housing within the project. Built on about five acres of land, Auburn Court in Cambridge, Massachusetts, is a large development with 230 units, about a third of which is moderate- to low-income housing. By varying house styles and colors, the designers of Auburn Court were able to achieve the appearance of an older, well-established Cambridge neighborhood. To attain the mix of housing types and densities, the city created a special zoning district for the site, a process that took 15 years. Once the project was complete, however, Auburn Court proved to be successful in both physically and socially integrating itself into its surroundings (Linn, 1997).

While many sites can potentially be developed into infill housing, a careful "reading" of the neighborhood is required before the design process can begin. This reading should take into account the physical conditions of the site, including its size, zoning, grading, and the presence and condition of existing infrastructure. In addition to the site's physical state, however, the social and economical conditions of the surrounding area must also be looked into.

Planning for High Density

Raising the density of a project increases its affordability. It can, however, be a detriment to the quality of both the project itself and the area around it. Successful, affordable infill housing projects, therefore, must reconcile reducing costs through increased density while maintaining a design that will be attractive and desirable for residents and neighbors. As discussed above, there are several ways to measure housing density. *Net density* is based on areas pertaining directly to the dwellings themselves, including footprints, outside spaces belonging to the project, and parking for the project. *Gross density*, however, includes the same area as net density, but it also includes shops, community centers, and parks. At the level of infill housing, net density is the more appropriate measure of density, as the scale of infill is usually too small to include shopping centers and large parks (Goodchild, 1997).

Given the extremely varied and diverse nature of infill housing, no exact formula exists for determining an optimal net density. For public transportation to be practical and affordable, the general rule of thumb is a minimum of seven dwellings per acre (17 units per hectare) for a bus to run every 30 minutes (Duany et al., 2000). Studies have indicated that low-rise schemes below 80 bedrooms per acre (200 per hectare) can produce high levels of satisfaction (Goodchild, 1997). Another strategy for maintaining high densities and resident satisfaction is to create a balanced mix of users age groups within a project.

Ultimately, however, notions of social acceptability are essentially local, and density relative to a particular site often proves to be a better indicator of satisfaction. The density of a project in comparison to respectable and typical nearby housing will determine whether the new project will stand out as unusual or be easily stigmatized (Goodchild, 1997). Therefore, the best way to increase the acceptable density of an infill project is to select sites that are in areas of high density already. In addition, as density rises, parking becomes an increasingly important and difficult problem. Traditional towns and neighborhoods often handled parking with a rear lane where residents of apartments and row houses parked (Duany et al., 2000). For higher densities or for areas in which a rear lane cannot be developed despite higher cost, underground parking should be provided.

URBAN AND ARCHITECTURAL FIT

As previously noted, characteristic of infill projects is the fact that they are woven into an existing urban, architectural, and social fabric. The need to be familiar with those factors prior to the project's design is highly important. Another consideration will be the image of the proposed project. Past government-funded affordable housing initiatives stigmatized developments by concentrating large numbers of low-income people in sad-looking buildings. Low-cost public housing projects such as St. Louis, Missouri's Pruitt Igoe and Chicago's Cabrini Green are testimony to how poorly designed housing can contribute to (or even promote) social deterioration. In light of these past failures, one of the most important goals of affordable housing today is to ensure that it looks like any other project.

Affordable infill housing designers should create buildings that embrace the materials, colors, and style of the neighboring buildings. Well-designed projects that successfully complement their surroundings will help to garner support and lower opposition from existing communities. Further, by creating an environment that is physically integrated into the existing community, infill housing can lay the foundation for a sense of social unity and acceptance between new and current community residents. This integration can be achieved in a variety of ways, but it must begin with a thorough reading and understanding of the physical structure and characteristics of the existing community.

Figure 9.2 The urban grid of the Le Village neighborhood originated from a plan devised in 1783.

In an intensive urban infill study of the neighborhood of Le Village in the town of Cornwall, Ontario, Canada, the author developed guidelines for successful integration of infill housing at both the community and individual unit levels through a systematic approach and analysis (Friedman, 1999). While the exact framework of the study may not be compatible with all infill projects, its general principles and methodology can provide a useful starting point from which to begin an examination of a site's surroundings.

Starting with establishing patterns for the community as a whole, the urban investigation focused on Le Village's urban morphology and community structure, the community facilities, the industrial buildings, parking, alleys, and the waterfront area (Friedman, Lin, and Krawitz, 2002). The research first focused on Cornwall's lot layout, which originated from a 1783 plan. The plan called for a square-mile area to be divided into 81 square blocks and for each of these blocks to be subdivided into 24 lots. The farmland surrounding the block was divided into grids of long, narrow lots. The two grids and an overlapping transition zone linking the two formed the overall block pattern for Cornwall (Figure 9.2). The urban structure of the community was determined by its main traffic artery and a complex of buildings along it. Industrial buildings were located and their potential for redevelopment noted, and parking and back lane patterns were also examined.

From these observations, the study area was divided into eight zones based on the morphology of the lots, their functions, and importance within the community. These divisions allowed for much more accurate generalizations about lot typology and, therefore, permitted the formulation of more appropriate guidelines. Analysis of each zone yielded the general character and urban pattern of the neighborhood, upon which foundation guidelines could be developed. By comparing and analyzing data such as land coverage and floor area ratio, the general condition of land use and configuration in Le Village was obtained. Then, this information was synthesized, and the character of each zone established, taking into account various urban features, including lot size and setback, parking, and building heights (Figure 9.3). From this data, guidelines specific to each zone and building type could be developed to ensure that infill projects are consistent with the existing character of the community—that they "fit in." This careful analysis of the community as a whole allowed for more educated planning of the optimal locations for infill projects.

The creation of architectural guidelines for new buildings in Le Village followed a similar process. The investigation began by surveying the form and construction of the typical houses in the area and dividing them into principal types: single detached narrow front, single detached wide front, semidetached, duplex, fourplex, and commercial building with residential use. Architectural details were documented next, since they comprise the main visual articulation of the buildings and influence the image of both private and public areas. The various elements surveyed include: front and back porches, enclosures, doors and windows, additions, accessory buildings, decorative woodwork, landscaping, and fencing.

The analysis and synthesis of the collected data began with the common features of building volumes and roofs. Most of the houses in Le Village are rectangular boxes with porches at the front and back, and they are one-and-a-half to

Existing urban conditions

Lot	- 29.5' x 108.3' (9.0 m x 33.0 m) - 24.7' x 9.8' (7.5 m x 3.0 m)
Parking	- Access through the alley - Rear of the lot for parking - Curb parking (wide streets)
Land use	- Residential: duplex, triplex, multiplex
Grow space	- No alley wall - Spontaneous growth - No clear specified use
Additions	- Additions do not respect the limit
Sections and heights	- No backyard limit regulations

Proposed urban guidelines

Lot	- Side setback: 0.9 m (min.) on both sides
Parking	- Curb parking only (wide streets)
Use	- Residential: single family, duplex
Grow space	- 1.5 (multi-use building) - Attached to a corner
Additions	- Respect the growth limit, street wall and additions limit
Sections and heights	- New trees in alley
Corner buildings	- Buildings located on corners should relate the sides of the house to the street - Commercial use on corners is allowed

Figure 9.3 Synthesis (left) and proposed urban guidelines (right) for one of the zones in Le Village, Cornwall, Ontario, Canada.

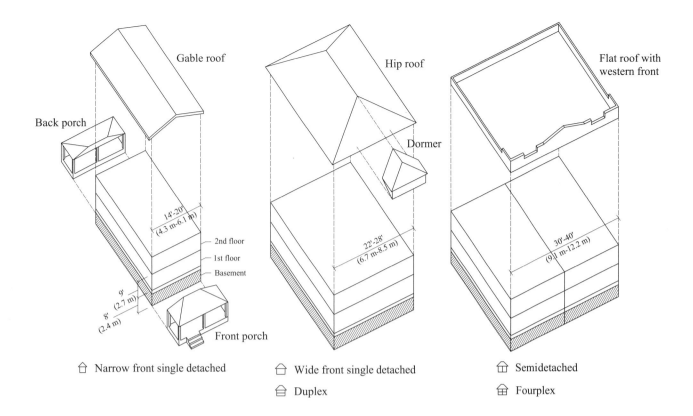

Gable roof

Back porch

14'-20'
(4.3 m–6.1 m)

2nd floor
1st floor
Basement

9'
(2.7 m)

8'
(2.4 m)

Front porch

Hip roof

Dormer

22'-28'
(6.7 m–8.5 m)

Flat roof with
western front

30'-40'
(9.1 m–12.2 m)

⌂ Narrow front single detached

⌂ Wide front single detached

⌂ Duplex

⌂ Semidetached

⌂ Fourplex

two-and-a-half stories tall, with simple roof forms. Three volume-composition types and three house-roof types were identified: gable, hip, and flat roof with parapet (Figure 9.4). Typical floor plans revealed that public spaces are located on the lower floor, and private spaces are configured along the two deep sides of the floor in the one-story units. Additions to houses are built in the rear, on the side and on upper floors. They are used for storage, for housing cars, and for additional living space.

With regard to doors and windows, a large variety of window types were identified in both the single and grouped categories. Windows in Le Village are generally rectangular with a vertical orientation. Doors were similarly categorized, with eight types each of entry and storm doors. The most typical cladding materials used were wood clapboard siding; brick, for walls; and concrete and stone, for foundations. In many instances, aluminum, vinyl, or fiberboard siding has been used to replace the original wood or brick cladding, as well as simulated brick and stone asphalt shingles.

The architectural guidelines for the construction of new dwelling units were developed at two levels: the first to provide the general requirements of the housing type and to cover issues such as the form and style of houses, and the second to address the technical requirements of architectural elements such as windows, cladding, and landscaping. All houses in Le Village were categorized according to volume composition, and the guidelines were organized according to volume, height, width, and floor area. In this manner, the guidelines reduced arbitrary forms to new homes in Le Village (Figure 9.5). As the Cornwall project demonstrated, many aspects of a design determine its ability to integrate within

Type	Porch Enclosures	Additions	Accessory Buildings	Infill Units
Materials	- Existing open porches that contain original elements of historical or heritage value shall be restored and maintained - Enclosure of such porches shall not be allowed - Porch enclosures shall be clad in horizontal wood or fibre cement siding as per the material requirements for exterior walls	- Additions shall be clad in wooc or fibre cement siding or brick as per the material requirements of exterior walls - The total number of cladding materials including that of additions shall not exceed two	- Accessory building shall be clad in wood or fibre cement siding or brick as per the material requirements of exterior walls - The total number of cladding materials including that of accessory buildings shall not exceed two	- Infill units shall be clad in wood or fibre cement siding or brick as per the material requirements of exterior walls - The total number of cladding materials including that of infill units shall not exceed two
Configuration	- Porch enclosures may be of another allowable material than that of the main building - Window sills in porch enclosures shall be located 2'6" to 3'0" (0.8 m - 0.9 m) above the porch floor - The total glazed area shall be a minimum of 80% of the allowable wall area for glazing	- In cases where additions continue or extend existing faces of exterior walls, the new cladding shall match that of the existing wall (including material, scale, colour, finish, and texture) - Additions to the rear of the house are permitted up to the required rear yard setback. On lots 35' (10.7 m) or more in width, additions are permitted to the side of the house up to the required side yard setback - The height of additions shall nct exceed that of the principal building	- See Urban Guidelines for location, height, and use requirements of accessory buildings	- See Urban Guidelines for location, height, and use requirements of infill units
Details	- Windows and doors in porch enclosures and additions shall conform to the same guidelines as for the main building - All exterior walls of porch enclosures and additions shall conform to the same detail guidelines as for the main building		- Windows and doors in accessory buildings and infill units shall conform to the same guidelines as for the main building - All exterior walls of accessory buildings and infill units shall conform to the same detail guidelines as for the main building	
Illustrations	 ELEVATION	 PLANS ELEVATIONS	 SECTIONS	

Figure 9.5 Proposed architectural guidelines for porch enclosures, additional accessory buildings and new infill units.

an existing community, both visually and socially. The following sections identify additional important features of infill design.

Lot Size and Setback

As demonstrated above, to create an infill project that visually fits into an urban pattern, the existing lot sizes should be acknowledged and their patterns respected. Often, affordable infill housing projects introduce a higher-density development into a lower-density area. When this is the case, efforts should be made to ensure that the new project emulates the scale of the existing lots and the dwelling sizes. This can be achieved through front-yard landscaping or by varying the massing of the street façade and breaking up the volume of the proposed project into a scale more appropriate to the surrounding buildings. When a large project made of several buildings is designed, it is best to line-up the façades of the new buildings with the old. By introducing a different setback or changing the urban pattern, the designer runs the risk of proposing a fabric that does not fit.

In general, front-yard setbacks for infill developments need to be equivalent to the existing properties. Where existing setbacks vary, the infill project should reflect a similar pattern in its own setbacks (Figure 9.6). The setback should provide space for an entry, front stoop, and landscaping between the public sidewalk and the private home. A minimum of 6.5 to 10 feet (2 to 3 meters) setback from the property line is desirable to provide for services and privacy when parking is located at the rear of the project. When parking is located at the front, however, a minimum setback of 20 feet (6 meters) is necessary (City of Toronto, 2003).

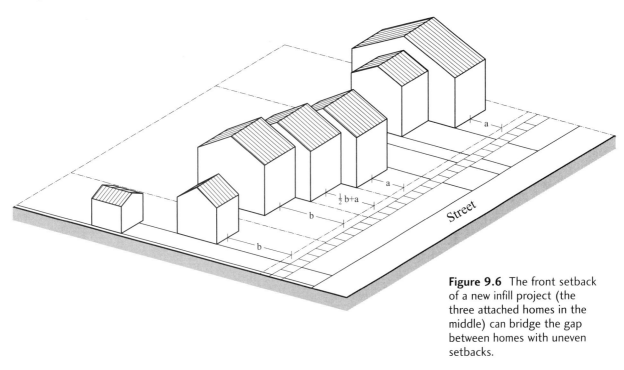

Figure 9.6 The front setback of a new infill project (the three attached homes in the middle) can bridge the gap between homes with uneven setbacks.

Circulation and Parking

Streets can be regarded as the threads that hold the new and the old together. Streets help delineate individual lots and blocks within the urban fabric and provide a setting for social interaction and neighborhood activities, as well as serve as connective, linear open spaces (City of Toronto, 2003). When possible, infill housing should be placed facing existing roads and take their address from these streets. Doing so will give existing neighborhoods and streets better definition.

When new streets need to be constructed for an infill project, the present street pattern should be extended to create a smooth transition between existing and infill houses and to maintain public pedestrian access to both. To create strong visual and physical links with adjacent neighborhoods, the landscaping, sidewalk treatment, and street furniture of new streets needs to match the existing streets. To maintain affordability, any new road construction should be public, adhering to local codes to take advantage of city waste and snow removal, as well as providing access for emergency vehicles. Otherwise, these responsibilities will have to be shared among the project's residents and higher monthly maintenance costs paid. When a parking space is provided at the rear of each dwelling, the street system can be designed to allow a common, shared entry road for all the homes rather than to a small group of dwellings.

Parking for infill housing, especially in a dense urban setting, should not dominate the streetscape. Ideally, infill projects will be designed to allow underground parking garages or in the rear on individual units (Figure 9.7). Placing parking in the front of infill projects poses a number of practical problems and lends the project a poor visual image. Providing front parking, whether through carports or garages, requires curb cuts and driveways that increase cost. Also, according to the City of Toronto: "Multiple curb-cuts and driveways jeopardize safety and comfort for pedestrians and precludes curbside parking and tree planting" (City of Toronto, 2003). In addition, the overwhelming presence of cars in front of dwellings detracts from the city streetscape, and the increased paving in the front yard reduces soil available for attractive landscaping.

Front driveways should only be considered when underground or rear parking options are not available due to shallow blocks or sites with problematic topography. When this is the case, front driveways require a minimum setback of 20 feet (6 meters) from the front property line to the garage door. Additionally, individual units should be at least 20 feet (6 meters) wide, to provide front yard widths sufficient for driveways. The driveway width should be minimized to allow for more landscaping and pedestrian walkways to the front door. Approximately 10 feet (3 meters) is sufficient to accommodate a single car leading to a one-car garage. By ensuring that driveways are spaced at least 20 feet (6 meters) apart, some on-street visitor parking can be provided (City of Toronto, 2003).

Creating a private lane leading to rear parking for groups of dwellings is a much nicer alternative to front-yard driveways. This option greatly reduces the number of curb cuts and the amount of front-yard space dedicated to pavement. Private lanes also allow for a larger amount of short-term visitor parking on the street. Rear parking allows for narrower dwelling units, which can be reduced from a minimum of 20 feet (6 meters) to 14 feet (4.2 meters) (City of Toronto,

Indoor parking in end units

Common outdoor parking

Common outdoor parking

Parking under rear deck

Figure 9.7 Alternative parking options in a high-density infill project (indicated with the dotted line).

2003). Responsibility for maintenance of the private driveway to rear parking will be shared by the project's residents. For larger infill projects, underground garages can be constructed, although rear access to parking is still preferred. Underground garages, however, are likely to cost much more than outdoor parking.

In addition to safe, attractive sidewalks along streets, publicly accessible paths may need to be created as the development on a block intensifies. Public walkways provide safe, well-lighted access ways to important community destinations, such as schools, transit stops, or parks. Walkways should be landscaped in a manner that creates a physical and visual connection to streets and sidewalks, to clearly designate them as public spaces. Buildings adjacent to pedestrian paths will be designed so that light can reach the walkways during midday, and windows overlooking the walkways will provide informal surveillance (City of Toronto, 2003).

Open Spaces and Amenities

Similar to new, affordable housing projects on undeveloped land, as the density of the development increases, the availability of open spaces and community amenities become essential to providing a high quality of life to residents of an infill project. Shared open spaces in infill projects can increase affordability by eliminating the need for certain services to each unit. Regardless of the fact that infill projects can vary greatly in size and shape, open spaces must be centrally located to allow quick and direct access from all dwellings and help strengthen a sense of community. Open spaces also allow for higher densities by ensuring that each unit gets plenty of light and air. For larger developments, however, wide, central open spaces can lack safety, privacy, and ownership necessary for them to be used successfully. In addition, it may not be possible for dwelling units to face the open space, as they would be fronting the street instead; so the backs of units and service areas would surround the open space, potentially creating an undesirable visual environment.

Creating a series of smaller, more private open spaces is a better alternative. It would help reinforce privacy and security of each unit (Wei, 2002). These small spaces can be located in between individual units or at the center of clusters. Care must be taken to ensure that the buildings are laid out to allow for sunlight to penetrate open areas. Windows from surrounding dwellings should look onto the space to provide informal surveillance and create a sense of safety, especially for children.

When designing open spaces, healthy trees and shrubs already existing on the site should be preserved and protected to increase the site's appeal and save on planting costs. The design should work around trees, or alternatively arrangements should be made to relocate the trees before construction. Existing park areas can be preserved or extended into new infill developments and help ease the existing community's acceptance of the new project and its residents. These strategies can also be applied to revitalized industrial sites where remnants of the site's former function, such as brick walls or steel structures, can become gardens and trellises that give a space a unique character and identity while saving on landscaping costs (City of Toronto, 2003).

Utilities and Servicing

One of the notable advantages of infill housing is the ability to spend less on public utilities and servicing, since they are already in place. Branching with these utilities needs to be done however, with great care to save additional costs. The preferred location of such utilities is, of course, underground; yet unfortunately they are at times installed above grade. In high-density developments, visible power, telephone, or cable TV lines may have a negative effect and should be avoided.

Garbage disposal and recycling services can be located in areas where they do not negatively affect adjacent properties, or they should be integrated into the design of the building, so they are not visible from the street or from adjacent open spaces and parks. Screening of such areas with attractive fences or landscaping, when a smooth integration into the building is not possible, can also be effective. Public garbage pick-up and recycling must be from a public street (City of Toronto, 2003).

Flexibility and Balance of Dwelling Types

With increasingly diverse population and household types, infill developments present a unique opportunity to provide nontraditional, affordable housing for different groups. A single infill project, for example, can vary dwelling types and sizes to provide housing for elderly residents, single-parent families, as well as university students. This mixture of housing types can contribute to neighborhood revitalization by bringing in residents who can support a greater variety of businesses and cultural activities. Furthermore, such infill projects can house people of different cultures, incomes, and ages and foster interaction, which strengthens the social bonds essential to any community.

Providing a wide range of housing types can also help revitalize a rundown area by attracting a mixture of people to patronize local businesses and amenities throughout the entire day. For example, neighborhood parks in an area with mainly young families usually remain fairly vacant during the day while children are at school. By providing infill housing for the elderly nearby, these parks can be better utilized. This quality of constant and diverse use and users is crucial to the success and vitality of both parks and city centers (Jacobs, 1961).

Before such mixed populations can benefit an infill project, one must first ensure that the surrounding area can sustain diverse groups of people. Creating infill housing for the elderly in an area with a poor public transit system and few amenities within walking distance will not prove successful. Planning for local amenities to be conceived as part of the housing project itself will allow for a greater variety of residents.

A dwelling type commonly used in high-density infill projects is the row house. It can be constructed in a variety of forms, such as rows facing a street or clusters with individual open spaces. Flexibility can also be offered through internal floor arrangements. The same structure can be a home to a single person or several families. Widths of the units can also vary. The changing widths can help fit row houses into a variety of sites, and when appropriate they can be constructed as freestanding structures.

Designing for Mixed Use

Infill housing is often only one aspect of a much larger, overall community economic revitalization process. Through mixed-use development, an infill project can more directly and efficiently play a role in district economic development. By merging commercial and residential spaces, infill developments can become income generators, helping to mitigate property and construction costs and providing more successful and diverse environments for residents (Wei, 2002).

In addition to helping ease construction costs, mixed-use projects also help prevent sprawl and reduce dependency on automobiles. Even the simple provision of a convenience store for daily needs can significantly reduce residents' trips to commercial centers. By including a dry cleaner or video rental store within a project, for example, the pressure to drive can be eased. Such small businesses will serve only a small market at first and will not be highly profitable until the community matures. To help such businesses survive through this initial period, developers can provide commercial and retail spaces at a reduced rent until the businesses are self-sustaining (Duany et al., 2000).

A popular model for mixing residential and retail spaces that has proven successful in infill projects is the ground-floor shop with apartment housing above. The growth of "just-in-time" ordering patterns for some small businesses has greatly reduced the need for large storage spaces, freeing up the floors above shops for housing. As long as a separate entrance for these upper floors is designed, their cost can be kept quite low (Goodchild, 1997). The introduction of housing into predominantly retail areas can help counter neighborhood dereliction and revitalize abandoned commercial districts. Furthermore, housing provides the "eyes and ears on the street" that reduce crime and increase a sense of security for the businesses after closing hours. Having dwellings above shops also improves the site's property value and provides rental income for business owners (Goodchild, 1997).

CONVERSION DESIGN

Brownfield Conversion

Another approach to revitalizing city centers and reducing urban sprawl can be favoring the development of *brownfields* over greenfields. While building housing developments in brownfields can be beneficial to the area around it, many financial, environmental, and political factors need to be considered prior to its beginning. The first issue facing brownfield development is site clean-up. Often, little or no information about the type and extent of contamination on a site is known. Private owners may choose not to get a site evaluated and tested and will avoid disclosing such information to the public (Wright, 1997). When the contamination status of brownfields is undertaken by governments, potential developers will be in a position to better assess the cost of decontamination as well as the overall project's cost. Such knowledge can accelerate planning and approval processes and help attract initiators (National Round Table on the Environment and the Economy, 2003).

Due to all the challenges facing brownfield redevelopment, strategies on the local or national level are necessary to ensure that the opportunities these sites possess are not lost. Some sites can be set aside for new industrial use; however, it is not reasonable to assume that the demand for new industrial sites will reclaim all brownfield sites (Wright, 1997). Sites that are near downtown, attractive waterways, or other amenities and have minor contamination are usually best-suited for residential development. If brownfield revitalization programs already exist in an area, they can help initiators find funding for projects. Due to a shortage of affordable housing, many cities eager to see brownfield sites developed pay for their decontamination.

Converting Buildings to Affordable Housing

In industrial and commercial building conversion, part or all of an existing structure is maintained and either incorporated or converted into a housing. Like brownfield redevelopment, the conversion of these buildings comes with its own set of challenges. Many opportunities to create unique, affordable housing that preserves the character of existing neighborhoods and enhances the quality of the urban environment do exist. Such projects will be initiated only if the housing market in an area is significantly better than the market for industry or office space, and the building can be easily converted.

Conversion of underused industrial buildings to affordable housing was undertaken by the author and his colleagues (Friedman, Drummond, and Sheppard, 1995). The Mayor Building is an industrial building that makes up Montreal's Fur District. Over the years, the building's main occupants have been fur manufacturers, and the structure has supported light industrial activities. The building remained vacant, as its occupants moved to other locations.

In accordance with the objective of converting the Mayor Building to mixed use, the lower three floors remained commercial and the upper eight floors were designed for residential use. A typical upper floor was served by two elevator shafts near the two far apart entrances, which were linked by a corridor. The structural bay sizes varied between 18 feet by 16 feet 8 inches (5.5 meters by 5.08 meters) and 23 feet 6 inches by 17 feet 8 inches (7.16 meters by 5.39 meters), and the structure itself was judged to be in good condition. When designing a typical floor, a cost-effective strategy was to offer potential buyers a choice of unit sizes, subject to a predetermined price scale that was set by the developer. The number of dwelling layout choices were limited to better manage the unit's sale. Buyers were also offered a choice of bathrooms and kitchens, and the option to leave their spaces either open or partitioned, according to their lifestyle.

The unit's design proceeded in several stages. First, the sociodemographic composition of potential buyers was determined. Then, the number of units and price ranges were decided to maintain the project's economic viability. Design flexibility was achieved by creating open spaces with predetermined wet walls. The design process at this point becomes one of adapting a generic volume to the buyer's particular spatial and economic specifications. The clients selected kitchens and bathrooms from a menu of offerings, and then decided on their location in the purchased spaces. The result was a range of affordable dwelling units that met the space needs and means of the buyer and were profitable to the initiator.

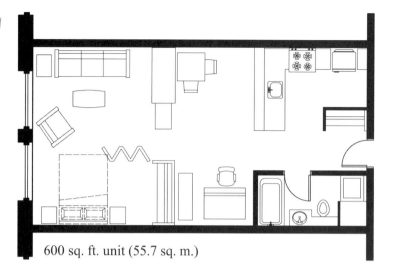

600 sq. ft. unit (55.7 sq. m.)

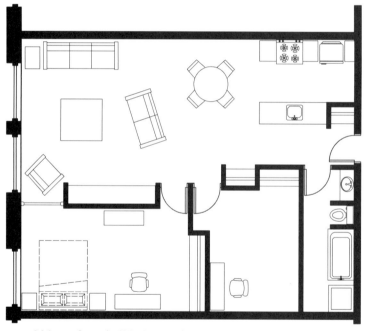

Figure 9.8 Two typical units designed for the Montreal fur district's Mayor Building.

900 sq. ft. unit (83.6 sq. m.)

To demonstrate the project design and sale process, two model units were designed (Figure 9.8). A 600-square-foot (56-square-meter) unit was conceived for a single person who worked at home. There was no formal living room, and the front of the apartment was a combination bedroom and living room. The 900-square-foot (84-square-meter) unit was designed for a couple. Much of the partitioning in this unit was eliminated by using storage units to create a separation between the living and the sleeping areas.

KEY CONSIDERATIONS

- Societal and economic changes make consideration of infill housing projects, primarily in the urban core, highly relevant. Perhaps the greatest contribution of building on vacant land is the possibility of curbing rampant urban sprawl.

- A potential benefit of infill housing is its effect on the surrounding area. Well-designed infill housing can help revitalize the neighborhood in which it is built.

- Soil contamination is a challenge in infill, affordable housing developments. When the site is the former location of a manufacturing plant or storage facility, poisonous materials that have found their way into the ground may pose a risk to the people who will inhabit future homes.

- Infill housing projects need to be woven into the physical and social fabric of an existing community. Proposing a project for low-income users, for example, in an area with costly services and amenities is a poor decision.

- For infill sites with a larger amount of housing, effort should be made to vary the types and costs of housing within the project.

- Successful, affordable infill-housing projects must reconcile reducing costs through increased density while maintaining a design that will be attractive and desirable for residents and neighbors.

- The best way to increase the acceptable density of an infill project is to select sites that are already in areas of high density.

- Affordable infill-housing designers should create buildings that embrace the materials, colors, and style of neighboring buildings. Such designs will help to garner support and lower opposition from existing communities.

- By varying the massing of an infill project's street façade and breaking up its volume, a closer fit can be achieved between new and old.

- A minimum of 6.5 to 10 feet (2 to 3 meter) setback from the property line is desirable to provide for services and privacy when parking is located at the rear of the project (City of Toronto, 2003).

- When new streets need to be constructed for an infill project, the present street pattern should be extended to create a smooth transition between existing and infill houses and to maintain public pedestrian access to both.

- Creating a private lane leading to rear parking for groups of infill dwellings is a much nicer alternative to front-yard driveways. Lanes will greatly reduce the number of curb cuts and the amount of front-yard space dedicated to pavement.

- Providing shared open spaces in infill projects can increase affordability by eliminating the need to provide certain services to each individual unit. Creating a series of smaller, more private open spaces, where possible, is an alternative.

- When designing open spaces, healthy trees and shrubs already existing on the site should be preserved and protected to increase the site's appeal and to save on planting costs.

- Creating infill housing for the elderly in an area with a poor public transit system and few amenities within walking distance will not prove successful.

- By merging commercial and residential spaces, infill developments can become income generators, helping to mitigate property and construction costs (Wei, 2002).

c h a p t e r

10

Projects

T he previous chapters dwelled on different aspects of designing and constructing affordable homes and communities. Each chapter focused on a number of issues within a defined topic, describing a range of possible alternatives. These issues are all considered jointly in the design of a project. Certain strategies will be rendered impractical while others will become the foundation of the project's identity and affordability. Several projects have been featured in this chapter to illustrate a comprehensive design process. The projects have been selected because they cover a range of issues, concerns, and approaches to the design of affordable community. Some of the projects are small in scale, whereas others are large and comprehensive. An in-depth description of the decision-making process involved in their design as well as their outcomes are made in each case.

Infill À La Carte

Name of Project: Le Carré Saint-Antoine (Phase I and II)

Builder: Anobid Construction, José Di Bona, President

Design: Architect: G.S.N. Parent; Designer: Paul-André Gagnon, based on the author's Next Home concept.

Location: Downtown Montreal, Quebec, Canada

Site Area: Approximately 26,400 square feet (about 0.6 acres/0.24 hectares)

Number of Units: 11 structures built in a row, 18 units in total

Project Type: Urban infill

Density: Net: 44 units per acre (109 units per hectare)

Parking: On-street, individual interior garages, rear of units
Unit Type: 2 triplexes, 3 duplexes, 6 townhouses

Unit Size: triplexes and duplexes average 1,000–1,200 square feet (90–110 square meters)

Type of Ownership: Condominium

Cost: $53,000–$75,000 (C$70,000–$100,000)/unit at time of construction (1998)

Cladding Materials: Brick and wood siding

Users: Small families, single persons, and students with a need for affordable housing

---

LE CARRÉ SAINT-ANTOINE is an 11 structure, three-story row townhouse, urban infill project, located near the edge of downtown Montreal. Despite close proximity to the city's commercial district and many cultural facilities, the project is separated from the downtown core by a highway overpass and a steep slope. Lower land cost contributed to the project's affordability, permitting buyers to trade the quality of their immediate living environment for homeownership. Builder José Di Bona recognized the ability of the downtown site to attract a variety of non-traditional households, so he created a project that could easily be adapted to different buyers' space needs and budgets. Di Bona sold the units by the floor, and buyers were able to participate in deciding the layout and choosing finishing for the interior. By taking advantage of the existing infrastructure, construction costs were lowered as well (Figures 10.1a, b, and c).

PLANNING CONSIDERATIONS

Due to the infill nature of this project, the configuration of the roads was in place when the project's design began. The designers were able to reduce the units' cost by linking the project with existing infrastructure (Figure 10.2). Instead of creating one large parking lot, several smaller solutions were found. According to local bylaws, off-street parking is required for at least one car per unit. To satisfy

(a) Close-up: Saint-Antoine Facade

(b) Lusignan Street Facade

(c) Saint-Antoine Avenue Facade

Figures 10.1a, b, and c Le Carré Saint-Antoine is a multifamily infill housing project composed of 11 structures built in a row.)

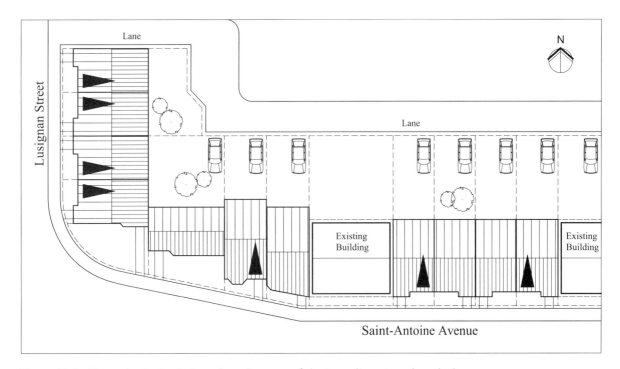

Figure 10.2 The project's circulation takes advantage of the two adjacent roads and a lane.

this, the builder offered buyers the choice of a unit with an individual interior garage or a reserved parking spot in the lot's rear, with access through a service lane. On-street parking was provided for residents with more than one car and for visitors along both sides of Saint-Antoine Avenue.

The location of Le Carré Saint-Antoine also provided several opportunities for convenient public transit. An advantage of the project was the location's proximity to downtown places and the many amenities within walking distance. For residents who prefer to avoid walking the steep slope to the downtown area, bus and subway stations are located near the project as well.

Since the project is small in size and fits into an existing urban pattern, few options were available for open-space design. Small backyards were created for the units and enclosed with wooden fences to provide privacy and security. These fences allow the yards to be used as outdoor storage and provide a safe play space for children. While Le Carré Saint-Antoine does not have large open green spaces, the location of the project takes advantage of existing neighborhood parks that compensate for the lack of on-site space. Residents have access to playgrounds, baseball diamonds, lawns, and benches, all within walking distance.

DWELLING CHOICES

To appeal to a diverse market, the structures of Le Carré Saint-Antoine were sold as duplexes, triplexes, and single-family, three-story townhouses (Figure 10.3). The flexibility of the interiors, especially the location of a kitchen and bathroom on each floor, allowed for a greater arrangement of living conditions within the townhouses. Families could purchase all three floors of a unit to create a three-to four-bedroom townhouse, while small households could purchase a single floor to live in as a studio apartment. The lower floors were left largely unpartitioned, permitting their use as a home office or studio. The entrances to the units were such that each lower level could be accessed directly, accommodating mixes of private and public space.

Prior to construction and occupancy, buyers participated in a process of making modifications to the interior and, at times, to the building envelope itself. The builder presented buyers with plans for each floor that they could accept or alter according to their needs. Buyers were also offered a menu of priced finishing options. For example, the menu listed a finished basement painted and carpeted, for $4,000 (C$5,300) and a powder room with toilet, sink,

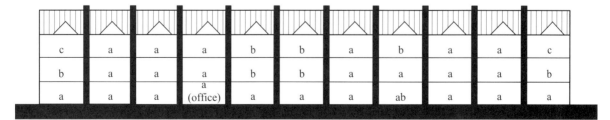

Figure 10.3 To appeal to a diverse market, the three-story structures of Le Carré Saint-Antoine were sold as single-family townhouses, duplexes, and triplexes. The letters represent various households.

mirror, and vinyl floor for $1,460 (C$1,950). By listing design options with their cost, buyers could see what options they could afford and prioritize their selections accordingly.

The structure at the south end of Lusignan Street, for example, was originally intended to house one family. The owner, however, purchased and altered its interior layout to create a triplex. He rented out the two upper units and then moved into the ground floor. The owner also made preconstruction alterations to the building envelope, straightening a beveled side to facilitate the arrangement of furniture and adding several windows to the exposed side façade to increase natural light penetration to the interior. The flexibility offered by the builder during this preconstruction design phase allowed the owner to shape the building according to his own needs and budget, increasing postoccupancy satisfaction.

The flexibility of the Le Carré Saint-Antoine project also accommodated unique lifestyles. One structure, designed as a duplex, was purchased by two young women who shared the ground floor, and each lived in one of the above floors (Figure 10.4). This arrangement allowed the owners to remove the original design's second staircase, freeing additional interior space. The dwelling's livable space was further increased by extending the length of the building from the original 32 feet to 40 feet (10 meters to 12 meters) at the request of the women. The ground floor was redesigned to accommodate a two-car garage, powder room, and laundry facilities. The upper floors reflect the different lifestyles of each of the occupants. One woman opted to have a smaller bedroom and bathroom and use the saved area as a work space and possible guest room. The other selected a larger bedroom and bathroom with a separate shower stall and tub (Huang, 2003).

A variety of methods have been used to create a sense of the occupant's identity in Le Carré Saint-Antoine on both the macro and micro levels. The consistent use of red brick and wood paneling throughout the project created coherence among the eleven row houses. To avoid monotony, the front façade of the dwellings are varied slightly, some have areas of wood paneling, others do not. The fenestration pattern also varies from house to house, with some having prominent bay windows. Additionally, an existing row house in the center of the Saint-Antoine side of the project was preserved, further breaking up the project and helping to integrate it into the community. This controlled variation allowed the project as a whole to achieve a distinct identity while permitting residents to personalize individual dwellings. Some units have been further personalized with small gardens or other landscaping in the front. One resident displayed a brightly colored ceramic-tile mosaic of the home's address above the dwelling's standard black number.

STRATEGIES FOR AFFORDABILITY

Several strategies allowed the builder to offer quality flexible housing at affordable prices. The location of the project next to a highway overpass and railway tracks kept land costs low, yet provided easy access to public transportation and downtown. Money saved on land costs was invested in accommodating buyers' needs. By providing a menu of interior options and engaging buyers in the

Figure 10.4 Original floor plans of a single-family town-house that was converted to a two-family structure, with one resident occupying the lower, two floors and another the top third of the house.

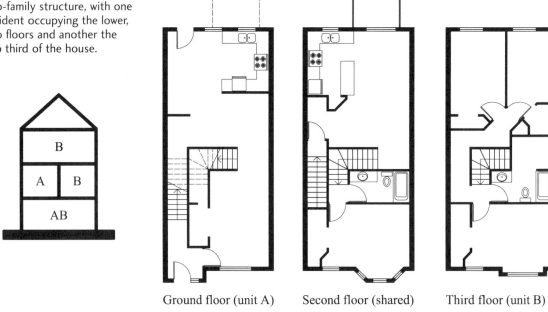

Ground floor (unit A)　　Second floor (shared)　　Third floor (unit B)

Original plans - A two family Duplex

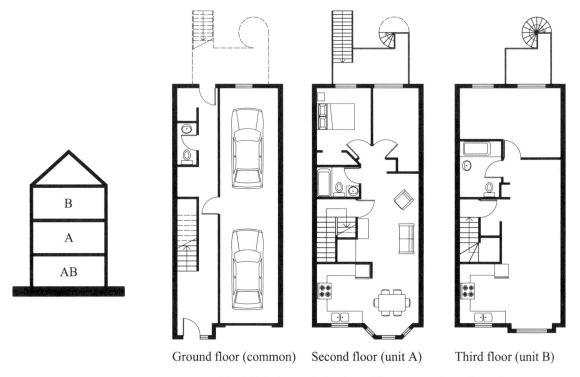

Ground floor (common)　　Second floor (unit A)　　Third floor (unit B)

Modified plans - A Duplex with rearranged configuration

design process, the cost of each unit could be tailored to the occupant's unique lifestyle and budget. For example, those who enjoyed cooking could select a larger, higher quality kitchen while those who preferred to eat out could save money by purchasing a modest one.

Spaces could be left largely unpartitioned, reducing costs, and buyers could finish the interiors at their own pace. Additionally, by regarding each townhouse as a three-story volume and then selling layers of that volume, buyers could select the number of layers that best fit their needs and budget. Some buyers purchased all three floors and then resided in one, leaving the other floors to be rented. This arrangement generated extra income and further diversified the potential occupants of the project, making dwellings available for short-term residents while ensuring that the buildings would be cared for by long-term owners.

The infill nature of the project also created opportunities for affordability. Because roads and a rear service lane already existed, infrastructure costs were reduced. A row house in the block's center along Saint-Antoine Avenue was preserved, adding to the quality of the street façade without incurring significant additional costs.

A Balancing Act

Name of Project: Cité-Jardin Fonteneau

Architect: Cardinal, Hardy and Associates Architects

Location: Northeast Montreal, Quebec, Canada

Site Area: 300,000 square feet (6.9 acres/2.8 hectares)

Number of Units: 110 (36 semidetached, 74 row houses)

Project Type: High-density urban infill

Density: Net: 48 units per acre (120 units per hectare), gross: 38.2 units per acre (94.4 units per hectare)

Road Area: 60,000 square feet (5,600 square meters) (20%)

Parking: On-street, individual garages (with individual access or shared access lane), and off-street, grouped parking

Unit Type: Single-family semidetached and row houses

Type of Ownership: Freehold and condominium

Cost: $70,000–$83,000 (C$93,000–$110,000) (47%), $96,000 (C$128,000) (38%), under $143,000 (C$190,000) (15%) (in 1992)

Cladding Materials: Brick and stucco

Users: low- to moderate-income households

Cité-Jardin Fonteneau is a 110-unit, affordable, single-family housing project in northeast Montreal. The design won a city-sponsored design and build competition in 1991 and was constructed in 1992. The project explores the ideals of the nineteenth-century Garden City concept, meshing public and private domains through the creation of a network of green spaces. Despite being located close to Sherbrooke Street, a major city arterial road, the project achieves a parklike sense of tranquility and attractiveness, while creating efficient and pleasant housing for low- to moderate-income families. As an infill project, Cité-Jardin Fonteneau succeeds in creating a smooth transition between the existing detached houses of the surrounding neighborhood. Also, the architects placed single-family, semidetached housing on the periphery of the project and increased the density in the center of the project, through short rows of houses. The project's circulation system proves exemplary, separating vehicular and

(a) Suspended deck over a parking entrance

(b) Pedestrian path

(c) Joseph-Rodier Street

(d) Narrow private street

(e) Facade of a row house

Figures 10.5a, b, c, d, and e The Cité-Jardin Fonteneau is a 110-unit, affordable, single-family housing project.

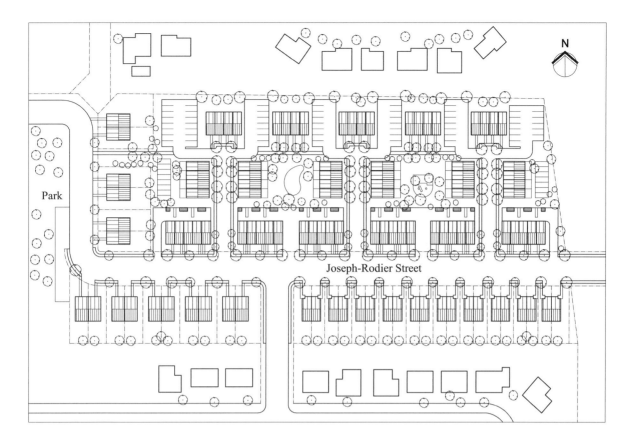

Park

Joseph-Rodier Street

N

pedestrian traffic and providing parking for every unit without creating unsightly lots or expensive underground garages. The project foregoes elaborate forms and finishes, focusing instead on the fundamentals: well-organized streets and open spaces, efficient and attractive parking, and well-proportioned rooms with access to natural light.
[Figures 10.5 and 10.6]

Figure 10.6 Site plan of Cité-Jardin Fonteneau. The semidetached dwellings are freehold-owned, and the occupants of the rows are associated as condominiums.

PLANNING CONSIDERATIONS

Much of the success of the Cité-Jardin Fonteneau project can be attributed to the architects' creation of a road and walkway scheme that separates pedestrian and vehicular traffic. This separation links different areas of a community together through a series of public green spaces and seeks to minimize the physical and visual presence of the automobile. Two distinct types of roads were proposed in Cité-Jardin Fonteneau: a main collector road and private streets. There is also a paved pedestrian path. Each of these serves a different purpose and adds to the organization and efficiency of the circulation within the community (Figure 10.7).

Joseph-Rodier Street, the collector, is 36 feet (11 meters) wide and accommodates parking on both sides. Although the street is slightly narrower than a typical residential main street, it is wide enough to permit on-street parking and two-way traffic. When informally surveyed, residents had few complaints about

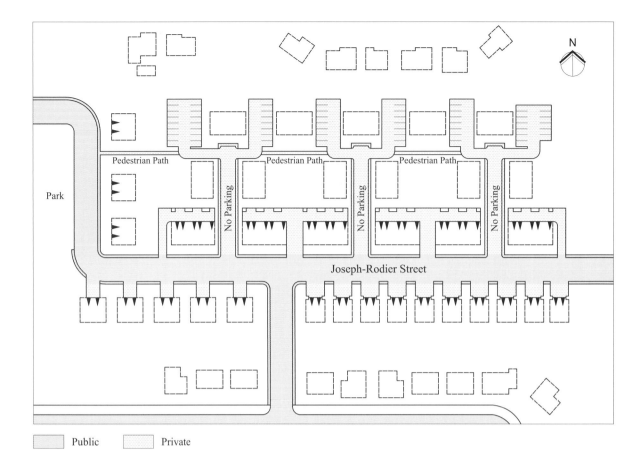

Park

Pedestrian Path

Pedestrian Path

Pedestrian Path

No Parking

No Parking

No Parking

Joseph-Rodier Street

N

Public   Private

Figure 10.7 Circulation network and parking in Cité-Jardin Fonteneau.

the narrowness of this street and believed that the parking on both sides alerted drivers to slow down because it visually reduced the street width. A sidewalk runs along the portion of the street that passes through the project, forming a clear indication of place and identifying this road's public nature. Trees planted along the sidewalk create an attractive streetscape that recalls the atmosphere of a traditional, urban neighborhood. Additionally, Joseph-Rodier Street is faced by three different unit types: semidetached, narrow semidetached, and row houses, which add variety and interest to the streetscape.

The second type of road in the Cité-Jardin Fonteneau project are the private roads that access the rear portion of the project. These roads are 18 feet (5.5 meters) wide with no sidewalks or on-street parking. This narrow width and lack of sidewalks and parking help to distinguish it from the more public Joseph-Rodier Street. Additionally, the narrow width helps to reduce construction costs and frees more land for housing and open spaces. It is these narrow private streets that make the entire layout of the project feasible by permitting innovative site planning and higher densities in the inner portion of the project. A pedestrian path is another means of circulation. The path runs parallel to Joseph-Rodier Street, providing access to green spaces, parking lots, and every residence without meeting the roads. When used in conjunction with one another, all these roads create an efficient and cost-effective network that not only contributes to the project's affordability but also to the community's appearance.

As housing density increases, so too does the number of parking stalls needed. This condition often leads to costly underground garages, large expanses of unsightly paved lots, and on-street parking that detracts from the streetscape. In the Cité-Jardin Fonteneau project, however, the architects effectively solved the problem of providing attractive parking for the 110 units with a ratio of 1.5 cars per dwelling unit with four prototype parking solutions.

The first type of parking in the project is individual garages in the basements of the semidetached houses. The semidetached houses are situated along the north and east sides of Joseph-Rodier Street and occupy a 60-foot-deep (18-meter-deep) stretch of land. This depth makes off-street parking behind the houses impossible, a solution considered to be cost-effective for affordable community design. Given the higher cost of a semidetached house, these homebuyers were assumed to be able to afford the additional expenses of an indoor garage (Zhang, 2002).

The second type of parking is the individual garage at the rear of each row, with a shared access driveway at the side. This solution is provided for the five clusters of row houses along the south side of Joseph-Rodier. In this solution, two rows of five units each share one access driveway to individual garages, reducing construction costs and dividing maintenance fees. This arrangement also places the garage doors at the rear and avoids a negative visual effect on the streetscape.

For dwellings that are not directly accessible from Joseph-Rodier, parking is provided in the form of off-street grouped parking on the southern edge of the project. This solution serves the lower cost dwellings by reducing construction cost and minimizing the stalls' negative visual impact on the project. The grouped parking is enclosed by the side walls of three rows of houses, preventing them from being seen from main street (Zhang, 2002). The final type of parking in Cité-Jardin Fonteneau is the on-street parking along Joseph-Rodier Street. This solution provides parking for visitors and families with a second car. The on-street parking not only provides a parking solution but also encourages motorists to decrease their speed and identifies its public nature.

While the project created a parklike environment that belies its urban setting, access to a thorough public transit system remains within walking distance of the project. Residents are a five-minute walk away from a subway station and a bus depot, which provides access to a transportation network that covers almost all of Montreal Island. In addition, there are many stores a short walking distance away, which lowers the need to rely on cars for daily shopping.

To achieve the desired densities, the open spaces were designed to provide maximum amenity for a small area. A large community park is located just west of the project, and the open spaces within the project are developed with this in mind, forming a well-balanced network (Figure 10.8). Two central courtyards constitute the main open spaces of the project, catering to types of residents who are less likely to use the larger park on a regular basis. One of these spaces provides a small play area for toddlers, with swings and a sandbox as well as several benches for parents. The other features a small pond with a waterfall. The play areas accommodate families with young children who may not wish to walk to the neighborhood park. The benches allow parents to supervise children comfortably. The pond, on the other hand, provides a peaceful area for the older res-

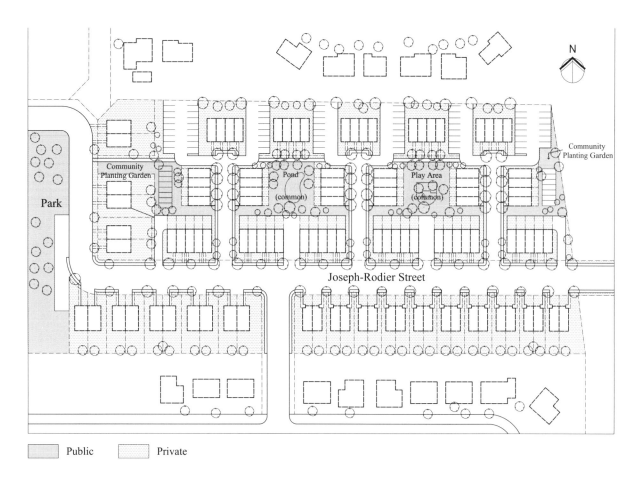

N

| | Public | | Private |

Figure 10.8 The open spaces provide a variety of amenities in this high-density project.

idents of the community to sit and read or to chat with neighbors. While each of these open spaces is quite small in size, they provide facilities for those most in need of outdoor space within the project. Older children can follow the pedestrian walkway to the community park, keeping noisier activities away from dwellings' backyards (Figure 10.9).

In addition to the courtyards, communal planting gardens are located at the east and west extremes of the project. Residents in the community can reserve a lot in a garden to plant and grow vegetables. These gardens have been very successful, providing a leisure activity that strengthens community bonds, as well as supplying inexpensive produce to residents.

Private outdoor spaces for individual units supplement the shared open spaces. The quality and quantity of this private space varies with the different housing types. The freehold semidetached homes have large backyards that can be accessed from the side. Many residents have chosen to fence in this outdoor area to increase its privacy. The row houses have a small deck or a concrete slab to accommodate a typical outdoor table and chairs, which is the function most residents have allotted to these spaces. A possible drawback to these areas is that they border the common spaces and thus possess little privacy. Some residents have addressed this concern by planting hedges or other tall plantings to screen the private area; however, most of these spaces remain open to the common courtyard.

(a) Play structure   (b) Pond

Figures 10.9a and b Clusters of row housing enclose communal and private open spaces.

The architects successfully created a strong sense of identity for the community as a whole and allowed residents to personalize the dwellings to some
degree. This sense of community is strongest at the project's center, off the public street, where residents take part in condominium ownership. A masonry wall
sign along the middle secondary access lane displays the developments' name,
creating a subtle demarcation between the public realm and the project. It is
interesting to note that the semidetached units are located beyond this sign,
reinforcing their more autonomous freehold status.

Cité-Jardin Fonteneau employs many strategies to create a sense of cohesiveness throughout the project. The part of Joseph-Rodier Street that runs through
the project is adorned with trees and streetlights that continue along the private
streets. A distinct and welcome absence of electric lines and posts can be noted
throughout the project, separating it from the surrounding area. The materials
and fenestration of the façades are treated in a manner that provides cohesiveness while avoiding monotony through a system of ordered variation in which
consistent forms, materials, and colors are repeated in a variety of ways. A uniform system clearly displays house numbers, and similar front entry stairs add
to the strong sense of identity of this community.

THE DWELLINGS

The combination of two types of ownership, freehold and condominium,
allowed the project to attract a diversity of residents. The condominium row
houses appeal to first-time homebuyers, such as young families and seniors who
previously rented, and provide them with lower-cost housing. The semidetached
houses attracted more established buyers, such as families with children, who
had some savings yet did not own a home before (Figure 10.10).

The project, with five different unit designs, was meant to meet the different
needs and budgets of different households. The interiors of Model A houses are
left unfinished, with minimal partitioning, exposed concrete block walls, and
unfinished flooring. These homes are the least expensive and are geared toward
young families, with or without children, who wish to finish the interior progres-

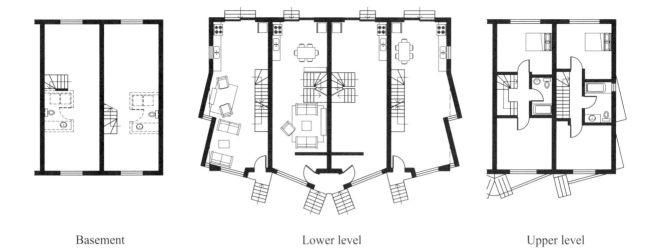

| Basement | Lower level | Upper level |

Figure 10.10 Floor plans for typical row house units.

sively themselves. In fact, part of the buyers' property legal obligations requires that they finish their interior. Model B, a finished version of Model A, was meant to attract young families who lack the time or desire to finish the interior. This model provides minimal partitioning, utilizing an open-plan concept.

Model C homes are designed for households who wish to have a garage and a large backyard. These homes are located along Joseph-Rodier Street in groups of five, with shared access to individual garages. The interior space has a more traditional organization, with a separate living room, dining room, and a kitchen in the rear that looks onto the backyard, providing easy surveillance of playing children. Model D also caters to young households who wish to obtain the level of autonomy normally associated with home ownership. The interior layout is similar to that of model C, with an adjustment for access to a front garage. Model E homes are designed to appeal to move-up buyers. These houses feature large backyards, individual garages, and a greater level of privacy than other homes in the project. By offering such a variety, the architects were able to appeal to a diversity of households, ensuring a community that is socially and economically diverse, vibrant, and integrated.

During the project's marketing phase, the buyers were offered a range of interior layouts and finishes. Front or back dormers in the attic were one of the features offered, and it currently serves as an architectural feature that fosters individual identity. In the interior, a number of residents have chosen to leave the joists exposed, contributing to a greater sense of spaciousness.

STRATEGIES FOR AFFORDABILITY

The architects employed a variety of strategies to ensure the affordability of Cité-Jardin Fonteneau while maintaining a high-quality living environment. Through careful site planning, densities could be increased in the inner portion of the project, while lower densities along the project's periphery created a smooth transition between the project and the surrounding single-family detached houses. By differentiating between collector roads and the private streets, road widths could be decreased accordingly and paving costs reduced. Incorporating a variety of parking solutions that corresponded to different income levels further reduced paving and helped enhance the visual quality of the community. Similarly, by providing different interior layouts and degrees of finishing, the dwellings appeal to a more socially and economically diverse market. The open spaces were carefully developed to provide the maximum benefit to the community while occupying a minimum amount of land, accommodating higher densities. By taking advantage of the site's proximity to ample public transportation, the project did not have to force extending roads, thereby preventing sprawl. Overall, the success and affordability of the Cité-Jardin Fonteneau project can be attributed to the architects' focus on maximizing the quality of the basic needs that form the foundation of a community, such as parking, roads, and quality outdoor spaces, and providing well-designed interior spaces that respond to the budgets and lifestyles of the residents.

Affordability by Process

Name: Benny Farm Redevelopment

Developer: Canada Lands Corporation (CLC), a government agency

Architect: Master plan by Saia and Barbarese Architects; unit designs by various architects, including the author assisted by Dong An, Min Shu, and Jiahui Wu

Location: Notre-Dame-de-Grace, Montreal, Quebec, Canada

Total Site Area: 18 acres (7.3 hectares)

Number of Units: 535 in total, design options for the author's section range from 89 to 125

Project Type: Urban infill, redevelopment

Density: 40–48 units per acre (99–144 units per hectare)

Parking: On-street, interior garages, outdoor rear parking, underground garages

Unit Type: Single-family row houses, duplexes, triplexes, two- or three-unit walk-ups

Unit Size: 700–1,400 square feet (65–130 square meters)

Cost: $53,000–$150,000 (C$70,000–$200,000) per unit, with a lower-cost majority

Cladding Materials: Brick, vinyl siding, stucco

Users: Low- to middle-income single persons and family households

BENNY FARM was built between 1946 and 1947 to house World War II veterans. Consisting of several walk-up apartments, the development had 312 units. The project stood out from the surrounding area due to its size, layout, and generous green spaces. As time passed, the housing ceased to meet the needs of veterans and failed to attract new occupants, eventually becoming largely abandoned. In the early 1990s, Canada Housing and Mortgage Corporation (CMHC), which had owned the land since 1947, announced plans to demolish the existing apartments and construct 1,200 rental units in six-story buildings. Local opposition to the plan arose, followed by Canada Lands Company's (CLC) purchase of the site in 1999. This Crown corporation is responsible for disposing of surplus federal property, and the corporation began construction of two more buildings on the site. A community task force organized and eventually a compromise was reached. CLC agreed to develop the site for low- to moderate-income households and sold several of the existing buildings to community and nonprofit organizations for renovations. The rest of the site will be developed according to a comprehensive master plan (Figures 10.11 and 10.12).

The author was one of the architects who was invited to participate in the design of a portion of the site, which focused on providing affordable market housing. Working within the layout set forth by the master plan, a study of the socioeconomic and architectural character of the surrounding neighborhoods was conducted to develop housing solutions that would prove affordable and fit

(a)

(b)

(c)

(d)

Figures 10.11 a, b, c, and d The Benny Farm project site is a mix of renovated and new infill, affordable housing development in the heart of an established neighborhood.

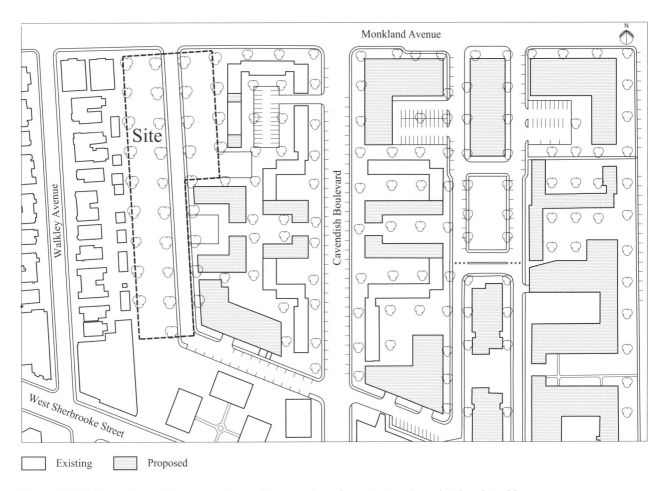

Figure 10.12 Benny Farm's Master Plan. The author's portion of the site is indicated with a dotted line.

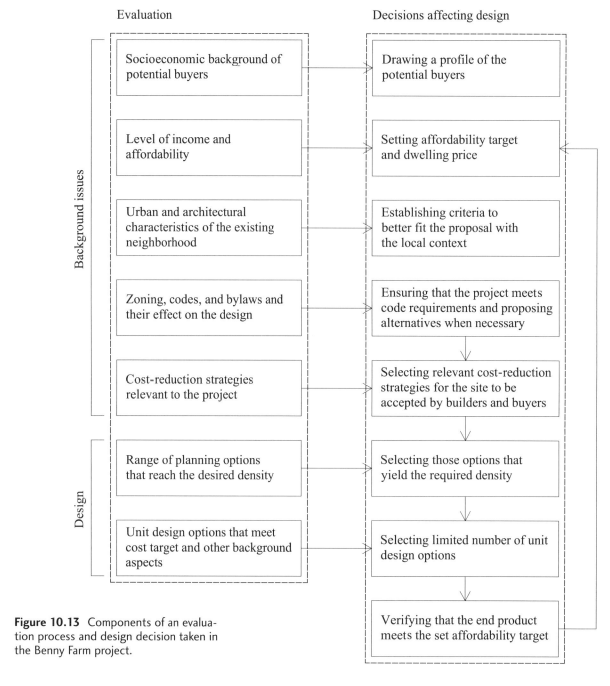

Evaluation

Decisions affecting design

Background issues

| Socioeconomic background of potential buyers | → | Drawing a profile of the potential buyers |

| Level of income and affordability | → | Setting affordability target and dwelling price |

| Urban and architectural characteristics of the existing neighborhood | → | Establishing criteria to better fit the proposal with the local context |

| Zoning, codes, and bylaws and their effect on the design | → | Ensuring that the project meets code requirements and proposing alternatives when necessary |

| Cost-reduction strategies relevant to the project | → | Selecting relevant cost-reduction strategies for the site to be accepted by builders and buyers |

Design

| Range of planning options that reach the desired density | → | Selecting those options that yield the required density |

| Unit design options that meet cost target and other background aspects | → | Selecting limited number of unit design options |

| | | Verifying that the end product meets the set affordability target |

Figure 10.13 Components of an evaluation process and design decision taken in the Benny Farm project.

the existing character of Notre-Dame-de-Graces (Figure 10.13). This segment outlines an approach to developing the different aspects of an affordable housing project, adhering to the most important design objectives while making compromises in other areas. The process is especially pertinent to infill projects, as the design had to fit into an existing set of project objectives laid out by the master plan, as well as the architectural framework of the surrounding community. After conducting a study, six different design alternatives were offered, each with its own advantages and drawbacks.

DRAWING PROFILES AND SETTING TARGETS

Prior to the project's planning and housing design, a systematic evaluation of socioeconomic characteristics was investigated to draw a profile of the potential homebuyers to address their needs (Figure 10.14). A household composition study demonstrated that the share of small, young families in the area is substantial. The proposed homes will also have to address the needs of seniors who constitute 19 percent of the population in the area. Studies also demonstrated that there is a high percentage of renters who may be interested in acquiring a unit. Additional aspects that were looked at were cost of homes sold most recently in the community, type of existing and new units currently offered, and the rents paid. The collected data helped draw a profile of a buyer for whom the design would be oriented.

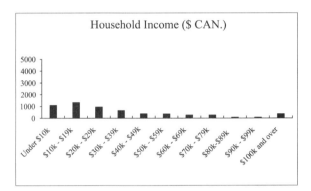

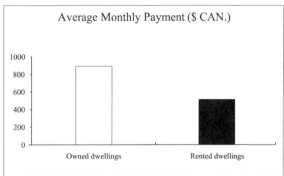

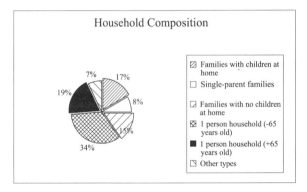

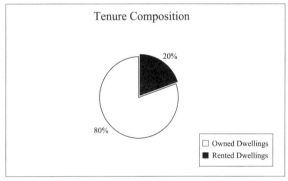

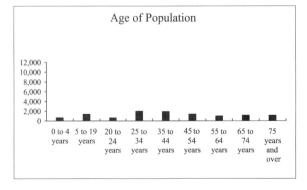

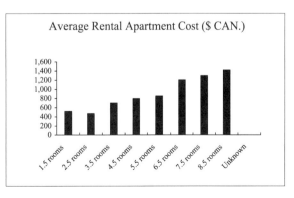

Figure 10.14 Socioeconomic factors that were studied to draw a profile of potential buyers.

Setting an affordable cost target was another necessary step. By examining the income of lower-end buyers and in consultation with the client, a range from $19,000 to $45,000 (C$25,000 to $60,000) was established. Based on these targets, and procedures used by private lenders that included an assumed down payment, the dwelling costs were determined. The target costs provided a first indication of the type and size of unit possible for the site based on a rough cost per unit area estimation.

In studying local zoning and bylaw requirements, the author was aware that the project would be submitted for city approval as a "planned unit development" (PUD). Despite the fact that current requirements can be altered, to avoid delays, attempts to adhere to as many zoning bylaws as possible was attempted. The aspects that were paid attention to included building width, building lines and setbacks, size of opening and dimensions of projections, and parking, which is a critical issue in high-density projects. Then several recommendations were made, a kind of zoning synthesis for the site.

Due to the infill nature of the Benny Farm project, the creation of a distinct identity was secondary to the project's assimilation into the surrounding area of Notre-Dame-de-Grace. To develop an accurate assessment of the architectural context of the site, a survey was conducted of the architectural character of the housing on the streets surrounding the site. Two main building types were identified as forming the area's building typology: the single-family dwelling and the duplex. The buildings can be further distinguished as detached or semidetached structures. As noted previously, the building heights and setbacks were also documented and taken into consideration when recommendations for these qualities in the new units were developed. This survey also examined the parking to provide solutions for the new units consistent with those of the surrounding area. Existing types included street parking, indoor front garages, rear parking structures with a shared driveway between buildings, and indoor parking with a side entrance.

The exterior building coverage in the surrounding area consisted of three main materials: brick, stucco, and stone. To maintain a degree of coherence with the larger community, the survey recommended that the new housing contain at least 80 percent masonry on the street-facing façade, excluding openings, in combination with a less-expensive cladding, such as stucco or vinyl siding, to reduce costs. Similarly, the buildings of the surrounding area frequently sprouted balconies. These balconies are an important part of Montreal and Notre-Dame-de-Grace dwelling culture and are commonly featured in the design of façades. Balconies, however, can be costly to construct. For the Benny Farm project, it was recommended that the builder offer buyers the option of a first- or second-story front balcony or, alternatively, a deck. Decisions about what will be offered should depend on the overall cost target.

Studying means and ways to reduce cost was the next aspect considered. There are several cost-reduction strategies, not all of which are applicable to any one location. Some depend on locally accepted traditions of building and others on what the builders believe the market will be receptive to. When potential cost-reduction strategies were listed for the Benny Farm area, the author undertook a similar process of identifying those most relevant measures that can bring costs down significantly. Some of these measures were considered "macro." They targeted the entire building and its surroundings. Other measures were considered "micro," since they investigated the dwelling interior and the building subcomponents.

The topics that were examined under the "macro" banner were the type of dwellings most suitable for the site, the effect of the unit's width on cost, the preferred number of grouped units, parking alternatives, whether to have a basement or not, and the type of roof to be chosen, and its use. In the "micro" category, the unit's level of interior completion, choice of number and location of wet services, and choice of façade coverage material were examined. The study also looked into the cost of balconies, the dwellings' interior layout, and the type and quality of finishes offered. By systematically laying out all the options and categorizing them, a selection was made among the strategies that would be most suitable for the project. Once the profile of most likely buyers was drawn up, their affordability targets set, local zoning studied, architectural context studied, and most suitable cost-reduction strategies selected, it was time to plan the site.

PLANNING CONSIDERATIONS

Six planning options, with gradually increasing densities, were prepared for the site (Figure 10.15). Three aspects were studied in each alternative: the type of units, parking solutions, and the amount of open spaces. These aspects will affect not only the cost of each unit but the community's curb appeal.

As density increases, attractive parking solutions for a project become more difficult to find. In lower-density options two and three, parking in an interior garage with front access was suggested, especially for single-family units, as this arrangement allows for a more attractive backyard area, and an individual interior garage is the preferred solution for single-family dwellings. It was noted that rear parking via an access lane is also a viable alternative for these units; however, this arrangement would compromise the quality of the backyards. For the triplex units in options two and three, some parking will also be outdoors at the rear.

In the fourth option, zipper lots were introduced to further increase densities. By increasing the efficiency of land use, however, less land is available for outdoor space, especially at the rear, and so parking access must be located at the front of units in interior garages. Front parking for narrow-front row houses leads to a large proportion of paving in front setbacks, creating a less attractive streetscape. In the fifth option, a larger portion of the west row is made up of duplexes and triplexes, creating a higher density and increasing the parking challenge. It was suggested that to maintain this higher density, all parking for units on the western side be outdoors at the rear. This solution comes at the expense of backyard space, which is significantly reduced. Option six increases density by augmenting the proportion of triplexes along the western side. As with the previous option, parking must be outdoors at the rear and access through a shared lane. Again, this solution comes at the expense of backyard space.

For all the options, parking for the walk-up apartments, along the eastern side of the project, will be located in underground garages, most of which will be accessed through a common driveway. This alternative is more expensive than

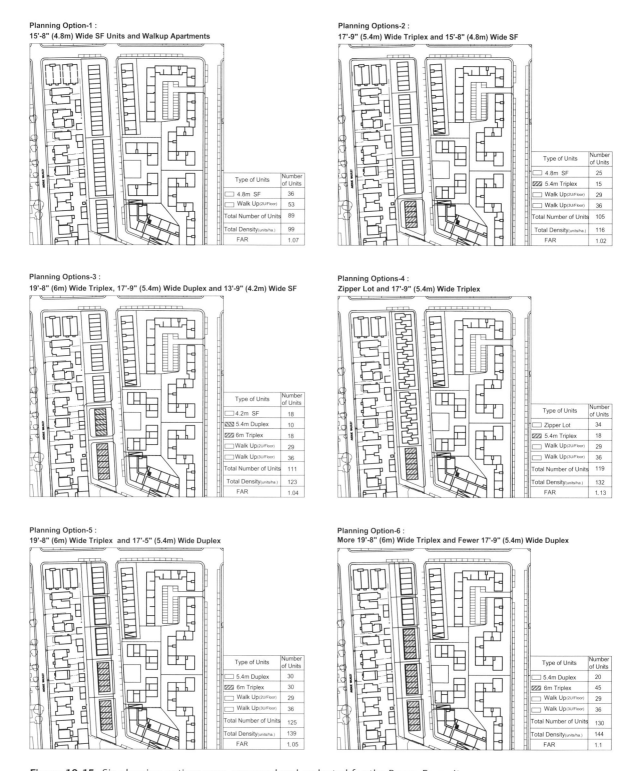

Planning Option-1:
15'-8" (4.8m) Wide SF Units and Walkup Apartments

Type of Units	Number of Units
4.8m SF	36
Walk Up(2U/Floor)	53
Total Number of Units	89
Total Density(units/ha.)	99
FAR	1.07

Planning Options-2:
17'-9" (5.4m) Wide Triplex and 15'-8" (4.8m) Wide SF

Type of Units	Number of Units
4.8m SF	25
5.4m Triplex	15
Walk Up(2U/Floor)	29
Walk Up(3U/Floor)	36
Total Number of Units	105
Total Density(units/ha.)	116
FAR	1.02

Planning Options-3:
19'-8" (6m) Wide Triplex, 17'-9" (5.4m) Wide Duplex and 13'-9" (4.2m) Wide SF

Type of Units	Number of Units
4.2m SF	18
5.4m Duplex	10
6m Triplex	18
Walk Up(2U/Floor)	29
Walk Up(3U/Floor)	36
Total Number of Units	111
Total Density(units/ha.)	123
FAR	1.04

Planning Options-4:
Zipper Lot and 17'-9" (5.4m) Wide Triplex

Type of Units	Number of Units
Zipper Lot	34
5.4m Triplex	18
Walk Up(2U/Floor)	29
Walk Up(3U/Floor)	36
Total Number of Units	119
Total Density(units/ha.)	132
FAR	1.13

Planning Option-5:
19'-8" (6m) Wide Triplex and 17'-5" (5.4m) Wide Duplex

Type of Units	Number of Units
5.4m Duplex	30
6m Triplex	30
Walk Up(2U/Floor)	29
Walk Up(3U/Floor)	36
Total Number of Units	125
Total Density(units/ha.)	139
FAR	1.05

Planning Option-6:
More 19'-8" (6m) Wide Triplex and Fewer 17'-9" (5.4m) Wide Duplex

Type of Units	Number of Units
5.4m Duplex	20
6m Triplex	45
Walk Up(2U/Floor)	29
Walk Up(3U/Floor)	36
Total Number of Units	130
Total Density(units/ha.)	144
FAR	1.1

Figure 10.15 Six planning options were proposed and evaluated for the Benny Farm site.

the others mentioned, but the cost is shared among a greater number of units, and this solution effectively conceals vehicles underground, allowing generous open spaces to be developed despite the higher densities.

The layout of open spaces for the entire project was largely determined by the master plan. Open spaces for each dwelling, however, in the form of private backyards or balconies were decided by the unit design and the corresponding parking solutions for each option. The main challenge in designing the open spaces for the individual units was providing adequate parking for units as well. As discussed above, providing rear entry to parking garages reduces usable backyard space. Also, the introduction of outdoor rear parking virtually eliminates the backyard altogether.

A compromise between parking solutions and private outdoor space had to be reached through the unit design. By recommending front-access parking in the form of interior garages for single-family dwellings, the design ensured that users who have a great need for private outdoor space will have it, even if the streetscape is somewhat impaired. For multifamily units, backyard space is less practical as it usually serves only the ground-floor occupants. For these dwellings, rear parking is recommended, and private outdoor space can be provided through decks and balconies.

DWELLING DESIGN

To reach the project's affordability targets, several dwelling design principles were followed. The unit size was minimized, and their layout maintained simple, rectangular footprints. Additionally, the buildings were designed taller rather than wider. This narrow frontage allowed a greater number of units to share infrastructure costs. The structures were joined together in groups that were small enough to avoid visual monotony but allowed significant cost-savings through shared walls and energy conservation (Figure 10.16).

Innovative measures were taken to reduce costs within the building envelope as well. Buyers were offered a choice of dwelling layouts and interior finishes that could be tailored to their individual needs and budgets. Offering these options in a menu form facilitated the selection process by making choices clear and accessible. Furthermore, some interior spaces could be left unfinished and completed when the buyer had sufficient time and money. Back-to-back wet functions and plumbing further reduced interior costs.

To achieve maximum suitability, both the entire project and the units were regarded as a flexible system. Reversibility was a principal guideline in all of the proposed designs, allowing kitchens to be placed in the front or rear of the dwellings. In the 20-foot (6-meter) wide triplex and the three-units-per-story walk-up apartments, buyers could purchase two floors or adjacent units that could be combined to form a single dwelling. It was also recommended and demonstrated that arrangements be made to house occupants with reduced mobility.

While not a primary focus of this project, several qualities of all of the design options contributed to energy conservation. The units' small sizes led to a reduction in energy consumption. All of the structures possess varying degrees of attachment with those around them, minimizing exterior wall exposure, which

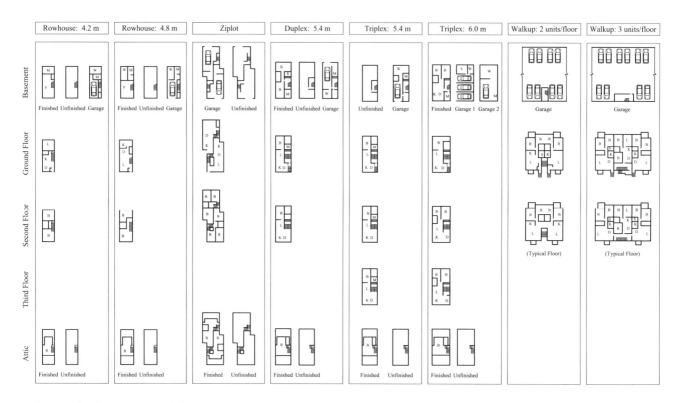

Figure 10.16 Prototypes of the Benny Farm project's selected dwellings and their interior layout options.

reduces heat loss. In addition, the master plan calls for trees to be planted around the dwellings to create shade in the summer leading to reductions in cooling costs, since the trees act as a wind break in wintertime.

STRATEGIES FOR AFFORDABILITY

The Benny Farm project was a systematic investigation of a wide range of cost-reduction strategies. The most effective strategies in this project, however, were those that reduced the width of buildings, favored multifamily housing types over single-family types, built units in groups, and parked cars outdoors. By building up rather than out, infrastructure costs were shared among more units. Keeping the footprint of dwellings a simple rectangle reduced construction costs and allowed for a more flexible interior. By leaving a portion of the interior unfinished, the initial cost of a unit can be reduced, and homeowners can take an active role in completing and personalizing their home as means become available.

The systematic identification of the buyers' socioeconomic characteristics and the setting of affordability targets were instrumental parts of the project's design. In fact, the client had to withdraw the original idea of building single-family townhouses. Instead, multifamily duplexes and triplexes were chosen, which made the project accessible to a wider range of lower-income households.

A Walkable Neighborhood

Name of Project: Quartier Jardins

Developer: Immobilière du Chemin du Golf Ltée.

Architects: Avi Friedman and Jean-Pierre Lagace

Location: L'Assomption, Quebec, Canada

Site Area: 102 acres (41 hectares)

Number of Units: 889

Project Type: New medium-high-density community

Density: gross: 9.66 units per acre (23.88 units per hectare)

Road Area: 1,245,000 square feet (115,636 square meters) (28% of the total area)

Parking: Outdoor group lots, individual interior garages, outdoor front

Unit Type: Single-family (80), semidetached (284), triplexes (48), duplexes (60), row houses (297), other (120)

Unit Size: 900–2,000 square feet (85–185 square meters)

Cost: $90,000–$100,000 (C$120,000–$130,000) for single family, $60,000–$90,000 (C$80,000–$120,000) for an apartment at time of construction (2002)

Cladding Materials: Masonry, siding

Users: Varied, majority expected to be first-time homebuyers

L'ASSOMPTION is a town, with a population of 16,000, east of Montreal Island. The Assomption River forms a loop that surrounds the community. From its founding in the middle of the nineteenth century, the town provided commercial and administrative services to the surrounding farms. With a steady shift away from an agricultural lifestyle and as a result of increased demand for housing in neighboring cities, many, primarily young, first-time homebuyers are looking to settle in L'Assomption.

A local private developer who owned a large plot decided to build a new community, where the majority of buyers, it was assumed, would be young households. They would be joined by retirees who in the coming years might sell a large single-family home in town and move into a condominium apartment. The need to lower housing cost required increased density. Yet the rural character of the area demanded that a good balance be established between the newly built neighborhood and the surrounding environment. The size of the development and its ultimate number of occupants permitted design of a self-contained community with its own services and amenities, such as a school, shopping facilities, play area, and library.

The design of the Quartier Jardins embodies an alternative to typical suburban design. In fact the impetus for this project was a private builder's desire for a walkable, market-friendly alternative to traditional suburban development. This project is an attempt to demonstrate that affordable housing need not only respond to economic necessity but can also accommodate changing societal trends (Figure 10.17).

PLANNING CONSIDERATIONS

The creation of an efficient and attractive circulation system proved crucial in the design of Quartier Jardins. Several strategies were used to minimize the presence of the automobile and ameliorate the road's appearance and efficiency. The most noticeable departure from a traditional street layout was a series of looped cul-de-sacs along the northwest portion of the project. These cul-de-sacs are designed to separate a majority of dwellings from through-traffic in order to create a safer and more attractive environment. A small green space that can function as a garden or a play area for children occupies the center of each of these loops. This arrangement allows vehicles to enter and to exit the housing clusters safely without having a large paved area that detracts from the community's curb appeal.

The roads along the southern portion of the site were designed to point to important features of the neighborhood. On their south end, the roads lead to L'Assomption River and a proposed commercial center. To the north, the roads lead to a large open space that will serve as a community park and, ultimately, a local school. Many of the cul-de-sacs in the plan also point to this central open space, establishing its importance within the community. This centralized park and school location also ensures that they will be within walking distance for all residents. A path running east to west, through the southern portion of the site, creates a pedestrian network through open spaces and away from vehicular traffic.

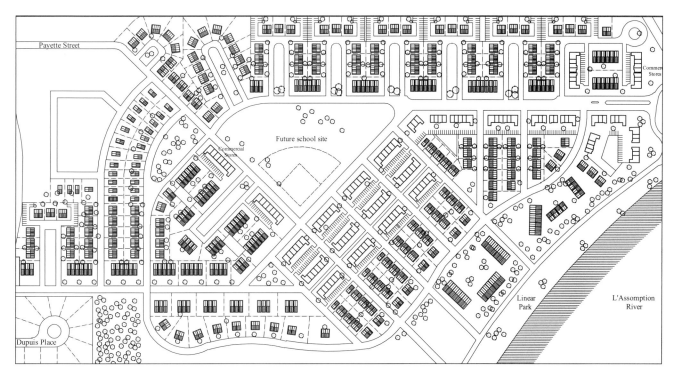

Text labels within the image:
Payette Street
Future school site
Commercial Stores
Commercial Stores
Dupuis Place
Linear Park
L'Assomption River

Figure 10.17 Site plan of Quartier Jardins.

The proposed plan also reduces the presence of the automobile by using a variety of parking alternatives that successfully "hide the car" while maintaining the project's affordability. Indoor parking was designed in many of the semidetached houses, as occupants would be expected to own at least one car and able to afford the extra cost of an interior garage. Some semidetached houses have outdoor front parking for families who cannot afford interior garages. Similarly, in a typical group of four row houses, some interior garages were offered. When front access to parking was provided, the proportion of the paving in the front setback was reduced, making the sidewalks safer and increasing curb appeal.

Multifamily dwellings, duplexes, and triplexes have exterior group parking, which corresponds to the lower unit costs of the multifamily dwellings. The solution was carefully arranged to ensure that no dwelling looked onto a parking lot. Additionally, group lots were located out of sight from the streets, preserving an attractive streetscape and maintaining the project's curb appeal. The lots were distributed with enough frequency to ensure practical walking distances from cars to dwellings while preventing paved areas from dominating the landscape.

Due to its rural location, only a limited amount of public transportation exists outside of the town's center of L'Assomption. The major roads that surround the proposed site are serviced by local bus routes, which provide transportation into town several times daily. Once in town, transit hubs provide more extensive bus routes within the town and the surrounding area. As the project develops, it is assumed that higher frequency bus service will be integrated into the community.

The project also seeks to ease general reliance on the automobile. The unit designs facilitate home offices, largely allowing more people to work from home. The layout of the project places important destinations centrally in the plan and puts key spaces within walking distance of all units.

Two types of open spaces were designed in Quartier Jardins: a large communal park and the open spaces close to the housing clusters. The central open space serves as a large park; ultimately a school will be built on a portion of the area, along with playing fields. This space serves as a focal point for the community and facilitates activities that require a large open area, such as children's sports and games. The open spaces at the center of housing clusters and the green area of the cul-de-sacs provide more private open spaces that can be supervised from individual units. These spaces were conceived as places for young children's play as well as the pleasure of older residents. As construction of the project progresses, more public green spaces will be developed.

The public and semiprivate open spaces are augmented by private outdoor spaces for most of the dwellings. Units on the ground floor have access to private decks or backyard areas. Some units without ground floor access have private terraces or balconies that provide outdoor space that is more appropriate for small households in an affordable housing project.

The project incorporates several design features that ensure a strong sense of identity on both the community and unit levels. Most of the units, which vary in size and type, have façades of masonry cladding, giving a sense of cohesiveness to the project as a whole. Within this material, however, buyers will be able to select from a variety of colors, allowing for a degree of personalization that adds visual interest to the streetscape without detracting from the overall cohesion.

The school and central park area will become a communal focal point used by most of the residents, whether through recreation at the park or attendance at school. The smaller open spaces particular to housing clusters, on the other hand, foster a local, more intimate sense of identity for the residents of each cluster. With these spaces, residents can select their landscaping, allowing a greater sense of ownership and personalization to develop.

THE DWELLING UNITS

Unlike common suburban housing typology and to increase the project's potential market, Quartier Jardins was designed to accommodate gracefully a variety of housing types. Unlike the neighboring suburban developments that offered only single-family detached housing, this project strives to incorporate various unit types that appeal to the demographic composition and budgets of today's diverse households. The housing types range from a small number of single-family detached and semidetached houses to multifamily row houses, duplexes, and triplexes.

The different housing types are distributed throughout the project in a manner that ensures the intermixing of unit types and a smooth transition between the project and the adjacent neighborhoods. The project's density is highest along the main roads and around the central school and park area. In the school-park area, the row houses and multiplexes frame the park in a manner that increases the park's appeal and provides the units with excellent views. Furthermore, the large open space of the park reduces the visual impact of the higher-density buildings. Beyond the "inner ring" of high-density unit types, the density decreases to semidetached houses. These units provide a greater degree of autonomy than the row houses and multiplexes, even as they share common areas with nearby multifamily housing types. Along the western side of the project that abuts the existing development, single-family detached and semidetached units provide a gradual decrease in density that prevents visual tension between the new and the old from developing.

The variety of unit types allows a greater demographic diversity of buyers to live in the same community. Young couples wishing to start a family can purchase a semidetached house that offers the same advantages as a typical suburban home—e.g., interior garage, backyard, and basement—while maintaining a greater degree of affordability. More established households can upgrade to a detached house and enjoy the benefits of living in a more diverse community, and singles can begin their experience of homeownership with smaller, more affordable units.

The units were designed to allow for flexibility and adaptability, and as a result, affordability. For each of the different unit types, a typical module was created. By creating a module that facilitated changes, adaptability could be maintained while the cost of customization was avoided. In a typical row house

Basement

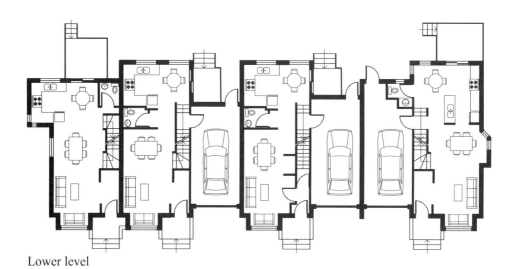

Lower level

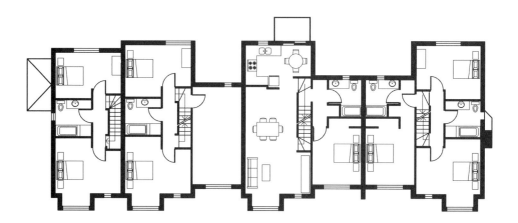

Upper level

Figure 10.18 Floor plans of a typical single-family, row-house unit.

group, four or five modules were repeated, each with an interior layout that can be determined by a buyer. Buyers purchase a slice of the group and are given the option of purchasing a "link," which provided the project and the buyer with an added degree of flexibility in terms of both spatial arrangements and costs. At the ground level, this link can become a garage, providing individual interior parking and extra storage space for a unit. Since indoor parking is not required by the city, this space can also become a home office. The second story of the link can function as a home office if the ground floor link is being used as a garage. For families with children, the upper story of the link can be turned into a master suite, freeing the second story for children's bedrooms and a separate bathroom (Figures 10.18 and 10.19).

These links also offer the possibility of two-generations housing. Families who cannot afford to or choose not to place their parents into nursing homes can invite them to live with them. The link creates a unique opportunity to provide a home for an elderly parent that facilitates regular care but maintains a distinction between family spaces, becoming a sort of "granny flat."

Similar design options were available for the semidetached and multiplex units. In all dwellings, buyers had the opportunity to select from several interior layout options Several options for size and layout of kitchens and bathrooms were offered, including space-finishing alternatives. With this information and flexibility, buyers could prioritize different elements and areas of their home, achieving a higher degree of personalization and satisfaction while ensuring affordability.

Figure 10.19 A typical single-family row house.

The design of Quartier Jardins also employs several energy-saving strategies. As with other affordable housing projects discussed above, the attached and semiattached nature of many of the units results in a reduction of exposed exterior walls, which reduces heat loss and therefore energy consumption. Four blocks along the southern portion of the site capitalize on direct southern exposure, which can increase their passive solar gain potentials. Additionally, the streets in this portion of the development that runs north to south allow cool river breezes to penetrate into the community center, helping to maintain a cooler microclimate within the development in summertime.

STRATEGIES FOR AFFORDABILITY

Although this project employs a variety of strategies to increase affordability, its lower land cost and high density is most responsible for keeping units' prices down. By utilizing long, narrow lots instead of more square ones, infrastructure costs could be shared among more dwellings, greatly reducing costs. These long, narrow lots lend themselves to narrow-front row houses and semi-detached dwellings, which reduces the need to spread out horizontally. This spatial configuration lowers foundation and roofing costs and makes the homes affordable. Within the individual units, flexibility in layout and finishing permits a greater degree of buyer participation without raising costs and leads to dwellings that satisfy buyers' needs while fitting comfortably within their budgets.

The project's master plan also contributes to the overall affordability of the project by keeping costs low and curb appeal high. Cost-efficient outdoor group parking lots are provided for many of the units. By ensuring that no units face these lots and that they are surrounded by vegetation, however, the group lots are able to provide affordable parking without detracting from the quality of the project's open space. By preserving existing trees and vegetation and placing maintenance responsibilities into the hands of the condominium associations, Quartier Jardins will reduce landscaping costs and achieve a gardenlike quality.

Name of Project: Quartier du Parc Madaire

Developer/Builder: Jag-Do Construction

Architects: Avi Friedman, David Morin, Francois Dufaux

Location: Aylmer, Quebec, Canada

Site Area: 345,700 square feet (32,120 square meters)

Number of Units: 119

Project Type: High density, urban infill

Density: Gross: 15 units per acre (37 units per hectare), net: 25.7 units per acre (63.5 units per hectare)

Road Area: 101,700 square feet (9,451 square meters)

Parking: Outdoor parking in rear lots (9.57% of total area), individual interior garages

Unit Type: Row houses, triplexes, and semidetached houses

Unit Size: Row houses 1,500 square feet (140 square meters), including basement

Cost: $51,500 (C$68,000) (in 1991)

Cladding Materials: Masonry, vinyl siding

Users: Primarily first-time homebuying households

THE SITE IS LOCATED within the former village of Deschênes, which is now part of the City of Aylmer, in the province of Quebec, Canada. The site was developed during World War I and housed the employees of the British North American Nickel Company plant. The homes in the village of Deschênes were largely self-built by their occupants, most of whom worked at the plant, and consisted of cottages and single-story homes. Despite the regular gridlike plan, the settlement grew informally as witnessed by the irregular setbacks and lot dimensions (Figure 10.20).

In the 1980s, years after the plant closed, the brownfield site was purchased by a developer who replaced the contaminated topsoil and changed its zoning to residential. Located across the river from Canada's capital Ottawa, Ontario, the developer recognized a need for affordable housing in the area. Therefore, the design team was asked to propose a neighborhood with density and a number of units that would generate a home with a lower price tag.

From the outset, the developer and the architects encountered resistance to the project's introduction. The objections were voiced mostly by neighboring residents and their elected representatives. The design process became a tale of resisting NIMBY sentiments and seeking a compromise while still providing affordable housing.

Figure 10.20 Aerial photo of the site and its neighboring homes. The Ottawa River runs south of the site.

THE APPROVAL PROCESS

The approval process of new projects in the City of Aylmer is similar to other towns in the province of Quebec. A citizens' committee made up of elected community representatives needed to review and approve each project. Their recommendation is then passed on to the city's Planning Committee, which is made up of elected city councillors and representatives of the planning department. Once approved at this level, the project had to get a final go-ahead in a city council meeting clearing the way for enacting it as a bylaw.

The project was designed and submitted as a PUD. There were very few bylaws related to the site, which included primarily road width and parking requirements. It was, therefore, up to the designers to suggest a master plan and design for the units. The first plan was made of 149 14-foot (4.3-meters) wide units, arranged in rows. The design called for narrow streets, reduced setbacks, and common outdoor parking.

At a presentation to the Citizens' Committee, the design was rejected outright. The formal reason for the rejection was that the existing community, its road and infrastructure, could not accommodate a project of such high density. The unofficial reasoning, as was voiced by some committee members, was that buyers of affordable housing were also bound to be on social assistance and would not contribute to the community's well-being. Once blocked at this level, the proposal was rejected by the higher authority Planning Committee. Luckily, the developer was willing to persist and suggested that more options be prepared.

In meetings with the local city planner, several changes were recommended. They included reduction of density. The structure's width, still built in a row, was expanded from 14 feet to 17 feet (4.3 meters to 5.2 meters), the front setback was also slightly enlarged from 10 feet to 15 feet (3 meters to 4.5 meters). The city planners also suggested that the 10 percent public open space would be arranged as a park, open to the community at large, which may have eased objections to the project. Triplex structures have been suggested around the park and semidetached on the northern edge. Those changes brought the average price tag from $49,000 to $51,500 (C$65,000 to $68,000), still affordable in the Aylmer area.

Over a period of 12 months, several additional planning options were prepared, and presented to the Citizens' Committee until a final scheme was approved. The principal conclusion of the process is that compromise can be reached if there is a dialogue and collaboration between the parties. It requires more work on the part of the designers as well as an understanding of citizens' concerns. Many meetings were held with community groups in Aylmer. The meeting had educational objectives, and they meant to persuade concerned neighbors that affordable homes and their occupants do not pose risks of any kind to them or their property (Figure 10.21).

PLANNING CONSIDERATIONS

Although a wide right of way, from 49 to 66 feet (15 to 20 meters) is common in the village, the streets were only paved to a width of 23 feet (7 meters), and there

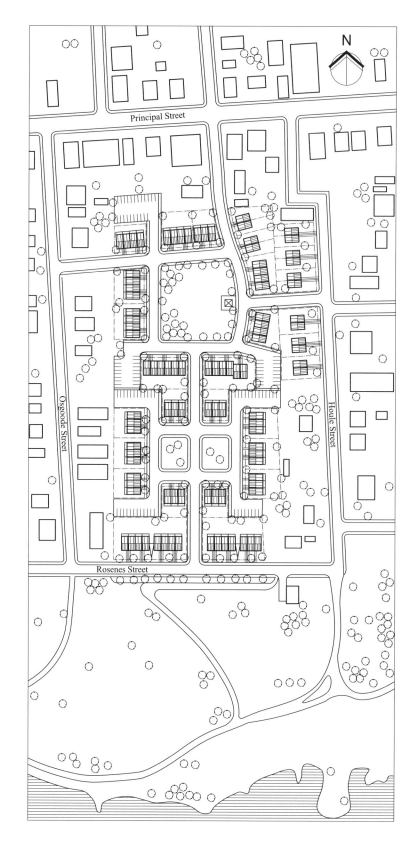

Figure 10.21 Site plan of Le Quartier du Parc Madaire.

are no sidewalks. As stipulated in the project's objectives, the design team incorporated this pattern of relatively narrow streets into their design proposals. The resulting project contains a series of narrow roads with sidewalks, which help to heighten a walkable environment. The narrowness of the roads also reduced construction costs for the project and created a more pedestrian- and children-friendly environment, as narrow roads tend to reduce vehicular speed. Additionally, the fragmented nature of the circulation layout discouraged through-traffic within the community.

Several parking solutions were offered in the design of Quartier du Parc Madaire. They vary in accordance with the different housing types. The more expensive semidetached houses have individual interior garages. As semidetached housing is more expensive than the other types offered in this project, these buyers are also expected to be able to afford the extra construction costs incurred with an interior garage. The row houses are provided with outdoor group parking in four shared lots. The lots are carefully located to provide convenient and efficient parking while detracting as little as possible from the overall visual environment. Although outdoor surface parking has a negative stigma, its low cost adds to the project's affordability and measures are taken to ensure that it does not detract from the project's visual quality. The row houses are positioned to minimize the number that face the parking lots, and landscaping further ameliorates this solution. The triplexes have a limited number of interior garage spaces and three surface parking lots. As with the lots for the row houses, the triplex lots were placed on the periphery of the site to minimize any negative effects that they might otherwise have on the project. These lots also succeed in drawing traffic and vehicles in general away from the central park areas of the community.

The sequencing of open spaces was a key consideration in the design of Le Quartier du Parc Madaire. Proper planning of private and outdoor spaces can encourage social interaction and increase a collective sense of security among community members. Accessing the public realm by moving directly from a private unit to the street by passing through semiprivate courtyard spaces can drastically affect individual maintenance costs, user satisfaction, and isolation from the surrounding areas. The large, central open spaces seek to provide a gathering place to all community members. To make this sense of openness available to all, the spaces are set apart from individual units by roads. This location requires that all residents cross a public road before entering the park, preventing certain areas of the project from feeling a greater sense of ownership. The central park is surrounded by taller triplexes that create a feeling of enclosure and security, while also mitigating the building's large size.

Complementary to the public open spaces, smaller semiprivate courtyards are scattered between clusters of row houses. They create intimate areas that are to be used primarily by residents in the surrounding units. In addition to the semiprivate spaces, most units are provided with private space in the form of a deck or balcony. To enhance a sense of identity, a limited range of brick colors was chosen so that each cluster of rows had its own character.

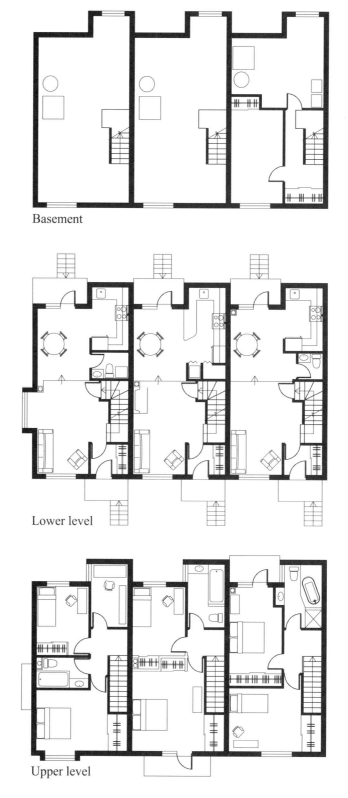

Basement

Lower level

Upper level

Figure 10.22 Floor plans of a typical row-house unit.

DWELLING DESIGN

All of the row housing units in Le Quartier du Parc Madaire employ "Grow Home" principles. The units' narrow fronts were instrumental in reducing the cost of expensive land and infrastructure. Within the dwellings, space is used efficiently, and partitions are minimized (Figure 10.22). Back-to-back plumbing fixtures also help to reduce costs. The lower level of multilevel units were left unpartitioned and, if the buyer chooses, unfinished, reducing the unit cost by another $3,800 (C$5,000) at the time of sale.

Although great efforts were made to reduce construction costs, certain high-quality products were introduced into the units to achieve a greater overall value. Quality kitchen cabinets enhanced the appeal of this critical area of the units, and better vinyl or tile floors similarly improved the bathrooms. Buyers were also offered choices in the layout and interior finishes. These choices were aimed at accommodating different budgets and increasing buyer satisfaction. Among these choices were a first-level powder room and a cantilevered bay window for end units, which added space and character to the living area without significantly increasing the dwelling's price tag.

To reduce costs, the building envelope is essentially a simple rectangle in shape. This form was modified, however, at the rear of the unit where the façade projects outward. This projection serves several functions. On the ground level, it creates a nook for the kitchen counter, increasing its efficiency. On the upper floor, it provides extra space for the bathroom. This bump-out also creates a protected niche for the back porch, providing more privacy for users. Some residents have made a postoccupancy decision to place a roof over this area, further enhancing its sense of protection and intimacy.

Strategies were also employed in Le Quartier du Parc Madaire to create identity on both the individual and community level. Within each unit, buyers were offered a variety of options to personalize the unit to their individual lifestyle and budget. On the exterior, different aspects of the uniform base unit, as expressed in different façade designs, could be altered to avoid monotony and further promote individuality among residents, such as dormer style and paint color (Figure 10.23).

STRATEGIES FOR AFFORDABILITY

Several design strategies contributed to the affordability of Le Quartier du Parc Madaire. The most important of these, however, proved to be its high density. By sharing land and infrastructure costs among a greater number of units, the overall unit price was significantly reduced. The buildings' footprints were also minimized and kept rectangular in shape, reducing construction costs for the foundation and roof. The attached nature of the units further eased construction costs and helped to conserve and to lower energy bills. The units were designed to be flexible in both layout and cost, making them affordable to a broader range of homebuyers. Funds were invested in key areas of the home, such as the kitchen and bathrooms, to increase significantly the quality of the living environment for the smallest increase in cost. Certain areas of the home,

Figure 10.23 Clusters of row-house units in Le Quartier du Parc Madaire.

mainly the basement, could be left unfinished, to be completed at a later time by the owner. Above-ground parking lots provided inexpensive parking for all the units on the site, and landscaping effectively minimized their visual impact.

KEY CONSIDERATIONS

- By choosing a site with a lower land cost, taking advantage of existing infrastructure, and selecting a dwelling unit where buyers can purchase the quantity of space that they need and can afford as well as participate in the choice of their interior finishes, the initiators of Le Carré Saint-Antoine achieved affordability.
- By balancing the areas allocated to public and private open spaces, creating a network of public and private roads, introducing a variety of parking solutions, proposing a mix of freehold and condominium ownership, allowing buyers to purchase dwellings with unfinished space, and offering them a menu of interior options, the initiators and the architects of Cité Jardin Fonteneau were able to achieve both affordability and curb appeal in this high-density community.

- The Benny Farm design followed a process that was meant to ensure that the homes built would address the economic and demographic profiles of the target users. By listing and evaluating cost reduction strategies, developing a range of planning and dwelling options and verifying their cost implications against a preset affordability target, the design objective was reached.

- Quartier Jardins' design is a demonstration that affordability and sustainability need not be opposing objectives. By building communal amenities, such as school and commerce in the neighborhood, creating a network of pedestrian paths and streets that lead to them, proposing housing prototypes that let people work from home, allowing bi-generational dwelling accommodation, a self-contained community with less reliance on cars was proposed.

- The Quartier du Parc Madaire project demonstrated how, through persistence, design flexibility, and compromise, NIMBY sentiments can be overcome. By maintaining a dialogue with the opposing side, involving local planning and elected officials, amending the design, and creating amenities that serve both the existing neighborhood and the new development, construction of affordable housing can begin and succeed.

Bibliography

Alexander, C., S. Ishikawa, and M. Silverstein. *A Pattern Language: Towns, Buildings, Construction.* New York: Oxford University Press, 1977.

Allen, E. *Fundamentals of Building Construction Material and Methods.* New York: John Wiley & Sons, 1990.

An, D. *Cost Effective Building Forms for Affordable Homes* (Unpublished M.Arch. Report). McGill University School of Architecture, Montreal, 2003). Advisor: Avi Friedman.

Archer, J. The Problem with Parking at Medium and High Density Housing, *Habitat*, 24, 2 (1981): 4–9.

Arendt, R. G. *Conservation Design for Subdivision.* Washington, D.C.: Island Press, 1996.

Bradford, S. "For Starters." *Builders*, January (1991):170.

Builder. "Framing Alternatives." February (1993).

Calthorpe, P. *The Next American Metropolis.* Princeton Architectural Press, 1993.

Canada Mortgage and Housing Corporation (CMHC). *Habitable Attics*, 1991.

———. *Making a Molehill Out of a Mountain II: Implementing the Three R's in Residential Construction.* Ottawa, 1991.

———. *Parking Advisory Document.* Ottawa, 1980.

———. *Residential Site Development Advisory Document*, Ottawa, 1981.

Canada Mortgage and Housing Corporation (CMHC). *New Made-to-Convert Housing.* Ottawa, ON, 1988.

Canadian Banker's Association, The. *Mortgage Wise: A Guide for Home Buyers*, 1984.

Carstens, D. Y. "Housing and Outdoor Spaces for the Elderly." in *People Places: Design Guidelines for Urban Open Spaces*, C. Cooper Marcus and C. Francis, eds. New York: Van Nostrand Reinhold, 1992.

Childs, C. M., *Parking Spaces: A Design Implementation and Use Manual for Architects, Planners and Engineers.* New York: McGraw-Hill, 1999.

City of Toronto. "Toronto Urban Design Guidelines: Infill Townhouses." Toronto: City of Toronto Urban Development Services, 2003.

Conrad, T. *Small Spaces: Inspiring Ideas and Creative Solutions.* New York, NY: Clarkson Potter/Publishers, 2001.

Dear, M. "Understanding and Overcoming the NIMBY Syndrome." *Journal of the American Planning Association*, Vol. 58, No. 3, Summer 1992.

Deng, J. *The Alley and Affordable Housing in Montreal* (Unpublished M.Arch. Report). McGill University, School of Architecture, Montreal, 2003. Advisor: Avi Friedman.

Diamond, J. "Residential Density and Housing Form," *Journal of Architectural Education*, Vol. 3, February, 1976.

Department of Municipal Affairs, Province of Prince Edward Island. *Residential Subdivision Design Handbook.* 1979.

Devereaux, W. and S. Bradford. "Natural Causes." *Builder*, July, 1991.

Duany, A., E. Plater-Zyberk, and J. Speck. *Suburban Nation: The Rise of Sprawl and the Decline of the American Dream.* New York: North Point Press, 2000.

Energy, Mines and Resources, Canada (EMR). *Heating and Cooling with Heat Pump.* Ottawa, 1989.

England, J. "Residential Land and Prices in the City." *Habitat*, Vol. 23, No. 3, 1980.

Fine Homebuilding. "More than One Way to Plumb a System." February/March, 2003.

Fisher, S. *Landscape Alternatives for Cost Savings and Resource Conservation in Medium Density Housing* (Unpublished M.Arch. Thesis) McGill University, School of Architecture, Montreal, 1994. Advisor: Avi Friedman.

Fliess, H. *Site Planning Guidelines for Medium Density Housing.* Prepared for The Ontario Ministry of Housing, 1980.

Ford Foundation. *Affordable Housing: The Years Ahead.* New York, 1989.

Friedman, A. *Le Village: Retooling for the Next Century.* Prepared for Renaissance Waterfront Association. Cornwall, Ontario, August 1999.

———. *Planning the New Suburbia: Flexibility by Design.* UBC Press, 2002a.

———. *The Adaptable House.* New York: McGraw-Hill, 2002b.

———. *The Grow Home.* Montreal, QC: McGill-Queen's University Press, 2001.

———. "The Evolution of Design Characteristics During the Post-Second World War Housing Boom: The US Experience." *Journal of Design Housing*, Vol. 8, No. 2, pp. 131–146, 1995.

———. "Prefabrication Vs. Conventional Construction in Single-Family Wood-Frame Housing." *Building Research and Information*, Vol. 2, No. 4, 1992.

Friedman, A. et al. *Sustainable Residential Development: Planning, Design and Construction Principles (Greening the Grow Home).* Prepared for Canada Mortgage and Housing Corporation, McGill University, May 1993.

Friedman, A., D. Drummond, and A. Sheppard. "The Conversion of Under-used Industrial Buildings to Affordable Housing in Montreal, Canada." *Open House International*, Vol. 20, No. 3, pp. 3–11, 1995.

Friedman, A., Q. Lin, and D. Krawitz. "The Development Process of Urban and Architectural Guidelines for the Rehabilitation of an Inner-City Neighbourhood: Le Village, Cornwall, Ontario, Canada." *Journal of Urban Design.* Vol. 7, No. 1, pp. 5–34, 2002.

Gibson, S., "Engineered Lumber." *Fine Homebuilding*, October/November, 2002.

Goodchild, B. *Housing and the Urban Environment: A Guide to Housing Design, Renewal and Urban Planning.* Oxford: Blackwell Sciences, Ltd., 1997.

Govan, T. "Finding Space in Small House." *Fine Homebuilding.* August/September, 2003.

Granger, W.F. "The Joy of Raking Leaves." *Wildflower.* pp. 14–15, Autumn, 1991.

Grans, H. J. *The Levittowners.* New York: Pantheon Books, 1967.

Habitat for Humanity Canada. Affordable Home Ownership Background Discussion Paper, October, 2003.

Harris, R. W. *Arboriculture: Care of trees, Shrubs and Vines in the Landscape.* Englewood Cliffs, NJ: Prentice-Hall, 1983.

Haun, L. *Habitat For Humanity: How to Build a House.* The Taunton Press, 2002.

Hemp, P. "Framing with the Plumber in Mind." *Fine Homebuilding*, October/November, 1988.

Hill, P. "Children and Spaces." *Habitat.* 13.4. pp. 25–27, 1970.

Hinshaw, M., A. Scarfone, and J. Donnelly. *Model Code Provisions, Urban Streets &*

Subdivisions. Prepared for Washington State Community Trade and Economic Development, Olympia, Washington, October, 1998.

Housing and Urban Development (HUD). "Cost Saving Construction Opportunities and the HOME Program: Marking the Most of HOME Funds." *HOME Model Series,* December, 1994.

———. *Affordable Residential Construction: A Guide for Home Builders,* July, 1987.

Howard, E. *Tomorrow: A Peaceful Path to Real Reform.* London: Swan Sonnenschein & Co., 1898.

Huang, Q. *Pre-Occupancy Choices of Interior Layout in Montreal Housing* (Unpublished M. Arch. Report). McGill University, School of Architecture, Montreal, 2003. Advisor: Avi Friedman.

Jackson, K. T. *Crabgrass Frontier.* New York: Oxford University Press, 1985.

Jacobs, J. *The Death and Life of Great American Cities.* New York: Random House, 1961.

Jensen, D. "How to Win at the Zoning Table." *National Association of Home Builders of the United States,* 1984.

Johnson, A. W., "Basement Leaks." *Builder,* October, 1990.

Kicklighter, C., et al. *Architecture: Residential Drawing and Design.* The Goodheart-Wilcox Company, Inc. Tinley Park, Illinois, 2000.

Legget, R. F. "Groundwater." *Canadian Building Digest,* No. 82, National Research Council, 1966.

———. "Soil and Buildings." *Canadian Building Digest,* No. 3, National Research Council, March 1960.

Linn, C. "Affordable Housing: Auburn Court, Cambridge, Massachusetts." *Architectural Record.* pp. 112–113, July, 1997.

Litman, T. *Parking Requirement Impacts on Housing Affordability.* Victoria Transport Policy Institute, November, 1999.

Lynce-Tresch, R. "Renovating: Residential Landscape." *Habitat,* 27.2, pp. 19–24, 1984.

Lynch, K. *A Theory of Good City Form.* Cambridge, MA: MIT Press, 1981.

Macfadyen, D. *Sir Ebenezer Howard and the Town Planning Movement.* Manchester, UK: Manchester University Press, 1933.

Marshall Macklin Monaghan Limited. *Achieving Infrastructure Cost Efficiency/Effectiveness Through Alternative Planning Approaches.* Prepared for Canada Mortgage and Housing Corporation (CMHC), June, 1992.

———. *Making Choices, Alternative Development Standards: Guidelines.* Ontario Ministry of Housing, Ontario Ministry of Municipal Affairs, May, 1994.National Association of Home Builders (NAHB). *Cost Effective Site Planning: Single Family Development.* Washington, DC, 1986.

———. *Manual of Lumber and Plywood-Saving Techniques for Residential Light-Frame Construction.* NAHB Research Foundation, Inc., June, 1971.

_____. *Reducing Home Building Costs with OVE Design and Construction.* Guideline 5. NAHB Research Foundation, Upper Marlboro, MD, Washington DC, 1987.

National Round Table on the Environment and the Economy. *Clearing up the Past, Building the Future: A National Brownfield Redevelopment Strategy for Canada.* Ottawa, 2003.

New York State Council on the Arts. *Reweaving the Urban Fabric: Approaches to Infill Housing.* With an introduction by Peter Marcuse. New York: Princeton Architectural Press, 1988.

Numbers, M. J. "Sitting a House: Proper Sitting and Design Strategies Enhance Energy Efficiency." *Fine Homebuilding,* pp. 40–45, February/March, 1995.

Olmsted, F. L. *The Years of Olmsted Vaux and Company, 1865–1874,* Vol. 6 *of The Papers of Fredrick Law Olmsted.* Baltimore: John Hopkins University Press, 1992.

Ou, Y. *The Evolution of Prefabricated Interior Components for Post-Occupancy Modification* (Unpublished M.Arch. Thesis). McGill University School of Architecture, Montreal, 1999. Advisor: Avi Friedman.

Parsons, K. C. *British and American Community Design: Clarence Stein's Manhattan Transfer Planning Perspectives.* 7:191–210, 1992.

Petrowski, E. M., "Setting Houses in Hard Places." *Architectural Record,* April, 1999.

Pope, A. "Avoiding the Problem Building Lot." *Habitat,* Vol. 27, No. 3, 1984.

Pope, A. (With Brink, S.) "Living Comfortably With Traffic Noise." *Habitat,* Vol. 25, No. 3, 1982.

Radburn Association Archives. *Plans of Northwest and Southwest Residential Districts.* Fairlawn, NJ, 1929.

Roberts, C. J. B. "Home Buying U.S.A.: A System Analysis." *Industrialization Forum.* Vol. 1, No. 3, pp. 35–40, 1970.

Schoenauer, N. *Streetscape and Standards.* The Canadian Architect, December, 1963.

Skaates, G. "Drainage Systems." *Fine Homebuilding,* October/November, 1985.

Southworth, M. *Walkable Suburubs? An Evolution of Neotraditional Communities at the Urban Edge,* APA Journal, pp. 28–44, 1997.

Southworth, M. and P. Owens. "The Evolving Metropolis," *Journal of the American Planning Association,* Vol. 49, No. 3, Summer 1993.

Stein, C. S. *Toward New Towns for America.* New York: Reinhold, 1957.

Susanka, S. *Home By Design.* Newtown, CT: The Taunton Press, 2004.

———. *The Not So Big House,* Newtown, CT: The Taunton Press, 1998.

Svensson, O. *Planning of Low-Rise Urban Housing Areas.* SBI-Byplanlaeging 56: Danish Building Research Institute, 1998.

Tasker-Brown, J. and S. Pogharian. *Learning from Suburbia: Residential Street Pattern Design.* Prepared for Canada Mortgage and Housing Corporation, 2000 (Prepared for Fanis Grammenos).

The Model Code for Residential Development, Prepared by the Model Code Task Force of the Green Street Joint Venture, Commonwealth of Australia, 1990.

Tomalty, R., A. Hercz, and C. Warne. *A Guide to Developing a Municipal Affordable Housing Strategy.* Prepared for Canada Mortgage and Housing Corporation, 2001.

Wark, K. *Thermodynamics.* New York: McGraw-Hill, 1988.

Wei, C. *Infill Housing Projects in Inner City Rehabilitation* (Unpublished M.Arch. Report). McGill Unversity, School of Architecture, Montreal, 2002. Advisor: Avi Friedman.

Wei, J. *Open Spaces in High-Density Affordable Housing Communities in Montreal: Pattern, Design and Use* (Unpublished M.Arch Report). McGill University, School of Architecture, Montreal, 2003. Advisor: Avi Friedman.

Wentling, J. "Small Lot Housing Typology." *Progressive Architecture,* June, 1991.

Winter, S., Associates, Inc. *HVAC/Plumbing, Vol. 8 of the Rehab Guide.* Prepared for the U.S. Department of Housing and Urban Development Office of Policy Development and Research, August, 1999.

Wright, G. *Building the Dream: A Social History of Housing in America.* New York: Pantheon, 1981.

Wright, J. G. *Risks and Rewards of Brownfield Redevelopment.* Cambridge, MA: Lincoln Institute of Land Policy, 1997.

Wu, J. *Correlation Between Family Life Cycle and Space Adaptation in Affordable Single Family Homes* (Unpublished M.Arch. Report). McGill University, School of Architecture, Montreal, 2003. Advisor: Avi Friedman.

Zhang, J. *Cost Effective Circulation and Parking Design Strategies for Affordable Communities* (Unpublished M.Arch. Report). McGill University, School of Architecture, Montreal, 2003. Advisor: Avi Friedman.

Illustration Credits and Notes

Illustrations and photos not listed have been created or taken by the author and members of his team.

CHAPTER 1

Figure 1.1   Prepared by the author after consultation with private lenders at the Canadian Imperial Bank of Commerce and review of a publication by the Canadian Banker's Association, 1984.

Figure 1.2   Prepared by the author after consultation with private-sector home-builders and review of a publication by the Ford Foundation, 1989.

CHAPTER 2

Figure 2.3   Created after maps provided by the Planning Department, City of Regina, Saskatchewan, Canada, 2003.

Figure 2.7   Created based on data provided by the City of Hamilton, Ontario, Canada, and Statistics Canada On-line 2002 census information.

Figure 2.8   After the design by Kunfei Chen for the Heritage Site, City of Lethbridge, Alberta, Canada, 2004. Advisors: Avi Friedman and Louis Pretty.

Figure 2.9   After design by Ying Le for the Legacy Site, City of Lethbridge, Alberta, Canada, 2004. Advisors: Avi Friedman and Louis Pretty.

Figure 2.11   Courtesy of the City of Cornwall Planning Department, Ontario, Canada. ©1999.

Figure 2.12   After an illustration by the National Association of Home Builders (NAHB), 1986. Used with the permission of NAHB.

CHAPTER 3

Figure 3.11   After a design by An Dong for the Planning Department, City of Medicine Hat, Alberta, Canada, 2003. Advisors: Avi Friedman and Louis Pretty.

Figure 3.15   After Canada Mortgage and Housing Corporation (CMHC). *Habitable Attics,* 1991. All rights reserved. Reproduced with the consent of CMHC. All other uses and reproductions of this material are expressly prohibited.

Figure 3.16   After Canada Mortgage and Housing Corporation (CMHC). *Habitable Attics,* 1991. All rights reserved. Reproduced with the consent of CMHC. All other uses and reproductions of this material are expressly prohibited.

Figure 3.27   After Canada Mortgage and Housing Corporation (CMHC). *New Made-to-Convert Housing,* 1988. All rights reserved. Reproduced with the consent of CMHC. All other uses and reproductions of this material are expressly prohibited.

CHAPTER 4: INTERIORS

Figure 4.4   After a drawing by Jiahui Wu (2003). Courtesy of Jiahui Wu.

CHAPTER 6: LOTS

Figure 6.1   Used with the permission of Jack Diamond, 1976.

Figure 6.2   Used with the permission of the National Association of Home Builders (NAHB), 1986.

Figure 6.12   Howard, 1898.

Figure 6.13   Radburn Association Archives, 1929.

Figure 6.16   After a design by An Dong, 2003.

Figure 6.17   After a design by Jie Deng, 2003.

Figure 6.18   Used with the permission of the National Association of Home Builders (NAHB), 1986.

CHAPTER 7: CIRCULATION AND INFRASTRUCTURE

Figure 7.4   Used with the permission of Michael Southworth and Peter M. Owens. ©1993.

Figure 7.5   Courtesy of Tasker-Brown and Pogharian, 2000. Used with the permission of Julie Tasker-Brown.

Figure 7.8   Used with the permission of the National Association of Home Builders (NAHB), 1987.

Figure 7.9   Used with the permission of the National Association of Home Builders (NAHB), 1987.

Figure 7.11   Design of a housing project in the City of Gatineau, Quebec, Canada, by Avi Friedman, David Morin, and Francois Dufaux.

Figure 7.14   Used with the permission of the National Association of Home Builders (NAHB), 1987.

Figure 7.15   Used with the permission of the National Association of Home Builders (NAHB), 1987.

Figure 7.16   Used with the permission of Todd Litman, 1999.

Figure 7.17   Used with the permission of Todd Litman, 1999.

Figure 7.18   Source: Canada Mortgage and Housing Corporation (CMHC). *Parking Areas Advisory Document,* 1980. All rights reserved. Reproduced with the consent of CMHC. All other uses and reproductions of this material are expressly prohibited.

Figure 7.20   Used with the permission of Mark C. Childs, 2002.

Figure 7.21   Source: Canada Mortgage and Housing Corporation (CMHC). *Parking Areas Advisory Document,* 1980. All rights reserved. Reproduced with the consent of CMHC. All other uses and reproductions of this material are expressly prohibited.

Figure 7.26   Source: Canada Mortgage and Housing Corporation (CMHC). *Residential Site Development Advisory Document,* 1981. All rights reserved. Reproduced with the consent of CMHC. All other uses and reproductions of this material are expressly prohibited.

Figure 7.27   Used with the permission of the National Association of Home Builders (NAHB), 1987.

CHAPTER 8: OPEN SPACE

Figure 8.1   Olmsted, 1992.

Figure 8.2   After a design by Changhua Wei, 2003. Courtesy of Changhua Wei.

Figure 8.5   Used with the permission of Blandford Gates. Courtesy of Howard Fliess, 1980.

Figure 8.7   Used with the permission of Blandford Gates. Courtesy of Howard Fliess, 1980.

Figure 8.8   Used with the permission of Blandford Gates. Courtesy of Howard Fliess, 1980.

Figure 8.12   Source: Canada Mortgage and Housing Corporation (CMHC). *Residential Site Development Advisory Document,* 1981. All rights reserved. Reproduced with the consent of CMHC. All other uses and reproductions of this material are expressly prohibited.

CHAPTER 9: INFILL HOUSING

Figure 9.1   After design by Yan Ping for the Planning Department, City of Regina, Saskatchewan, Canada, 2002. Advisors: Avi Friedman and Louis Pretty.

Figure 9.2   Drawing by Richard Lu for the City of Cornwall, Ontario. Principal researcher: Avi Friedman.

Figure 9.6   Used with the permission of Robert Freedman. Courtesy of the City of Toronto, 2003.

CHAPTER 10: PROJECTS

Figure 10.1   Photographs used by permission of Qian Huang, 2003.

Figure 10.3   Used with the permission of Qian Huang, 2003.

Figure 10.4   Used with the permission of Qian Huang, 2003.

Figure 10.12   After Master Plan by Saia and Barbarese, Architects.

Index

optimal value engineering in, 103
  planned unit development, 133
Design consultants, 16
Design firms, 13, 15–16
Detached homes, 46, 130, 175
Developers, 15
Development:
  conservation, 198–203
  density-neutral, 200
  sustainable, 23
Development costs, 11
Di Bona, José, 232
Direct control, 27
Do-it-yourself (DIY) projects, 65, 102–103
Doors, 90, 92
Dormers, 57, 89
Double hip roof, 56
Double loaded streets, 145
Down payment, 6
Drainage systems, 121–123
Dufaux, Francois, 263
Duplexes, 62–63, 130
Du-Z-Lots, 138
Dwelling types, 41–73
  accessory structures, 70–72
  attachment, 45–52
  bungalow, 58–59
  density and FAR for, 130–131
  forms of dwellings, 42–45
  foundations, 53–55
  for infill housing, 225
  multifamily plex, 62–63
  multilevel, 58, 61–62
  one-and-a-half story, 58, 60
  rancher, 58, 59
  roof, 54, 56–67
  transformation of, 64–70
  two story, 58, 60–61
  walk-up, 58, 64

Economic changes, 3–4
Economy of scale, 32
Effectiveness (of energy use), 124
Efficiency. See also Energy efficiency
  designing for, 76–77
  and loss of open spaces, 186
  zoning within home, 77–82
Electric energy, 124–125
Energy conservation:
  designing open spaces for, 203–206
  solar energy for, 141
Energy efficiency:
  of attached homes, 46, 51–52
  and form of dwelling, 44–45
  with heating/cooling systems, 123–126
  and window types, 113–115
Entry/entryway, 83–84

Envelope, building, 45, 113
Equity Cooperative, 9
Equity in home, 5

Façades of homes, 162, 163
Families structure and lifestyle, 2, 4, 6
FAR, see Floor-area ratio
Faults, 35
Fences, 162
Financial institutions (in delivery process),
  13, 14
Financing, 3–4, 9, 11–12
Finishes, interior, 94–98
Flat roof, 56–57
Floating floors, 96–97
Flood plains, 35–36
Flood zone, 35
Floors:
  construction of, 108–109
  varying levels of, 89, 90
Floor-area ratio (FAR), 130, 131
Floor coverings, 96–97
Floor sheeting, 108–109
Floor trusses, 108
Flora and fauna, 37–38
Foam-core panels, 117
Footpaths, 177
Footprint, 42–45, 58
Forced-air systems, 123
Foreign competition, 4
Forms of dwellings, 42–45
For-profit sector, 8, 15
Foundations, 53–55, 103–107
Fourplexes, 63
Fragmented parallel streets, 155
Frames, window, 114
Framing, 107–108, 110
Freehold homes, 10, 45, 133, 134
Freestanding storage, 93
Friedman, Avi, 255, 263
Frost-protected shallow foundations, 105
Furnaces, 126
Furniture partitions, 92–93
Future demand, assessing, 30
Future planning flexibility, 33

Gagnon, Paul-André, 232
Gambrel roof, 56
Gambrel truss, 57
Garages, 70, 71, 76
Garbage areas, 225
Garden apartments, 131
Garden City, 142, 143, 186, 189
Gas-fired furnaces, 126
GDSR (gross debt service ratio), 6
General lighting, 98
Geothermal heat pumps, 125–126